D1681295

9781258223946

DESIGN MANUAL
FOR
HIGH-STRENGTH STEELS

BY

H. MALCOLM PRIEST

WITH THE COLLABORATION OF

JOHN A. GILLIGAN

RESEARCH AND TECHNOLOGY
UNITED STATES STEEL CORPORATION

Copyright, 1954

UNITED STATES STEEL CORPORATION

525 WILLIAM PENN PLACE

PITTSBURGH 30, PENNSYLVANIA

Third Printing, 1956

Publication Number ADUCO-215-56

PRINTED IN U.S.A. BY DAVIS & WARDE, INC., PITTSBURGH, PA.

Preface

ANYONE familiar with the design of structures fabricated with structural carbon steel should have no difficulty in designing for high-strength steels, since the fundamental principles of design are the same for all steels.

Structural carbon steel has long been used in many fields of construction and, to facilitate the work of practical design, some of the basic principles involved have been reduced to rules in design specifications in which principles and theory tend to become obscured. Such rules are nevertheless based on the fundamental theories, tempered by the wisdom of experience.

When the high-strength low-alloy steels were introduced, there were very few specifications that were adapted to designing for the best utilization of the higher strength of this group of steels. It became essential to re-examine the design specifications for structural carbon steel, particularly in regard to buckling and elastic stability, in order to modify the rules to take advantage of the properties of high-strength steels.

This Manual is an outgrowth of that earlier need, and endeavors to discuss the essential principles of structural design and to develop formulas, charts and tables which will assist engineers in designing for high-strength steels. It is not intended as a text book, but rather as a practical, working handbook. For the reader wishing more detailed information on the subject of structural analysis and design, there are numerous textbooks to which reference can be made.

It cannot be too strongly stated or emphasized that nothing in this text should be taken as a recommendation for any value of working unit stresses. The selection of such a value is a matter for the final judgment of the design engineer. However, the subject of design cannot be developed without a treatment of working unit stresses and accordingly, a commonly used factor of safety, 1.80, has been adopted for illustrative purposes in determining unit stresses from the formulas given in this Manual. This was done only for uniformity and not as an indication that the particular value of 1.80 should be used.

The applications of both structural carbon and high-strength steels are so varied and so wide-spread in industry that each designer must select those unit stresses which experience has indicated best meet the conditions prevailing in his particular field. For example, the requirements for a static structure are quite different from those for a large power shovel subject to shock and heavy abuse. No publication of this type could hope to evaluate all such variables, nor even presume to recommend unit stresses for the guidance of those with years of practical experience in their special fields.

The views expressed in this Manual are those of the authors and do not necessarily represent the position of the United States Steel Corporation.

Table of Contents

PREFACE	iii
LIST OF SYMBOLS	x
HIGH-STRENGTH STEELS	1
Engineering Considerations	3
Fundamental Characteristics	3
Tensile Strength	3
Yield Point	4
Fatigue Resistance	4
Notch Toughness	4
Abrasion Resistance	4
Corrosion Resistance	4
Formability	6
Amenability to Welding	6
Applications	7
Economics of Application of High-Strength Steels	8
USS High-Strength Steels	8
DESIGN CONSIDERATIONS FOR HIGH-STRENGTH STEELS	9
WORKING UNIT STRESSES	13
TENSION	15
COMPRESSION	18
Axially Loaded Columns	18
Eccentrically Loaded Columns	32
Flat Plates in Edge Compression	40
Interaction of Flat Plate Elements	49
Effective Width of Flat Plates	57
Stiffened Flat Plates	61
SHEAR	64
Rivets	64
Flat Plates in Shear	65

Table of Contents

Stresses in Beams 69
    Local Buckling of Compression Flanges 71
    Lateral Buckling of Beams 72
    Web Buckling 77
        Web Buckling Due to Compression 77
        Web Buckling Due to Shear 79
    Combined Compression and Transverse Loads . . . 82

Deformation and Deflection 89
    Beam Formulas 91

Formed Sections 93

Designing Against Corrosion 104

Appendix
    Beam Formulas 125
    Characteristics of USS High-Strength Steels . . . 159
    Bibliography 170

List of Tables

USS High-Strength Steels
1. Comparative Properties and Engineering Data for a Corrosion Resistant High-Strength Steel and Structural Carbon Steels . 8

Tension
2. Tensile Working Unit Stresses 15

Axially Loaded Columns
3. Column Formulas—Pinned Ends 24
4. Column Formulas—Riveted Ends 25
5. Allowable Stresses for Compression Members . . . 26

Flat Plates in Edge Compression
6. Values of Factors in Formula 8 (Critical Stress) . . . 42
7. Formulas for Critical Unit Stress in Flat Plates in Edge Compression 45
8. Specification Requirements—Maximum Values of Ratio b/t . 46

Rivets
9. Allowable Stresses for Structural Riveted Joints . . . 65

Flat Plates in Shear
10. Shearing Yield Points 66
11. Values of Factors in Formula 14 (Critical Stress) . . . 67

Stresses in Beams
12. Allowable Shearing Stresses 71

Local Buckling of Compression Flanges
13. Maximum Values of Ld/bt and L/r_y 75

Web Buckling
14. Maximum Values of h/t (Due to Compression) . . . 79
15. Limiting Values of h/t Without Stiffeners (Due to Shear) . 80
16. Spacing of Stiffeners 81

Formed Sections
17. Minimum Inside Radius of Bend for Cold Forming . . 94
18. Properties of Elements 95
19. Powers of t 96
20. Properties of Fillets ($R = 1.0t$) 98
21. Properties of Fillets ($R = 2.0t$) 99
22. Properties of Fillets ($R = 2.5t$) 100
23. Properties of Fillets ($R = 3.0t$) 101
24. Properties of Fillets ($R = 3.5t$) 102

List of Figures

Only those figures are given to which the reader may have occasion to refer frequently

High-Strength Steels
1. Time-Corrosion Curves for Steels in Industrial Atmosphere . 5

Axially Loaded Columns
4. Column Formulas 22
5. Comparison of Column Areas 33

Eccentrically Loaded Columns
7. Maximum Stress—Eccentrically Loaded Compression Members —$s_{\max}$ $(L'/r)^2 = 0$ to 900×10^6 psi 38
8. Maximum Stress—Eccentrically Loaded Compression Members —$s_{\max}$ $(L'/r)^2 = 0$ to 100×10^6 psi 39

Flat Plates in Edge Compression
11. Critical Compressive Stress for Flat Plates in Edge Compression 43
15. Plate Coefficient k—Webs of Box Section 53
16. Plate Coefficient k—Flanges of I and Channel Sections and Webs of U and T Sections 54
17. Plate Coefficient k—Webs of I and Channel Sections . . 55

Beams—Combined Compression and Transverse Loads
26. Compression Member with End Moments 84
27. Compression Member with Partially Distributed Uniform Transverse Load 85
28. Compression Member with Partially Distributed Uniformly Varying Transverse Load 86

List of Examples

AXIALLY LOADED COLUMNS
1. Determining column formulas 23
2. Allowable column load 31
3. Effect of different factors of safety and yield points on allowable column load 31

ECCENTRICALLY LOADED COLUMNS
4. Design of column—load eccentric to one axis only . . . 35
5. Maximum fiber stress—load eccentric to two axes . . . 37

FLAT PLATES IN EDGE COMPRESSION
6. Critical stress for plate elements of column section . . . 46
7. Critical stress for plate elements of column section—allowable column load 48
8. Critical stress for plate elements of formed section . . . 49
9. Critical stress for plate elements of formed section . . . 49
10. Example 7—Interaction of plates 56
11. Example 8—Interaction of plates 56
12. Ultimate load on plate—effective widths 59
13. Allowable column load—critical stress and effective width methods 60
14. Ultimate load on plate and stiffener combination . . . 63

FLAT PLATES IN EDGE SHEAR
15. Allowable shearing stress 68

LATERAL BUCKLING OF BEAMS
16. Allowable fiber stress 76
17. Maximum distance between lateral supports 76

WEB BUCKLING
18. Investigation of girder 81

COMBINED COMPRESSION AND TRANSVERSE LOADS
19. Investigation of member 87

BEAM FORMULAS
20. Design of beam—deflection at mid-span 92

ix

List of Symbols

A	Cross-sectional area
B, C, D	Constants in Formula 5
E	Modulus of elasticity in tension and compression
I	Moment of inertia
I_x	Moment of inertia about X axis
I_y	Moment of inertia about Y axis
K	Ratio of the effective column length to actual column length; torsional stiffness constant
L	Length of member; distance between supports
L'	Effective length of column
M	Bending moment; applied moment; and moment reaction
M_1, M_2	Moment reaction at left and right ends respectively
M_{max}	Maximum bending moment
N	Factor of safety
P	Concentrated load; and allowable column load
P'	Ultimate or critical column load
P_{cr}	Euler column load in Figs. 26, 27 and 28
P_{ult}	Ultimate load on plate; or on plate and stiffener combination
Q	Moment of area
R	Limiting slenderness ratio, L'/r, in Formula 5
R_1, R_2	Vertical reaction at left and right ends respectively
S	Section modulus
S_x, S_y	Section modulus about X and Y axes respectively
V	Total shear
W	Concentrated load
X, Y	Rectangular coordinate axes
a	Length of plate
b	Plate width; compression flange width
b_e	Effective width of plate
c	Distance to extreme fiber measured from neutral, or centroidal, axis; width of plate

LIST OF SYMBOLS

c_x, c_y	Distance to extreme fiber measured perpendicular to X and Y axes respectively
d	Depth of beam; distance between vertical stiffeners; width of plate
e	Eccentricity of application of load; elongation or total strain
e_x, e_y	Eccentricity of application of load measured perpendicular to X and Y axes respectively
h	Height of web
k	General plate buckling coefficient
k_c, k_d	Plate buckling coefficient referring to plate of c width and d width respectively
n	Constant in Formulas 8b and 14b
r	Radius of gyration
r_x, r_y	Radius of gyration about X and Y axes respectively
s	Allowable unit stress in tension or compression
s_{avg}	Average stress in plate width
s_{cr}	Critical compressive stress in plates
s_{max}	Maximum stress in tension or compression
s_y	Yield point in tension or compression
s_x, s_y	Maximum compressive stress in eccentrically loaded columns for bending about X and Y axes respectively
t	Thickness of plate
t_f	Thickness of element considered as a flange
v	Allowable shearing stress
v_{cr}	Critical shearing stress
v_y	Yield point in shear
w	Intensity of distributed load
x	Distance to beam section measured from left support
y	Distance to beam fiber measured from neutral axis
Δ	Beam deflection
Δ_x	Beam deflection at section x
θ	Beam slope
μ	Poisson's ratio

High-Strength Steels

HIGH-STRENGTH Low-Alloy Steels, commonly designated "High-Strength Steels," are a specific class of steels in which enhanced mechanical properties, and in most cases good resistance to atmospheric corrosion, are obtained by the incorporation of moderate proportions of one or more alloying elements, other than carbon.

These steels are generally intended for applications where savings in weight can be effected by reason of their greater strength, and where better durability is obtained because of their other desirable characteristics. These steels are supplied to minimum mechanical properties and are normally furnished in the as-rolled condition. Typical specifications for high-strength steels are ASTM A 242 and SAE 950.

High-strength steels owe their inception to a demand on the part of design engineers for a grade of steel that would make possible a reduction in the dead weight of structures. The first of these high-strength low-alloy steels, USS COR-TEN steel, was introduced in 1933. The practical service experience gained since that time has fully established the value of this class of steel for structural purposes.

These steels are characterized particularly by a considerably higher yield point than that of structural carbon steel—the mechanical property which gives the high-strength steels their great value in construction—and generally by a greater degree of resistance to atmospheric corrosion, the attribute which permits the use of thinner sections without the hazard of shortening life in service. Since only moderate amounts of alloying elements are required to achieve these characteristics, the mill price of high-strength low-alloy steels is only about 50 per cent more than that of structural carbon steel.

The combination of greater strength and low cost gives the high-strength steels definite economic advantages in many fields of industry and construction. The effective utilization of these steels depends, however, upon careful engineering analysis and design.

Today the designer is confronted with the challenge on the one hand of reducing the dead weight of equipment, and on the other hand, of obtaining longer service life together with lower maintenance costs. The constant demand for increases in the size and load-carrying capacity of mobile equipment has resulted in correspondingly increased dead weight when such structures are built of structural carbon steel. At the same time, the current high cost of labor makes it essential that equipment last as long as possible with a minimum of repairs.

High-strength steels may be used in thinner sections than those required with structural carbon steels, thus effecting a reduction in weight of the given structure. Reduction of dead weight is desirable from several points of view. In particular, movable structures, such as railroad rolling stock, trucks, buses, power shovels, earth movers, and machinery comprise a class in which pay load may be increased as the dead load is decreased. The power required to move such structures, or to increase their acceleration, may be favorably affected by reduction in weight. For a given application, the lesser weight of high-strength steel, as compared to structural carbon steel, results in narrowing the difference in total cost of the two materials, or in an actual saving. The lighter weight of members made from high-strength steels often brings about lower costs of transportation and of handling in fabrication and erection.

One common method of using high-strength steels in structures to obtain longer service life is that of maintaining the same thicknesses of material as those previously used with structural carbon steel. In some notable instances, greater thicknesses of the high-strength steels have been used. Two reasons for this procedure exist. Many structures are called upon to receive a great deal of mechanical abuse and the high-strength steels are of real value in making possible stronger, sturdier structures. Again, costs of replacement or repair of many types of equipment have mounted so high that longer life is a very important consideration. The superior corrosion resistance of some of the high-strength low-alloy steels, coupled with their ability to withstand abuse, make these steels an effective answer to many of the problems of present-day construction.

The choice between light-weight, standard, or heavier-than-standard construction must be decided on the basis of the economic factors involved. First cost of the structure is not always the sole criterion; maintenance and repair costs over the life of the structure can be even more important than initial cost. This initial cost must be considered concurrently with the economic benefits to be derived from the particular type of construction selected: for example, extra capacity with light-weight railroad hopper cars, standard capacity but longer life with standard-weight hopper cars, possibly slightly less capacity but longer life and less time out-of-service with heavier-than-standard hopper cars. High-strength steels offer these advantages in innumerable types of structures.

ENGINEERING CONSIDERATIONS

Since the yield point of the material usually serves to indicate the stress to which a structural member may be subjected without permanent deformation, it has become the generally accepted practice to base working unit stresses upon this important mechanical property. The minimum yield point of structural carbon steel, to Specification ASTM—A 7, is 33,000 psi; that of high-strength steel is generally 50,000 psi in thicknesses of $\frac{1}{2}$ inch and less. Hence, on the basis of the proportionality of their yield points, the working unit stress in tension employed with high-strength steel may be one and one-half times that used with structural carbon steel. It should be noted that in members where buckling can occur, the working unit stresses are modified to the extent necessary to insure stability. The use of higher working unit stresses permits reductions in the thicknesses of sections in the structure, with a consequent decrease in weight.

Subsequent sections of this Manual explain and illustrate the design calculations required to establish a sound application of high-strength steels in various types of structural members.

FUNDAMENTAL CHARACTERISTICS

A high-strength steel, to be of interest as a construction material, must have characteristics and properties which result in economies to the user when the steel is properly applied. Table No. 1 shows the comparative properties of a corrosion-resistant high-strength low-alloy steel and two widely used structural carbon steels. These properties will be discussed briefly, but for detailed information regarding a specific high-strength steel, reference should be made to data furnished by the producer.

Tensile Strength High-strength steels suitable for a wide range of structures in which weight reduction or increased strength is sought will have ultimate tensile strengths ranging between 70,000 and 85,000 psi.

Yield Point The yield point is of prime importance for the reason that it is the property upon which working unit stresses are generally based. The ratio of yield point to ultimate strength in tension is about 0.50 to 0.60 for structural carbon steel. This ratio is higher for high-strength steels, and generally is about 0.70. Most of the high-strength low-alloy steels have a minimum yield point of 50,000 psi in thicknesses up to and including ½ inch. A reduction in guaranteed minimum requirements is usually made for thicknesses over ½ inch.

Fatigue Resistance In most cases, the resistance to repeated loading (endurance limit or fatigue resistance) of materials is determined by laboratory tests of polished specimens. In these tests, the fatigue resistance of high-strength steels is greater than that of structural carbon steels. Likewise, the ratio of endurance limit to tensile strength is greater for high-strength steels than for structural carbon steel. The fatigue resistance of full size structures, however, is greatly affected by the presence of surface notches or discontinuities which act as stress raisers. Under conditions of service, therefore, the numerical values of endurance limit determined with polished specimens are not directly applicable. Results in service and a limited amount of data from tests of structural joints indicate that the use of high-strength steels results in an improvement in the fatigue resistance of structures.

Notch Toughness Toughness, as measured in a notched-bar impact test, is of interest because it reflects the behavior of the materials at notches in actual structures. High-strength steels exhibit notch toughness superior to that of structural carbon steels, whether the notch toughness be considered in terms of the amount of energy absorbed in breaking a specimen at room temperature or in terms of the refrigerated temperature to which they preserve their toughness. These advantages in notch toughness are reflected in superior performance of actual structures.

Abrasion Resistance There is general agreement that the resistance of various steels to abrasive action increases with strength, hardness and, to some extent, with carbon content. Service tests have demonstrated that the abrasion resistance of the high-strength steels, with their inherently greater strength, is higher than that of ordinary steel containing 0.15 to 0.20 per cent carbon.

Corrosion Resistance When section thicknesses have been reduced by the use of high-strength steel, it is important, in most

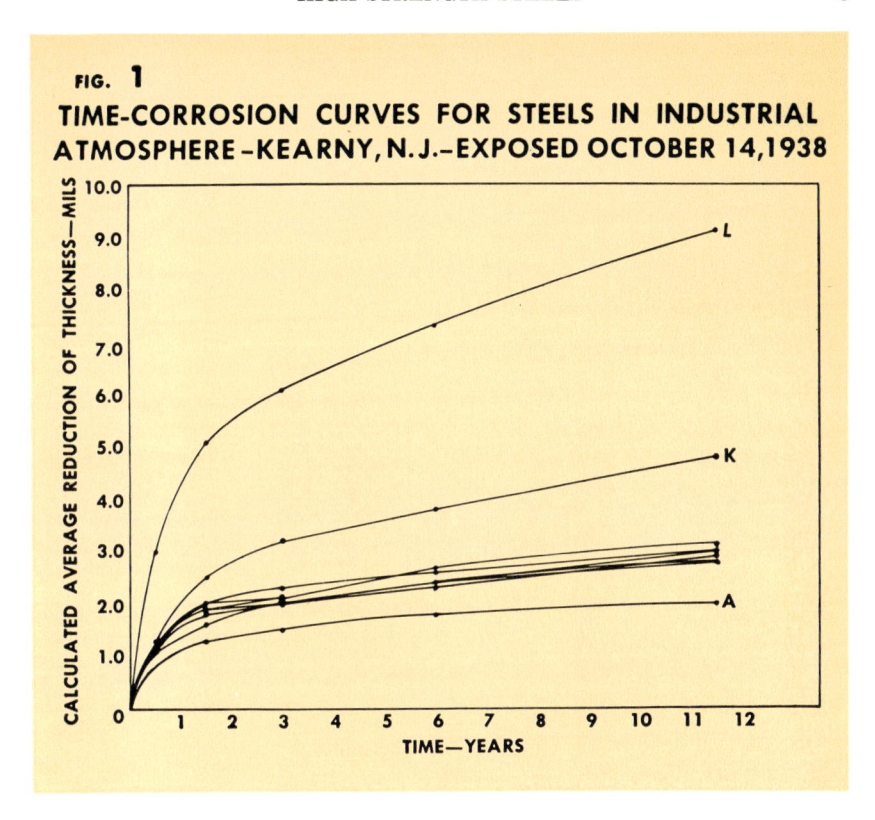

FIG. 1
TIME-CORROSION CURVES FOR STEELS IN INDUSTRIAL ATMOSPHERE – KEARNY, N.J. – EXPOSED OCTOBER 14, 1938

cases, that the steel have greater corrosion resistance in comparison with structural carbon steel if the high-strength steel structure is to have equal life. Unfortunately, the corrosion resistance of a material cannot be expressed quantitatively because it is only a relative term. Furthermore, no material is equally resistant to all the corrosive conditions to which it might conceivably be exposed. Its performance can only be compared with that of other materials under similar conditions. A large number of corrosion tests under many conditions of exposure, particularly atmospheric rack tests, have been conducted for the purpose of determining these relative values. Such tests differentiate between the performances of various steels and permit a close evaluation of the trends in weight loss due to corrosion.

The chart in Fig. 1 shows the losses in thickness for specimens exposed on racks in the industrial atmosphere of Kearny, N. J. for a period of nearly twelve years. Steel L is structural carbon steel with a low residual copper content. Steel K is a structural copper steel. The remaining curves represent the high-strength low-alloy steels made by various manufacturers in 1938, steel A being USS COR-TEN steel.

The atmospheric corrosion-resistance of steels varies with the amount and the characteristics of the alloying elements which they contain. It has been shown by numerous tests that combinations of certain alloying elements impart atmospheric corrosion resistance two to three times as great as that of copper steel. Some other combinations of alloying elements, while enhancing the mechanical properties of the steel, result in little or no improvement in the atmospheric corrosion resistance. The superior atmospheric corrosion resistance which most of the high-strength steels have shown in rack tests has been confirmed by their performance in many different kinds of service. This superiority is particularly evident in those applications in which the materials are subjected to atmospheric corrosion.

Formability High-strength low-alloy steels must have suitable plastic properties so that they can be cold formed or hot worked readily and economically into various parts for use in engineering structures. These materials are capable of being readily sheared, punched, reamed, coped, sawed, milled, drilled, riveted, gas cut and welded by the fabricator. Despite their higher yield points, high-strength steels can be satisfactorily worked in pressbrakes, drawbenches, presses and other equipment used for cold forming, even when these forming operations are quite severe.

Cold forming is the one operation in which there is a significant difference in behavior of the high-strength steel and structural carbon steel. This difference in behavior requires that more generous radii be used at the points of bending in high-strength steel. A broader discussion of this subject will be found in the section dealing with Formed Sections on pages 93 to 103.

Amenability to Welding Since welding is a general method of fabricating steel structures, it is very important that high-strength steels be readily welded. It is of even greater importance that the structure fabricated by welding have the required strength and ductility to withstand the conditions anticipated in service. The development of the present-day high-strength steels has paralleled the development of the various welding processes, and particular care was exercised to make certain that these steels possessed good welding characteristics. Suffice it to say that the high-strength low-alloy steels are considered readily weldable by the usual processes.

More detailed information regarding welding and other shop practices will be found in the publications mentioned on page 159 describing each of the USS High-Strength Steels.

Applications By far the largest single field of application of high-strength low-alloy steels has been in the construction of transportation equipment. Since 1934, more than 205,000 railroad freight cars and 6000 railroad passenger units have been constructed with one of the leading grades of high-strength steel, USS Cor-Ten steel. The railroads have obtained substantial economies in operating costs by using high-strength steels in somewhat reduced thicknesses to decrease the dead weight of their cars. In some cases, they have also increased the revenue per car trip by enlarging the light-weight car so that it can carry an additional amount of pay load equal to the reduction made in the dead weight. Similar benefits from weight reduction and from increase in capacity have been obtained with other mobile equipment, such as various types of trucks, trailers and buses.

Manufacturers of tractors and trailers, power shovels, cranes, ditchers, graders, farm machinery, conveyors and chutes have taken advantage of the qualities of the high-strength steels, usually to effect the economies possible with light-weight equipment. In some applications, the need for machines which would provide exceptional sturdiness and long service life led to the use of these steels in approximately the same sections as are used with structural carbon steel.

Generally, building construction does not provide a suitable field of application for high-strength steel because weight reduction in the structural members is not usually important or economical. However, in some notable instances, economies in shipping costs, in handling expenses and in erection charges have been obtained by the application of high-strength steels. In bridges with relatively long spans, reduction in the weight of the structure by the use of high-strength steel results in substantial economy of material. Satisfactory applications have also been made in deck or ballast plates of railway bridges, in blast plates and in highway bridges.

Miscellaneous applications of high-strength steels are numerous and greatly diversified. A few examples, suggestive of the wide range of uses in which the special properties of these materials prove valuable, are the inner bottoms, floors, tanks, sides and hatch covers of ore boats; hulls, other structural members and accessories of small tankers; the superstructures, auxiliary equipment and accessories of large ships; barges, tugs, launches and river boats; coal bunkers, cranes, derricks, powershovel booms and buckets, bulldozers, mine cars, lamp posts, pole line hardware, transmission towers, automobile jacks, cable reels, stokers, automobile bumpers and body parts, and air-conditioning equipment.

Economics of Application of High-Strength Steels The selection of high-strength steels in preference to other materials is usually based on one or more of three potential advantages: (1) minimum cost per unit of strength, (2) minimum cost per unit of service life, or (3) minimum overall cost due to operating savings and lower maintenance expense.

The first is based on the relatively low cost of the high-strength steels, approximately one and one-half times that of structural carbon steel.

The second advantage relates to increase of useful service life of many structures due to greater resistance to atmospheric corrosion.

The third is of particular significance in the face of ever-increasing labor costs in both operation and maintenance.

USS HIGH-STRENGTH STEELS

The United States Steel Corporation is currently producing four high-strength steels: USS Cor-Ten, USS Tri-Ten, USS Tri-Ten "E" and USS Man-Ten, which are supplied to minimum mechanical properties and are normally furnished in the as-rolled condition. Chemical composition, mechanical properties and additional typical properties for engineering guidance for these steels are shown on pages 160 to 169 inclusive. Typical specifications for these and other high-strength steels are ASTM A 242 and SAE 950.

Table I
USS COR-TEN STEEL AND STRUCTURAL CARBON STEELS
Comparative Properties and Engineering Data

MECHANICAL PROPERTIES ½ in. and Under in Thickness	USS COR-TEN STEEL	STRUCTURAL CARBON STEELS ASTM A 7	ASTM A 113
Yield Point, min, psi	50,000	33,000	27,000
Tensile Strength, psi	70,000 min	60/72,000	50/62,000
Elong. in 2 in., min, per cent	22		
Elong. in 8 in., min, per cent 0.180 in. and heavier	18	21	24
Cold Bend	180° D=1t	180° D=½t	180° Flat
Resistance to atmospheric corrosion (comparative)	4 to 6	1 (or 2 with copper 0.20% min)	1 (or 2 with copper 0.20% min)
Compressive Yield Point, psi	Tensile Y. P.	Tensile Y. P.	Tensile Y. P.
Shearing Strength, psi	¾ T.S.	¾ T.S.	¾ T.S.
Modulus of Elasticity, psi	28/30,000,000	28/30,000,000	28/30,000,000
Endurance Limit (as rolled, avg), psi	42,000	28,000	26,000
Charpy Impact, keyhole notch, (as rolled, room temp, avg), ft-lb	40	25	30
Coefficient of Expansion, per degree F, 70 to 200 F	0.0000063	0.0000063	0.0000063

Design Considerations for High-Strength Steels

DESIGN is concerned with the efficient and economical utilization of the materials of construction, as well as with the selection of the appropriate material for the project in hand. This Manual is concerned primarily with the use of a group of materials, commonly designated as high-strength low-alloy steels. The use of such steels requires no new principles of design, so that much of this discussion is equally applicable to structural carbon steel, though certain principles assume greater importance and must be given more extended consideration when designing for high-strength steels.

In evaluating materials of construction, the design engineer is mainly interested in the mechanical properties, especially the yield point, ultimate strength, elongation and modulus of elasticity—all readily obtainable from the tensile test. The yield point and modulus of elasticity in compression are usually taken as being the same as those in tension. The yield point, ultimate strength and modulus of elasticity in shear are also important and, in the absence of tests, may be approximated as a percentage of the corresponding tensile properties. Fatigue strength, impact strength and coefficient of expansion likewise enter into considerations of design. The effect of high and low temperatures on all these properties is of vital importance in some cases. Corrosion resistance is a significant property, particularly in connection with the use of high-strength steels.

An adequate design cannot be prepared without a background of knowledge relating to the methods of fabrication and the machines and equipment that are ordinarily employed. The engineer must have reliable information as to the performance characteristics of the steel as it passes through the various fabricating processes. Formability in press brake and die operations and the effect of welding cannot be neglected. Fortunately, only one consideration needs emphasis when cold forming high-strength steels. Experience has shown that a greater inside radius is required at all bends, in order to prevent cracking on the outer surface. The recommended practices for USS High-Strength Steels are given on pages 160 to 173. Hot forming requirements are the same as for structural carbon steel.

The basis of most design is stress analysis. The more completely and accurately the stresses can be determined, the more effectively can the engineer dispose the material to support the loads on the structures. With the recent development of electric strain gages and various electronic measuring devices, the analysis of stress by experimental means has broadened the field of stress analysis far beyond anything heretofore available to engineers. By photo-elastic examination of transparent models many facts have been brought to light regarding the internal distribution of stress and its concentration at discontinuities such as notches and sharp corners. Brittle lacquers which crack under strain can be sprayed on an actual structure and, when loads are applied, will reveal the presence and magnitude of stress in the steel. Dynamic stresses may now be studied and knowledge of this subject is continually expanding.

These introductory observations will perhaps indicate the breadth of knowledge which should be in the possession of a design engineer. In the routine work of ordinary designing, much of this knowledge has been reduced to clauses in specifications which, in time, tend to mask their technical significance. Where such knowledge is lacking, an engineer is frequently handicapped when confronted with the problems arising in industry today. The older methods of approximation, cut and try, of adding more material wherever weakness developed in a structure, are no longer sufficient.

Before the design of an engineering structure can proceed, a basis for proportioning the sizes of the members must be established. Such a basis is a set of specifications, which, in many instances, is a comprehensive document setting forth the allowable working unit stresses, certain limitations for proportioning members, and directions covering the fabrication of the structure—all intended to assure the production of a safe and satisfactory structure.

The function of any structure is to support or to resist loads and forces. In general, a structure must support its own weight, the super-imposed loads, and forces produced by wind, centrifugal action and the like. The term "load" is often used in the inclusive sense to cover all of the external forces acting on a structure.

When loads are applied suddenly, there is created a condition referred to as impact. The effect of impact is to increase the internal forces in the structure. Theoretically, the internal force may be doubled in a bar to which an axial load is applied suddenly, but in practice there are many parts of a structure which are more or less remote from the point of application of the load, and the augmentation of the internal force in such parts is considerably less than the theoretical maximum. Since designs are usually made on the basis of equivalent static load conditions, it is common practice to allow for the effect of impact-producing loads by the use of multiplication factors, rather than to reduce the allowable unit stress in the member.

Again, some of the loads may fluctuate or be applied repetitively over a great number of cycles. In view of the fact that steel, as well as many other materials of construction, exhibits a lower ultimate strength under such conditions, it is general practice to reduce the working unit stress for cyclic loading accordingly. The fatigue strength of steel depends upon the stress cycle followed, for example, whether the cycle is one of complete reversal from tension to compression, or whether it is one of minimum to maximum tension.

The ability of a member to resist the internal forces imposed upon it depends upon the mechanical properties of the material composing the member. As previously mentioned, the important properties which a design engineer needs to know are the values of the ultimate strength, the yield point, and the modulus of elasticity in tension and shear, and the yield point and modulus of elasticity in compression. Knowing these values, he can then proceed to determine the allowable working unit stresses.

Since this Manual is essentially intended for practical use, no extended treatment of stress analysis will be given. There are many excellent handbooks on that subject which may be consulted. Briefly, the first step in a design is to establish the outlines of the proposed structure and then determine the external loads and forces acting upon it. Next, the internal forces (often referred to by engineers as the stresses) are calculated. The final step is the proportioning of the members to resist these forces. When these forces are divided by the cross-sectional area of the member over which they are distributed, the result is the unit stress. A member is correctly proportioned when this unit stress does not exceed the allowable working unit stress for the material used in the member.

In subsequent sections of this Manual, each of the various kinds of stress to which a member may be subjected will be treated in detail. For most cases, the important factor will be unit stress, but in cases such as long, slender columns it will be found that the ultimate load is the controlling factor because such members fail by buckling. The text is so arranged that the designer may select a factor of safety, evaluate the conditions of the supports for the ends of columns or the edges of flat plates, and determine the sizes and proportions of the members required to withstand the anticipated stresses. In effect, he writes his own set of design specifications. As a matter of fact, this is what he is expected to do—bringing to bear his own experience and judgment in his particular field.

Structural carbon steel has long been the basic material of industry, and around it have developed innumerable design specifications and a wealth of practical knowledge regarding all phases of its fabrication and performance in service. It is natural, therefore, to compare high-strength steels with structural carbon steel.

There are two fundamental points of view from which to approach the design of structures of high-strength steels. One is to reduce the dead weight of the structure by taking advantage of the greater strength of the high-strength steels; the other is to maintain the same sizes as in structural carbon steel, utilizing the high strength to produce stronger, more rugged construction where severe service is encountered. Sometimes a compromise between these two methods provides the most satisfactory solution.

The service life of many types of structures, such as railroad hopper and gondola cars, trucks and earth moving equipment, is affected by the mechanical abuse they receive, and while lightweight construction is desirable from the standpoint of greater load carrying capacity, these advantages are sometimes outweighed by the necessity of providing in larger measure against excessive mechanical damage.

No rule can be established for selecting a particular approach to designing for high-strength steels. The conditions surrounding the service to which a structure will be subjected, and the economic factors involved will largely determine the selection.

Working Unit Stresses

A LLOWABLE working unit stresses are the basis for all structural design and their selection is a matter of prime importance. They must be of such magnitude as to assure the safety of the structure against failure. The determining factors are the mechanical properties of the material of construction, upon one or more of which depends the ultimate strength of any structural member.

In practice, a working unit stress is determined by dividing the strength of the material by a factor of safety. The mechanical properties which are considered to govern design will be discussed in subsequent sections of this Manual where the design of various types of structural members is treated. Since the factor of safety enters into every working unit stress, there is good reason to give it serious consideration.

Economy of material results from the use of a factor of safety with a value as low as sound engineering judgment and experience dictates. The following factors affecting the selection of the factor of safety are important:

  (a) The accuracy with which the loads assumed to represent service conditions are selected. If there is much doubt concerning these loads, the allowable working stress will necessarily have to be more conservative than under conditions where the loads are known with considerable accuracy.

  (b) The accuracy with which the stresses in the members of a structure are calculated. Many approximations are used in structural design, as well as more rigorous and exact methods, to estimate the stress distribution. The choice of a factor of safety should be consistent with the degree of accuracy of the analysis. The more precise the method the greater the allowable unit stress may be.

(c) The significance of the structure being designed. The designer must have in mind the relative importance of the structure and be able to appraise the possibility of its failure causing serious property damage or loss of life. The significance of the design in this respect will govern to a considerable extent the choice of a factor of safety.

The factors of safety used in designing most common types of structures are an outgrowth of experience gained from many applications, tests and even failures. The trend in recent years has been to reduce the factors of safety in line with improved quality of steel and increasing knowledge of stress distribution. Doubtless, further reductions may be made in the future as greater accuracy becomes possible and practicable. At present, it is well to be guided by current practice.

Any recommendation of factors of safety applicable to each of the innumerable fields of construction in which steel is used would be quite inappropriate for this Manual. However, throughout the text it has been necessary to use a value for illustrative purposes and a widely accepted value of 1.80 was adopted. In using this Manual, designing engineers should select those unit stresses which will result in structures best suited to meet the service conditions to be encountered.

Tension

THE working unit stress for tension members is commonly based upon the yield point of the steel, using an appropriate factor of safety. The required net area of the cross section of a tension member is determined by dividing the load or stress in the member by the selected working unit stress.

$$A = \frac{P}{s} \tag{1}$$

in which
A = required area, sq in.
P = total stress, lb
s = unit stress in tension, psi

In riveted construction, the area so determined is the net area after deducting for rivet holes.

The application of a factor of safety of 1.80 to a few selected yield points gives the working unit stresses shown in Table 2. The

Table 2
TENSILE WORKING UNIT STRESSES

Minimum Yield Point psi	Working Unit Stress Calculated psi	Working Unit Stress Rounded psi
33,000	18,330	18,000
45,000	25,000	25,000
50,000	27,780	27,500
55,000	30,560	30,500

column of rounded values gives them to the nearest unit of 500 psi, always on the conservative side.

It happens frequently that applications of high-strength steels are made in types of structures which have hitherto been fabricated with structural carbon steel. In such cases, the problem is one of substitution. The application of the same factor of safety results in working unit stresses in tension for the two steels in direct proportion to their respective yield points. For example, assuming that with carbon steel having a minimum yield point of 33,000 psi, it has been customary to use a working unit stress of 18,000 psi, the working unit stress for a high-strength steel with a minimum yield point of 50,000 psi would be $18,000 \times \dfrac{50,000}{33,000} = 27,270$ psi. The actual value of the ratio of the yield points is 1.515, but a convenient value to use is 1.50. Applying this value to the working unit stress of 18,000 psi for carbon steel gives 27,000 psi for high-strength steel.

Weight saving is one of the most important considerations in the use of high-strength steels and it becomes of interest to know the relative weights of a design in high-strength steel and one in structural carbon steel. The theoretical weight ratio for tension members is inversely proportional to the yield points of the two steels. Comparing steels with yield points of 50,000 psi and 33,000 psi, the former will result in an area equal to $33,000/50,000 = 0.66$ times that of the latter.

The theoretical weight saving is seldom exactly achieved in practical design since the cross-sectional areas of structural shapes are increased by definite increments and it is only by chance that the actual values agree with those called for by the calculations. However, a little care in design will produce results which approach the limit in weight saving. This is especially true when the members are bars, pressed sections, or of built-up, welded construction, where one has the advantage of selecting both width and thickness in the make-up of a member.

Since designs are based upon definitely determined working unit stresses, a nomographic chart, such as Fig. 2, can be constructed by which one may readily determine the theoretical weight ratio. Letting s_1 be the unit stress for carbon steel and s_2 that for high-strength steel, the ratio of s_1/s_2 will be the ratio of the area and weight of the high-strength steel to the area and weight of the carbon steel.

As an example, using Fig. 2, assume $s_1 = 16,000$ psi and $s_2 = 27,000$ psi. Laying a straight edge across the chart, as indicated by the dotted line, read the value of $s_1/s_2 = 0.59$. The calculated ratio is 0.593.

FIG. 2

RATIO OF s_1/s_2

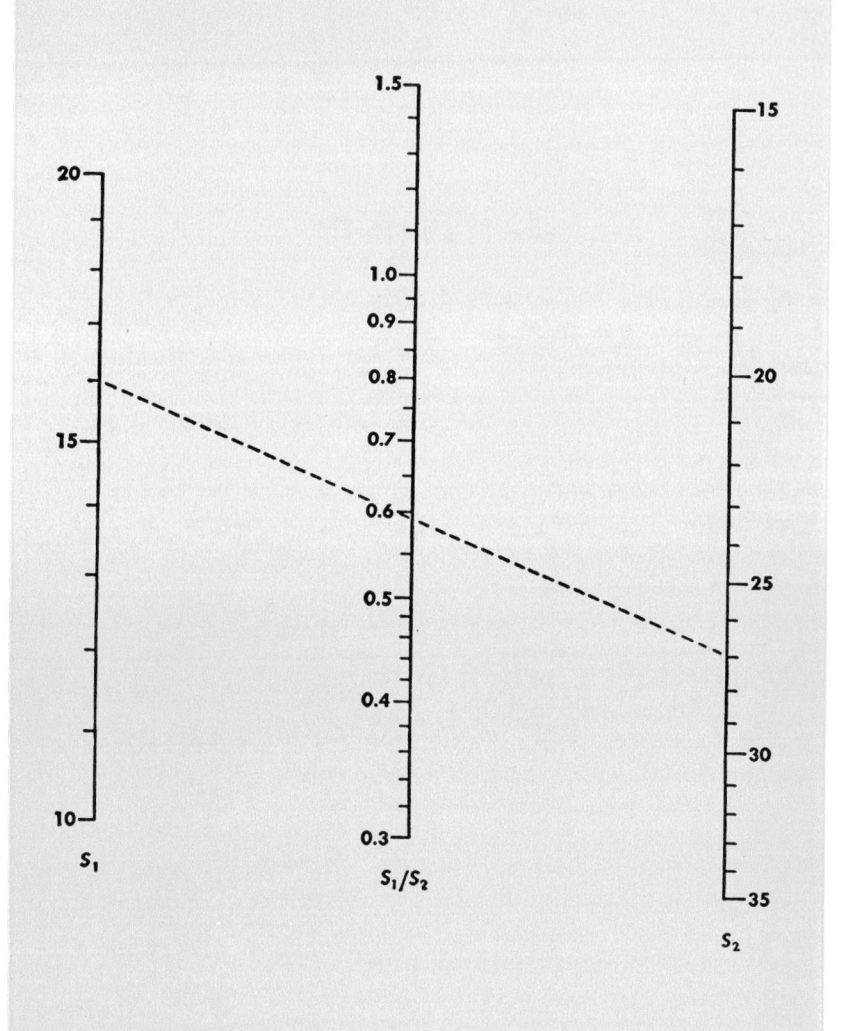

Compression

THE mechanical properties of steel in compression are not as clearly defined as those in tension. There is no definite ultimate strength, although there is a yield point (generally taken as equal to that in tension) beyond which marked plastic flow and lateral expansion of the steel occurs. Only relatively short compression members exhibit this behavior and for such members the basic working unit stress in compression may be taken equal to the working unit stress in tension. As the length of members increases, failure takes place by buckling at an average compressive unit stress progressively less than the yield point. It is with this latter class of members that the following sections on Columns will deal.

AXIALLY LOADED COLUMNS

By definition, a column is a straight member subjected to compression by forces acting in the direction of its longitudinal axis. Its unsupported length is great enough, compared to the dimensions of its cross section, for failure to take place by lateral bending, or buckling. Generally speaking, all column action is a combination of direct compression and bending. The determination of these effects is complicated by the inherent behavior of columns. Unlike tension and short compression members, the fiber stress in columns is not directly proportional to the load.

Technical literature is replete with information on columns and the classical formulas for ideal columns are given in all text books on strength of materials. In practice, one rarely deals with an ideal column, and it is in this field that there has developed a diversity of formulas for adapting the theoretical formulas to actual conditions.

In 1923 the American Society of Civil Engineers authorized a Special Committee on Steel Column Research. Engineers will find its first, second and final reports* of invaluable assistance in the study of columns and compression members. On the basis of extensive full-scale column tests, the Committee recommended the so-called secant formula as a rational one for design of columns.

This formula, based on the theoretical determination of the maximum combined stress in an eccentrically loaded column, is as follows:

$$\frac{P'}{A} = \frac{\text{Yield Point}}{1 + \frac{ec}{r^2} \sec\left[\sqrt{\frac{P'}{AE}}\left(\frac{L'}{2r}\right)\right]}, \tag{2}$$

in which
P' = ultimate column load, lb
A = cross-sectional area of member, in.^{2}
L' = effective column length, in.
E = modulus of elasticity, 29,000,000 psi
e = eccentricity of application of load, in.
c = distance from centroidal axis to most stressed fiber in compression, in.
r = radius of gyration, in.

For the practical application of the secant formula to axially loaded columns which are bent in single curvature, the Committee suggested that an eccentric ratio of $ec/r^2 = 0.25$ be used to include possible initial crookedness of the member and unintentional eccentric application of the load.

When Formula 2 is rearranged we have

$$\frac{P'}{A}\left\{1 + \frac{ec}{r^2}\sec\left[\sqrt{\frac{P'}{AE}}\left(\frac{L'}{2r}\right)\right]\right\} = \text{Yield Point}. \tag{3}$$

In this form, it will be recognized as the expression for the maximum combined stress, $s_{\max}$, due to the critical load, P'. The first term gives the average unit stress, while the second term gives the maximum unit stress produced at the extreme fiber by bending. When the ultimate strength of the column is reached, the sum of the two terms equals the yield point. When secondary plate buckling can occur before primary failure of the column as a whole, the value of $s_{\max}$ is generally reduced to the limiting value governed by the plate. (See page 40.)

The factor of safety as applied to columns is not based on the limiting fiber stress but on the critical load. Thus the working or

---
*Progress Report ASCE Transactions, Vol. 89 (1926); Second Progress Report, Vol. 95 (1931); Final Report, Vol. 98 (1933).

allowable load, P, equals P'/N, where N is the factor of safety.

It is well to have a clear understanding about the column length, since it is an important factor governing the strength of a column. As in all theoretical derivations for the strength of columns, the length, L', in Formula 2 is the length of a member whose end supports are ideally pinned and thus are free to rotate. This length is known as the effective length and is the basis upon which the strength of columns with varying end conditions is determined. As

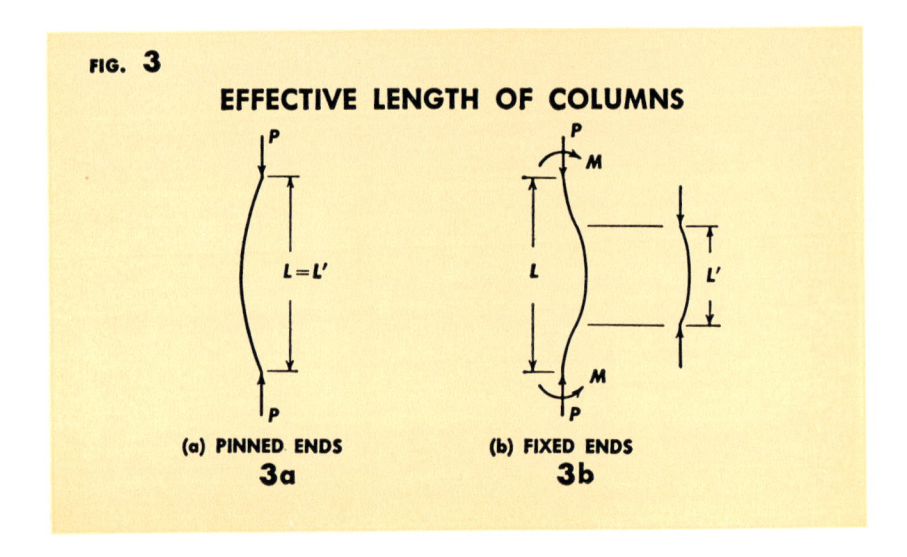

FIG. 3

EFFECTIVE LENGTH OF COLUMNS

(a) PINNED ENDS
3a

(b) FIXED ENDS
3b

shown in Fig. 3a, the effective length of an ideal pin-ended column is equal to the unsupported length of the column, L. For a column whose ends are fixed, Fig. 3b, the effective length is one-half the full length. In other words, in terms of strength, a fixed-ended column of length L could withstand the same load as an ideal pin-ended column of length $0.5L$. Similarly for a column with one end fixed and one end pinned, $L' = 0.7L$ and for the case where one end is fixed and one free, $L' = 2L$. Thus, the effective column length, L', is the length of the column which is equivalent to a pin-ended column and for which KL (K varying between 0.5 and 2.0) may be substituted in the column formulas.

In actual practice, the ends of columns are not frictionless hinges or pins, as there is always some restraint, either from the flat bearing or from the adjacent supporting members. The ASCE Committee recommended the following values of L':

$L' = 0.85L$ for columns with pinned ends,
$L' = 0.75L$ for columns with riveted ends.

These values, in effect, recognize that so-called pin-ended columns are not completely unrestrained, nor are fixed-ended columns fully restrained.

The column formulas in this Manual are based upon the above recommendations. Any engineer is at liberty to modify the value of K as his judgment and experience warrant.

The formula for the average working unit stress may be derived from Formula 2 by introducing the recommended value of 0.25 for the eccentric ratio, ec/r^2, and NP for P'.

Then
$$\frac{P}{A} = \frac{\overline{\text{Yield Point}}}{1 + 0.25 \sec\left[\sqrt{\frac{NP}{AE}}\left(\frac{L'}{2r}\right)\right]}, \tag{4}$$

in which
P = working column load, lb
N = factor of safety

and the other terms are as explained in connection with Formula 2.

Although the secant formula has both rational and experimental justification it is seldom used since for given values of L'/r the values of P/A can only be determined by successive approximations. Therefore more workable expressions of the type usually recognized as working column formulas have been determined for this Manual covering any grade of steel whose yield point or limiting stress lies between 30,000 and 60,000 psi. These expressions, which are based on the suggestions of the Special Committee on Column Research, have a maximum deviation from the secant formula of about two per cent. They take the form

$$\text{for } L'/r = 0 \text{ to } R \qquad \text{for } L'/r = R \text{ to } 200$$
$$\frac{P}{A} = B - C\left(\frac{L'}{r}\right)^2 \qquad \frac{P}{A} = \frac{B}{0.5 + \frac{1}{D}\left(\frac{L'}{r}\right)^2} \tag{5}$$

where
R = limiting value of L'/r
$\left.\begin{array}{c}B\\C\\D\end{array}\right\}$ = constants for a given limiting stress and factor of safety.

The values of B and C are functions of the limiting stress and factor of safety, while the values of D and R are functions of the limiting stress only, and all may be determined from the nomographic chart in Fig. 4. The following example illustrates the use of Fig. 4 for the determination of column formulas.

FIG. 4   COLUMN FORMULAS

Given the yield point of a steel and a factor of safety, the constants in the formulas for the average working unit stress in axially loaded compression members may be determined from this chart.

The formulas are:

$$0 < \frac{L'}{r} < R \qquad\qquad R < \frac{L'}{r} < 200$$

$$\frac{P}{A} = B - C\left(\frac{L'}{r}\right)^2 \qquad \frac{P}{A} = \frac{B}{0.5 + \frac{1}{D}\left(\frac{L'}{r}\right)^2}$$

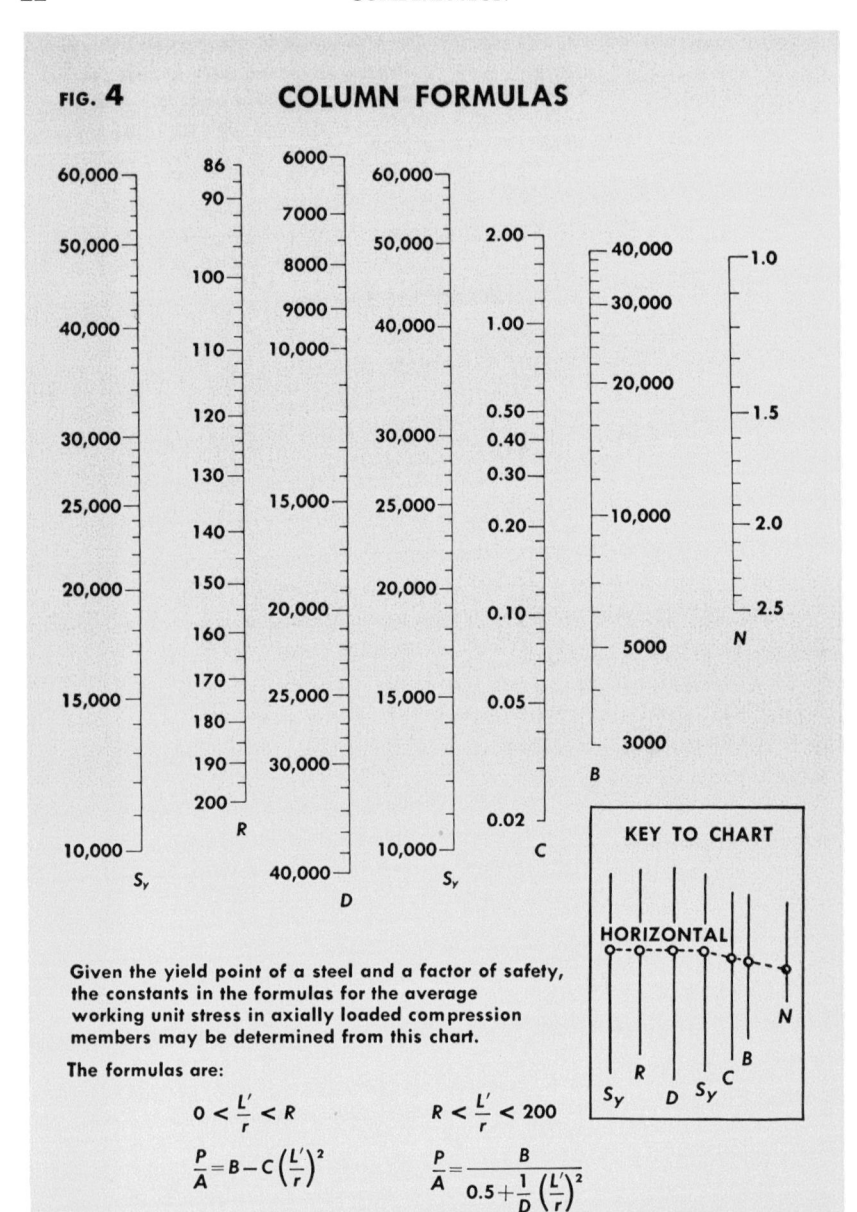

in which

P = working column load, lb
A = cross-sectional area of member, in.^{2}
L' = effective column length, in.
r = radius of gyration, in.
R = limit of L'/r

$\left.\begin{array}{l} B \\ C \\ D \end{array}\right\}$ = constants determined from chart

N = factor of safety
S_y = yield point, psi

KEY TO CHART

COMPRESSION

Example 1

Determine the column formulas in terms of the actual unsupported column length, L, for a steel with a yield point of 47,000 psi, and a factor of safety of 1.80.

From Fig. 4, read

$R = 99 \qquad B = 20{,}900 \qquad C = 0.88 \qquad D = 8100$

(a) *For a column with pinned ends:*

$L' = 0.85L$

$$0 < \frac{L}{r} < \left(\frac{99}{.85} = 116\right)$$

$$\frac{P}{A} = 20{,}900 - 0.88\left(\frac{.85L}{r}\right)^2 = 20{,}900 - 0.64\left(\frac{L}{r}\right)^2$$

$$116 < \frac{L}{r} < 200$$

$$\frac{P}{A} = \frac{20{,}900}{0.5 + \dfrac{1}{8100}\left(\dfrac{.85L}{r}\right)^2} = \frac{20{,}900}{0.5 + \dfrac{1}{11{,}200}\left(\dfrac{L}{r}\right)^2}$$

(b) *For a column with riveted ends:*

$L' = 0.75L$

$$0 < \frac{L}{r} < \left(\frac{99}{.75} = 132\right)$$

$$\frac{P}{A} = 20{,}900 - 0.88\left(\frac{.75L}{r}\right)^2 = 20{,}900 - 0.50\left(\frac{L}{r}\right)^2$$

$$132 < \frac{L}{r} < 200$$

$$\frac{P}{A} = \frac{20{,}900}{0.5 + \dfrac{1}{8100}\left(\dfrac{.75L}{r}\right)^2} = \frac{20{,}900}{0.5 + \dfrac{1}{14{,}400}\left(\dfrac{L}{r}\right)^2}$$

In everyday practice, high-strength low-alloy steels with definite minimum yield points will ordinarily be used. Column formulas for certain selected values of the yield point are listed in Table 3 for columns with pinned ends and in Table 4 for riveted ends. As a further aid to design, the values of P/A have been tabulated in Table 5 for yield points of 33,000 and 50,000 psi for both pinned and riveted ends. Both the column formulas and the tabulated average unit stresses are based on a factor of safety of approximately 1.80.

TABLE 3
COLUMN FORMULAS—PINNED ENDS

Yield Point	Limiting Values of L/r	Average Working Unit Stress
33000	0–140	$\dfrac{P}{A} = 15000 - 0.325\,(L/r)^2$
33000	140–200	$\dfrac{P}{A} = \dfrac{15000}{0.5 + \dfrac{1}{15860}(L/r)^2}$
45000	0–120	$\dfrac{P}{A} = 20500 - 0.605\,(L/r)^2$
45000	120–200	$\dfrac{P}{A} = \dfrac{20500}{0.5 + \dfrac{1}{11630}(L/r)^2}$
50000	0–110	$\dfrac{P}{A} = 22500 - 0.738\,(L/r)^2$
50000	110–200	$\dfrac{P}{A} = \dfrac{22500}{0.5 + \dfrac{1}{10460}(L/r)^2}$
55000	0–105	$\dfrac{P}{A} = 25000 - 0.902\,(L/r)^2$
55000	105–200	$\dfrac{P}{A} = \dfrac{25000}{0.5 + \dfrac{1}{9510}(L/r)^2}$

Formulas are based on the secant formula

$\dfrac{P}{A}$ is expressed in psi

Factor of safety = 1.80 approx.

TABLE 4
COLUMN FORMULAS—RIVETED ENDS

Yield Point	Limiting Values of L/r	Average Working Unit Stress
33000	0–155	$\dfrac{P}{A} = 15000 - 0.253\,(L/r)^2$
33000	155–200	$\dfrac{P}{A} = \dfrac{15000}{0.5 + \dfrac{1}{20370}(L/r)^2}$
45000	0–135	$\dfrac{P}{A} = 20500 - 0.471\,(L/r)^2$
45000	135–200	$\dfrac{P}{A} = \dfrac{20500}{0.5 + \dfrac{1}{14930}(L/r)^2}$
50000	0–125	$\dfrac{P}{A} = 22500 - 0.574\,(L/r)^2$
50000	125–200	$\dfrac{P}{A} = \dfrac{22500}{0.5 + \dfrac{1}{13440}(L/r)^2}$
55000	0–120	$\dfrac{P}{A} = 25000 - 0.702\,(L/r)^2$
55000	120–200	$\dfrac{P}{A} = \dfrac{25000}{0.5 + \dfrac{1}{12220}(L/r)^2}$

Formulas are based on the secant formula

$\dfrac{P}{A}$ is expressed in psi

Factor of safety = 1.80 approx.

TABLE 5
ALLOWABLE STRESSES FOR COMPRESSION MEMBERS

L/r	Y.P. = 33000 psi Pinned Ends	Y.P. = 33000 psi Riveted Ends	Y.P. = 50000 psi Pinned Ends	Y.P. = 50000 psi Riveted Ends
	psi	psi	psi	psi
0	15000	15000	22500	22500
1	15000	15000	22500	22500
2	15000	15000	22500	22500
3	15000	15000	22490	22490
4	14990	15000	22490	22490
5	14990	14990	22480	22490
6	14990	14990	22470	22480
7	14980	14990	22460	22470
8	14980	14980	22450	22460
9	14970	14980	22440	22450
10	14970	14970	22430	22440
11	14960	14970	22410	22430
12	14950	14960	22390	22420
13	14950	14960	22380	22400
14	14940	14950	22360	22390
15	14930	14940	22330	22370
16	14920	14940	22310	22350
17	14910	14930	22290	22330
18	14890	14920	22260	22310
19	14880	14910	22230	22900
20	14870	14900	22200	22270
21	14860	14890	22170	22250
22	14840	14880	22140	22220
23	14830	14870	22110	22200
24	14810	14850	22070	22170
25	14800	14840	22040	22140
26	14780	14830	22000	22110
27	14760	14820	21960	22080
28	14750	14800	21920	22050
29	14730	14790	21880	22020
30	14710	14770	21840	21980
31	14690	14760	21790	21950
32	14670	14740	21740	21910
33	14650	14720	21700	21870
34	14620	14710	21650	21840
35	14600	14690	21600	21800
36	14580	14670	21540	21760
37	14560	14650	21490	21710
38	14530	14630	21430	21670
39	14510	14620	21380	21630
40	14480	14600	21320	21580

TABLE 5—Continued
ALLOWABLE STRESSES FOR COMPRESSION MEMBERS

L/r	Y.P. = 33000 psi		Y.P. = 50000 psi	
	Pinned Ends	Riveted Ends	Pinned Ends	Riveted Ends
	psi	psi	psi	psi
41	14450	14570	21260	21540
42	14430	14550	21200	21490
43	14400	14530	21140	21440
44	14370	14510	21070	21390
45	14340	14490	21010	21340
46	14310	14460	20940	21290
47	14280	14440	20870	21230
48	14250	14420	20800	21180
49	14220	14390	20730	21120
50	14190	14370	20660	21070
51	14150	14340	20580	21010
52	14120	14320	20500	20950
53	14090	14290	20430	20890
54	14050	14260	20350	20830
55	14020	14230	20270	20760
56	13980	14210	20190	20700
57	13940	14180	20100	20640
58	13910	14150	20020	20570
59	13870	14120	19930	20500
60	13830	14090	19840	20430
61	13790	14060	19750	20360
62	13750	14030	19660	20290
63	13710	14000	19570	20220
64	13670	13960	19480	20150
65	13630	13930	19380	20070
66	13580	13900	19290	20000
67	13540	13860	19190	19920
68	13500	13830	19090	19850
69	13450	13800	18990	19770
70	13410	13760	18880	19690
71	13360	13720	18780	19610
72	13320	13690	18670	19520
73	13270	13650	18570	19440
74	13220	13610	18460	19360
75	13170	13580	18350	19270
76	13120	13540	18240	19180
77	13070	13500	18120	19100
78	13020	13460	18010	19010
79	12970	13420	17890	18920
80	12920	13380	17780	18830

TABLE 5—Continued
ALLOWABLE STRESSES FOR COMPRESSION MEMBERS

L/r	Y.P. = 33000 psi		Y.P. = 50000 psi	
	Pinned Ends	Riveted Ends	Pinned Ends	Riveted Ends
	psi	psi	psi	psi
81	12870	13340	17660	18730
82	12810	13300	17540	18640
83	12760	13260	17420	18550
84	12710	13210	17290	18450
85	12650	13170	17170	18350
86	12600	13130	17040	18250
87	12540	13090	16910	18160
88	12480	13040	16780	18050
89	12430	13000	16650	17950
90	12370	12950	16520	17850
91	12310	12900	16390	17750
92	12250	12860	16250	17640
93	12190	12810	16120	17540
94	12130	12760	15980	17430
95	12070	12720	15840	17320
96	12000	12670	15700	17210
97	11940	12620	15560	17100
98	11880	12570	15410	16990
99	11810	12520	15270	16870
100	11750	12470	15120	16760
101	11680	12420	14970	16640
102	11620	12370	14820	16530
103	11550	12320	14670	16410
104	11480	12260	14520	16290
105	11420	12210	14360	16170
106	11350	12160	14210	16050
107	11280	12100	14050	15930
108	11210	12050	13890	15800
109	11140	11990	13730	15680
110	11070	11940	13570	15550
111	11000	11880	13410	15430
112	10920	11830	13240	15300
113	10850	11770	13080	15170
114	10780	11710	12910	15040
115	10700	11650	12750	14910
116	10630	11600	12600	14780
117	10550	11540	12440	14640
118	10470	11480	12290	14510
119	10400	11420	12140	14370
120	10320	11360	11990	14230

COMPRESSION

TABLE 5—Continued

ALLOWABLE STRESSES FOR COMPRESSION MEMBERS

L/r	Y.P. = 33000 psi Pinned Ends	Y.P. = 33000 psi Riveted Ends	Y.P. = 50000 psi Pinned Ends	Y.P. = 50000 psi Riveted Ends
	psi	psi	psi	psi
121	10240	11300	11840	14100
122	10160	11230	11700	13960
123	10080	11170	11560	13820
124	10000	11110	11420	13670
125	9920	11050	11290	13530
126	9840	10980	11150	13380
127	9760	10920	11020	13240
128	9680	10850	10890	13090
129	9590	10790	10760	12950
130	9510	10720	10630	12800
131	9420	10660	10510	12660
132	9340	10590	10390	12530
133	9250	10520	10270	12390
134	9160	10460	10150	12260
135	9080	10390	10030	12120
136	8990	10320	9920	11990
137	8900	10250	9810	11860
138	8810	10180	9700	11740
134	8720	10110	9590	11610
140	8630	10040	9480	11490
141	8550	9970	9370	11370
142	8470	9900	9270	11250
143	8380	9830	9170	11130
144	8300	9750	9060	11010
145	8220	9680	8960	10900
146	8130	9610	8870	10790
147	8050	9530	8770	10680
148	7970	9460	8670	10570
149	7900	9380	8580	10460
150	7820	9310	8490	10350
151	7740	9230	8400	10240
152	7670	9150	8310	10140
153	7590	9080	8220	10040
154	7520	9000	8130	9940
155	7440	8920	8040	9840
156	7370	8850	7960	9740
157	7300	8770	7880	9640
158	7230	8690	7790	9540
159	7160	8620	7710	9450
160	7100	8540	7630	9360

TABLE 5—Concluded
ALLOWABLE STRESSES FOR COMPRESSION MEMBERS

L/r	Y.P. = 33000 psi Pinned Ends	Y.P. = 33000 psi Riveted Ends	Y.P. = 50000 psi Pinned Ends	Y.P. = 50000 psi Riveted Ends
	psi	psi	psi	psi
161	7030	8460	7560	9260
162	6960	8390	7480	9170
163	6900	8310	7400	9080
164	6830	8240	7330	9000
165	6770	8170	7250	8910
166	6700	8100	7180	8820
167	6640	8030	7110	8740
168	6580	7960	7040	8650
169	6520	7890	6970	8570
170	6460	7820	6900	8490
171	6400	7750	6830	8410
172	6340	7680	6760	8330
173	6280	7620	6690	8250
174	6230	7550	6630	8170
175	6170	7490	6560	8100
176	6110	7420	6500	8020
177	6060	7360	6440	7950
178	6010	7300	6380	7870
179	5950	7240	6310	7800
180	5900	7180	6250	7730
181	5850	7110	6190	7660
182	5790	7060	6140	7590
183	5740	7000	6080	7520
184	5690	6940	6020	7450
185	5640	6880	5970	7390
186	5590	6820	5910	7320
187	5550	6770	5850	7250
188	5500	6710	5800	7190
189	5450	6660	5750	7130
190	5400	6600	5690	7060
191	5360	6550	5640	7000
192	5310	6490	5590	6940
193	5270	6440	5540	6880
194	5220	6390	5490	6820
195	5180	6340	5440	6760
196	5130	6290	5390	6700
197	5090	6240	5340	6640
198	5050	6190	5300	6590
199	5010	6140	5250	6530
200	4960	6090	5200	6470

COMPRESSION

Example 2

A built-up column of high-strength steel whose cross section is shown in the figure is 10 feet long and acts as a pin-ended column. For a steel with a yield point of 50,000 psi, find the maximum axially applied load for the column, using a factor of safety of approximately 1.80 and assuming the column to be braced about the YY axis.

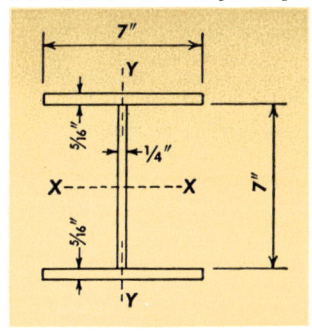

$A = 6.13$ in.^{2}
$I = 65.67$ in.^{4}
$r = 3.27$ in.
$$\frac{L}{r} = \frac{10 \times 12}{3.27} = 36.7$$

From Table 5, for Y.P. = 50,000 psi and pinned ends, interpolating for $L/r = 36.7$, $P/A = 21,500$ psi.

Therefore,
$$P = 21,500 \times 6.13 = 132,000 \text{ lb.}$$

If the factor of safety were 1.65, the allowable load would be $\frac{132,000 \times 1.80}{1.65} = 144,000$ lb.

Example 3

The cross section shown in the figure is to be used as a pin-ended column where the unbraced length is 10 feet about both the X and Y axes. For the purpose of further illustrating the use of the chart in Fig. 4, this example is divided into three parts, in each of which one of the factors is different.

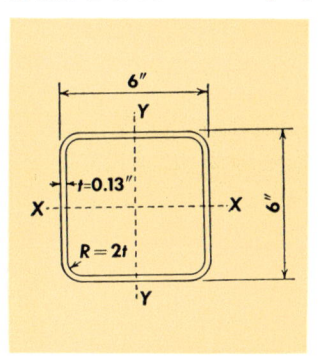

$A = 2.98$ in.^{2}
$I_x = I_y = 16.89$ in.^{4}
$r_x = r_y = 2.38$ in.

(a) Assume the maximum compressive unit stress to be 43,000 psi. With a factor of safety of 1.80, what would be the safe axially applied load on the column?

$$\frac{L'}{r} = \frac{KL}{r} = \frac{0.85 \times 10 \times 12}{2.38} = 42.9.$$

To obtain the proper column formula, enter the Column Formula Chart, Fig. 4, with $s_y = 43,000$ psi and $N = 1.80$. (Whenever the maximum limiting stress is less than the yield point of the steel it should be regarded as a reduced yield point.) It is seen that $\frac{L'}{r} = 42.9$ is less than $R = 103$, therefore the column will be in the range $0 < \frac{L'}{r} < R$ and the values of B and C are read as

$B = 19,100 \qquad C = 0.75$

$$\frac{P}{A} = 19,100 - 0.75\left(\frac{L'}{r}\right)^2$$

$$\frac{P}{A} = 19{,}100 - 0.75\,(42.9)^2 = 17{,}700 \text{ psi.}$$

$$P = 17{,}700 \times 2.98 = 52{,}700 \text{ lb max safe load.}$$

(b) If in part (a) the maximum compressive stress were limited to 33,000 psi, what would be the safe load?

From Fig. 4, with $s_y = 33{,}000$ psi and $N = 1.80$, $R = 118$.

$$0 < \frac{L'}{r} < 118, \quad \frac{P}{A} = 14{,}700 - 0.44\left(\frac{L'}{r}\right)^2$$

$$\frac{P}{A} = 14{,}700 - 0.44\,(42.9)^2 = 13{,}900 \text{ psi.}$$

$$P = 13{,}900 \times 2.98 = 41{,}400 \text{ lb max safe load.}$$

Note that the column loads are not proportional to maximum compressive stresses, i.e., $\dfrac{43{,}000}{33{,}000} \neq \dfrac{52{,}700}{41{,}400}$.

(c) If the conditions were the same as in part (a) except that the factor of safety is reduced to 1.65, what is the maximum safe load for the column?

From Fig. 4, with $s_y = 43{,}000$ psi and $N = 1.65$

$$\frac{P}{A} = 20{,}800 - 0.81\left(\frac{L'}{r}\right)^2$$

$$\frac{P}{A} = 20{,}800 - 0.81\,(42.9)^2 = 19{,}300 \text{ psi.}$$

$$P = 19{,}300 \times 2.98 = 57{,}500 \text{ lb max safe load.}$$

Note that column loads are proportional to factor of safety, i.e., $\dfrac{57{,}500}{52{,}700} = \dfrac{1.80}{1.65}$.

Considerable saving in the weight of compression members can be effected by the use of high-strength steels. In making an actual comparison of column strengths, comparable formulas (such as those in Tables 3 and 4) and the same factor of safety must be used.

A comparison of the possible savings in the cross-sectional area and weight of axially loaded columns, using high-strength steels, is shown in the chart of Fig. 5, where the base is ordinary structural carbon steel with a yield point equal to 33,000 psi. These savings are the averages obtained for columns with pinned ends and with riveted ends, using the formulas of Tables 3 and 4. In the range of $L/r = 0$ to 120, commonly specified for main compression members, the per cent saving in column areas is seen to be appreciable.

ECCENTRICALLY LOADED COLUMNS

In the discussion of columns thus far it has been assumed that the loads are axially applied and thereby do not produce any intentional bending in the column. Many columns are subjected to loading conditions which produce a definite bending moment in the

FIG. 5 COMPARISON OF COLUMN AREAS

X-axis: VALUES OF L/r (0 to 200)
Y-axis: SAVING IN COLUMN AREAS (per cent) (0 to 40)

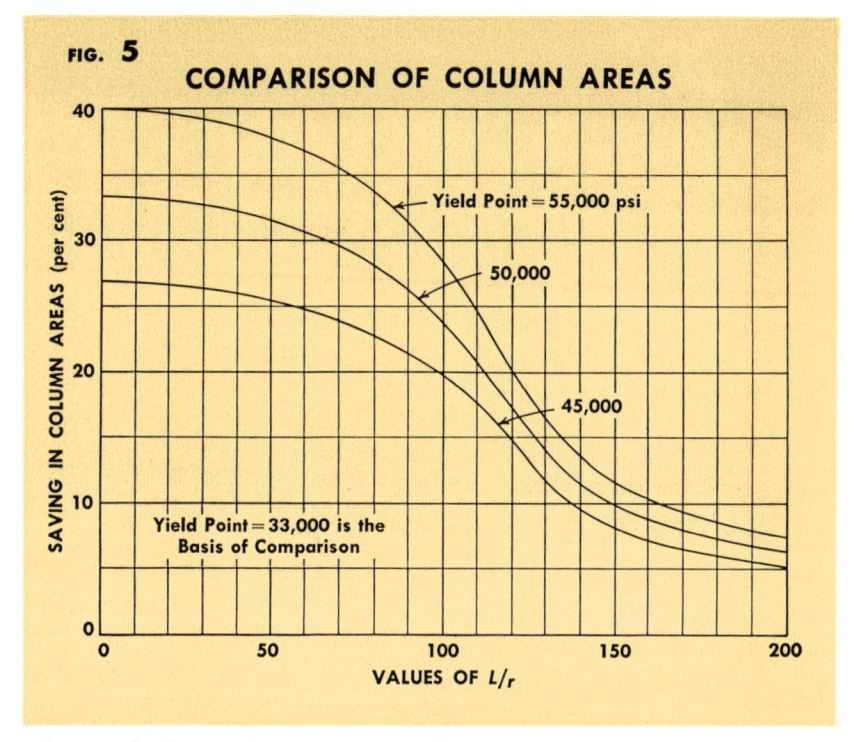

Curves shown for Yield Point = 55,000 psi; 50,000; 45,000. Yield Point = 33,000 is the Basis of Comparison.

column. Such members are treated as eccentrically loaded columns and include members which support compressive loads applied eccentrically to the longitudinal axis, as well as those subjected to end moments. Column loads may produce bending about one or both principal axes. The problem is treated as one of combined stress and, for the case of eccentricity about one axis only, the maximum fiber stress is given by Formula 3, substituting s_{max} for Yield Point,

$$s_{max} = \frac{P'}{A}\left\{1 + \frac{ec}{r^2}\sec\left[\sqrt{\frac{P'}{AE}}\left(\frac{L'}{2r}\right)\right]\right\}.$$

Any combination of column loads and end moments may be reduced to a single axial load P', equal to the sum of the loads, and a couple whose moment, $P'e$, is equal to the sum of the moments of the eccentric loads and end moments, where e is the equivalent eccentricity. Illustrations of this principle are shown in Fig. 6.

In the design of an eccentrically loaded column, it is best to deal with the ultimate loads, which may be readily obtained by multiplying the working loads by the factor of safety. Conversely, the working loads may be obtained by dividing the ultimate loads by the factor of safety.

FIG. 6
EQUIVALENT ECCENTRIC LOADS FOR COLUMNS

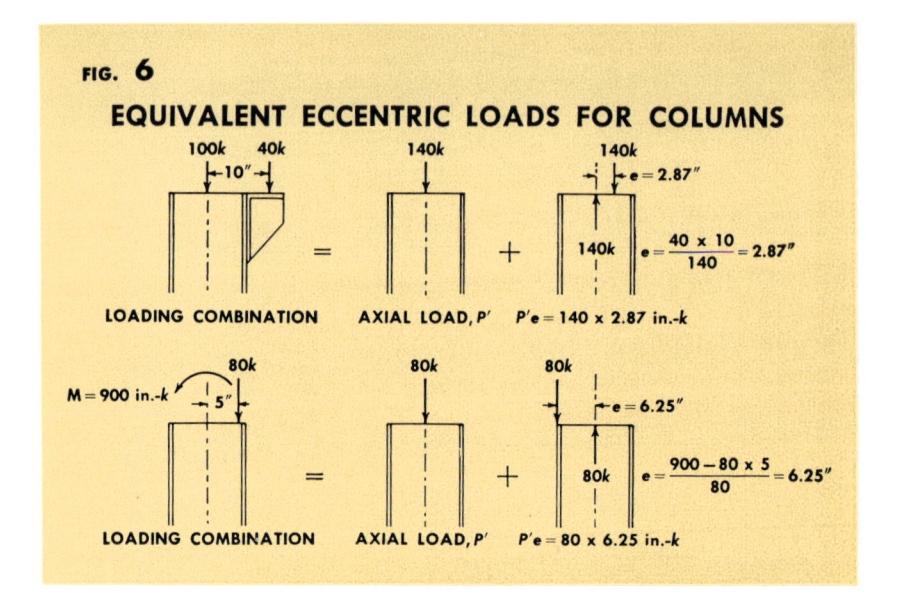

[Figure showing loading combinations equivalent to axial load plus eccentric load:

Top row: 100k + 40k at 10" offset = 140k axial + 140k with e = 2.87"
$$e = \frac{40 \times 10}{140} = 2.87''$$
$P'e = 140 \times 2.87$ in.-k

Bottom row: M = 900 in.-k with 80k at 5" = 80k axial + 80k with e = 6.25"
$$e = \frac{900 - 80 \times 5}{80} = 6.25''$$
$P'e = 80 \times 6.25$ in.-k]

The load P' in Formula 3 is the critical or ultimate load which will produce the limiting fiber stress, $s_{\max}$. In the eccentric ratio, ec/r^2, e is the eccentricity and the remainder of the term c/r^2 is numerically equal to the area of the section divided by the section modulus, S, on the axis about which the bending takes place. This ratio, A/S, is called the bending factor and its values for column sections are given in the "Steel Construction Manual of the American Institute of Steel Construction."

The value of ec/r^2, as calculated from the loading conditions, should be increased by the factor 0.25 which the ASCE Special Committee on Steel Column Research suggested as an allowance for initial crookedness and unintentional eccentricity.

The design of eccentrically loaded columns is a trial procedure in which column sections are analyzed until one is found which satisfies the secant formula as modified in Formula 3. Only a comparison of satisfactory sections will determine the one with the least weight. The labor involved in this procedure may be greatly simplified by the use of nomographs.

Formula 3 may be put in a form adapted to nomographic construction by multiplying the terms $s_{\max}$ and $\dfrac{P'}{A}$ by $\left(\dfrac{L'}{r}\right)^2$. The resulting expression is,

$$s_{\max}\left(\frac{L'}{r}\right)^2 = \frac{P'}{A}\left(\frac{L'}{r}\right)^2 \left[1 + \frac{ec}{r^2}\sec\sqrt{\frac{1}{4E} \times \frac{P'}{A}\left(\frac{L'}{r}\right)^2}\,\right]. \quad (6)$$

COMPRESSION

The three variable terms, $s_{max}\left(\dfrac{L'}{r}\right)^2$, $\dfrac{P'}{A}\left(\dfrac{L'}{r}\right)^2$ and $\dfrac{ec}{r^2}$ may be incorporated in such nomographic charts as those in Figs. 7 and 8. The first chart covers the range of $s_{max}\left(\dfrac{L'}{r}\right)^2$ from 0 to 900×10^6 psi. Since the lines joining low values of $s_{max}\left(\dfrac{L'}{r}\right)^2$ and $\dfrac{ec}{r^2}$ intersect the $\dfrac{P'}{A}\left(\dfrac{L'}{r}\right)^2$ scale at sharp angles, readings of the latter are subject to some inaccuracy. The supplementary chart in Fig. 8 covers the range of $s_{max}\left(\dfrac{L'}{r}\right)^2$ from 0 to 100×10^6 psi and provides for a more accurate reading of the value of $\dfrac{P'}{A}\left(\dfrac{L'}{r}\right)^2$. The use of these charts is illustrated in the following example.

Example 4

A 14 WF column with an effective length of 12 ft carries a concentric load of 300 kips and an eccentric load of 50 kips applied 18 inches from the major axis. Design the column using high-strength steel with a yield point of 50,000 psi and a factor of safety of 1.65 based on the critical load.

$$\text{Equivalent axial load } P = 300 + 50 = 350 \text{ kips}$$
$$\text{Equivalent eccentricity} = \frac{50 \times 18}{350} = 2.57 \text{ in.}$$
$$\text{Critical axial load } P' = 350 \times 1.65 = 577.5 \text{ kips}$$

The first step is the determination of an approximate value of $\dfrac{ec}{r^2}$. The value of $\dfrac{c}{r^2}$, which is equal to $\dfrac{A}{S}$, may be readily calculated by selecting an average column section, as for example a 14 WF 111, and using its area and section modulus, giving $\dfrac{A}{S_x} = \dfrac{32.65}{176.3}$ = 0.185. The radius of gyration for this section is $r_x = 6.23$.

$$\frac{L'}{r_x} = \frac{12 \times 12}{6.23} = 23.1 \qquad \frac{ec}{r_x^2} = 2.57 \times 0.185 = 0.475$$

$$\left(\frac{L'}{r_x}\right)^2 = 533.6 \qquad \begin{array}{l}\text{Allowance for} \\ \text{initial crookedness} = 0.250\end{array}$$

$$\text{Total value of } \frac{ec}{r_x^2} = 0.725$$

$$s_{max}\left(\frac{L'}{r_x}\right)^2 = 50{,}000 \times 533.6 = 26{,}700{,}000 \text{ psi.}$$

Since this value is less than 100,000,000 use the chart in Fig. 8, and read

$$\frac{P'}{A}\left(\frac{L'}{r_x}\right)^2 = 15{,}200{,}000 \text{ psi.}$$

COMPRESSION

Solving for the required area,
$$A = \frac{577{,}500 \times 533.6}{15{,}200{,}000} = 20.3 \text{ sq in.}$$

A 14 WF 74 section has an area of 21.76 sq in. and will be examined. For this section $r_x = 6.05$ and $S_x = 112.3$. When a specific section is being examined, calculate $\frac{P'}{A}\left(\frac{L'}{r}\right)^2$ and read $s_{\max}\left(\frac{L'}{r}\right)^2$ from the chart.

$$\frac{L'}{r_x} = \frac{144}{6.05} = 23.8$$

$$\left(\frac{L'}{r_x}\right)^2 = 566.4$$

$$\frac{ec}{r_x^2} = \frac{2.57 \times 21.76}{112.3} + 0.25 = 0.748$$

$$\frac{P'}{A}\left(\frac{L'}{r_x}\right)^2 = \frac{577{,}500 \times 566.4}{21.76} = 15{,}000{,}000 \text{ psi.}$$

From Fig. 8, read $s_{\max}\left(\frac{L'}{r_x}\right)^2 = 26{,}700{,}000$ psi.

$$s_{\max} = \frac{26{,}700{,}000}{566.4} = 47{,}100 \text{ psi} < 50{,}000 \text{ psi.}$$

Therefore, 14 WF 74 is satisfactory.

The next lightest column, 14 WF 68, gives a stress, $s_{\max}$, of 51,700 psi. Use 14 WF 74.

Had a 12 in. column section been selected the problem would have required a 12 WF 79, indicating that the 14 WF 74 is more economical.

The section should also be investigated about the weak axis, Y-Y. Since there is no intentional eccentricity of load application about this axis, the column should be treated as concentrically loaded. The formulas for the average stress may be determined from the chart of Fig. 4. As the investigation has been made for the critical load, the factor of safety, N, is equal to unity.

With $s_y = 50{,}000$ psi and $N = 1$:
$$\frac{NP}{A} = \frac{P'}{A} = 40{,}000 - 1.82\left(\frac{L'}{r}\right)^2.$$

For the 14 WF 74 section, $r_y = 2.48$ in.
$$\frac{L'}{r} = \frac{L'}{r_y} = \frac{12 \times 12}{2.48} = 58.1$$

$$\frac{P'}{A} = 40{,}000 - 1.82\,(58.1)^2 = 33{,}860 \text{ psi.}$$

The actual value of $\frac{P'}{A}$ is $\frac{577{,}500}{21.76} = 26{,}540$ psi $< 33{,}860$ psi.

Therefore the section is satisfactory about the weak axis.

COMPRESSION

In general, when the value of L'/r for the axis perpendicular to the bending axis is greater than the value of L'/r about the bending axis, the column section should also be investigated for the case of a concentrically loaded column having the greater value of L'/r.

When a column is loaded eccentrically with respect to both axes, the maximum stress becomes

$$s_{\max} = \frac{P'}{A}\left\{1 + \frac{e_x c_x}{r_x^2}\sec\left[\sqrt{\frac{P'}{AE}}\left(\frac{L'}{2r_x}\right)\right] + \frac{e_y c_y}{r_y^2}\sec\left[\sqrt{\frac{P'}{AE}}\left(\frac{L'}{2r_y}\right)\right]\right\}, \quad (6a)$$

in which the subscripts refer to the principal axes. This formula may also be solved by the use of Figs. 7 and 8. In doing so, the sum of the combined stresses found by considering each axis individually must be reduced by the value of P'/A. Thus,

$$s_{\max} = s_x + s_y - P'/A,$$

where s_x and s_y equal the combined stress as found by Formula 3 for column action about the X-X and Y-Y axes respectively.

Example 5

Determine the maximum fiber stress in the 12 WF 58 column due to a longitudinally applied ultimate load of 158 kips as shown in the figure. The effective length of the column is 15 feet for both axes.

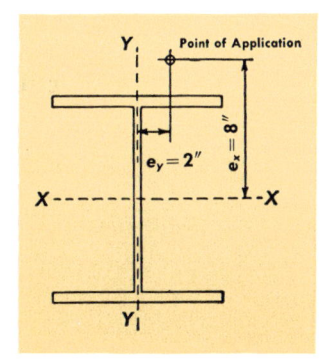

12 WF 58
$A = 17.06$ in.²
$r_x = 5.28$ in. $r_y = 2.51$ in.
$S_x = 78.1$ in.³ $S_y = 21.4$ in.³

Then $\dfrac{P'}{A} = \dfrac{158{,}000}{17.06} = 9260$ psi.

Bending about Axis X-X

$\dfrac{e_x c_x}{r_x^2} = \dfrac{8 \times 17.06}{78.1} + 0.25 = 1.998$

$\left(\dfrac{L'}{r_x}\right)^2 = \left(\dfrac{15 \times 12}{5.28}\right)^2 = 1162.2$

$\dfrac{P'}{A} \times \left(\dfrac{L'}{r_x}\right)^2 = 10.763 \times 10^6$ psi

From chart in Fig. 8,

$s_{\max}\left(\dfrac{L'}{r_x}\right)^2 = 33.3 \times 10^6$ psi

$s_{\max} = s_x = 28{,}650$ psi.

Bending about Axis Y-Y

$\dfrac{e_y c_y}{r_y^2} = \dfrac{2 \times 17.06}{21.4} + 0.25 = 1.844$

$\left(\dfrac{L'}{r_y}\right)^2 = \left(\dfrac{15 \times 12}{2.51}\right)^2 = 5142.8$

$\dfrac{P'}{A} \times \left(\dfrac{L'}{r_y}\right)^2 = 47.627 \times 10^6$ psi

From chart in Fig. 7,

$s_{\max}\left(\dfrac{L'}{r_y}\right)^2 = 157 \times 10^6$ psi

$s_{\max} = s_y = 30{,}530$ psi.

The total combined stress, $s_{\max} = s_x + s_y - P'/A$

$s_{\max} = 28{,}650 + 30{,}530 - 9260 = 49{,}920$ psi.

FIG. 7

MAXIMUM STRESS
ECCENTRICALLY LOADED COMPRESSION MEMBERS

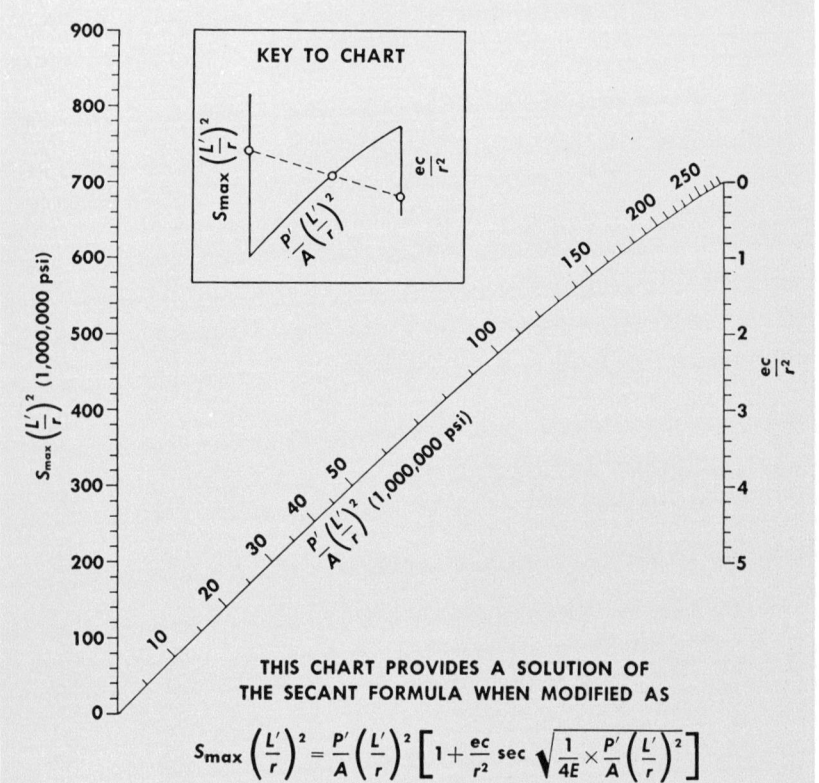

THIS CHART PROVIDES A SOLUTION OF THE SECANT FORMULA WHEN MODIFIED AS

$$S_{max}\left(\frac{L'}{r}\right)^2 = \frac{P'}{A}\left(\frac{L'}{r}\right)^2\left[1 + \frac{ec}{r^2}\sec\sqrt{\frac{1}{4E} \times \frac{P'}{A}\left(\frac{L'}{r}\right)^2}\right]$$

in which

S_{max} = maximum fiber stress, equal to yield point, unless governed by local or lateral buckling, (psi)

P' = ultimate column load, equal to working column load, P' times the factor of safety, (lb)

A = cross-sectional area of member, (in.²)

L' = effective column length, (in.)

E = modulus of elasticity, (29,000,000 psi)

e = total eccentricity of load, normal plus intentional (in.)

c* = distance from neutral axis to most stressed fiber in compression, (in.)

r* = radius of gyration, (in.)

*c and r are referred to the same neutral axis from which eccentricity, e, is given.

FIG. 8

MAXIMUM STRESS
ECCENTRICALLY LOADED COMPRESSION MEMBERS

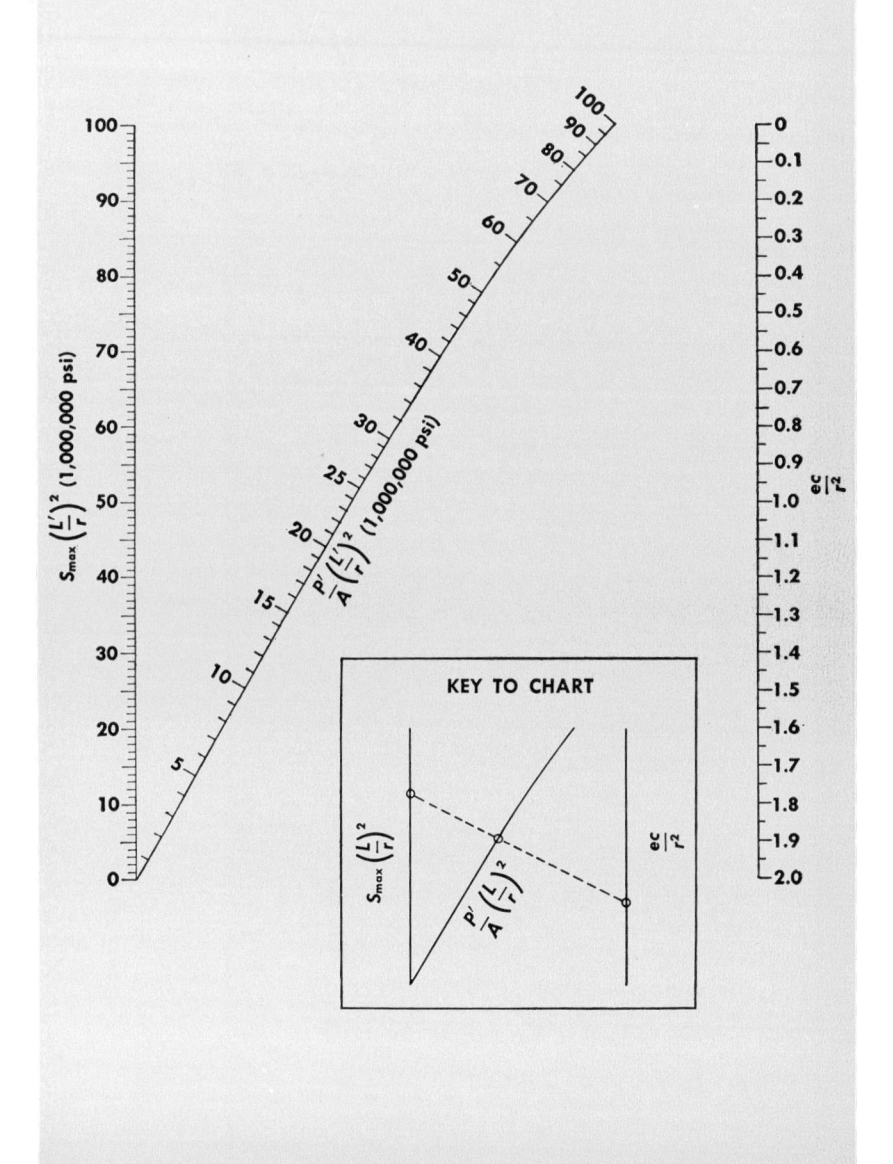

FLAT PLATES IN EDGE COMPRESSION

The treatment of compression members, thus far, has assumed that failure occurs by buckling of the entire member. When some of the component parts of a structural member are thin flat sections, it is possible for local buckling to occur in a short length of one such section, due to its elastic instability under the action of a compressive load. The buckling of a flat plate does not necessarily mean failure of the entire member, because it often occurs while the member is still capable of carrying additional load.

The problem in design can be treated in two ways, depending upon whether it is desired to prevent or to permit local buckling. The choice will depend upon the structure and the possible need, because of appearance, to prevent any buckles. Both methods will be treated in the text to follow.

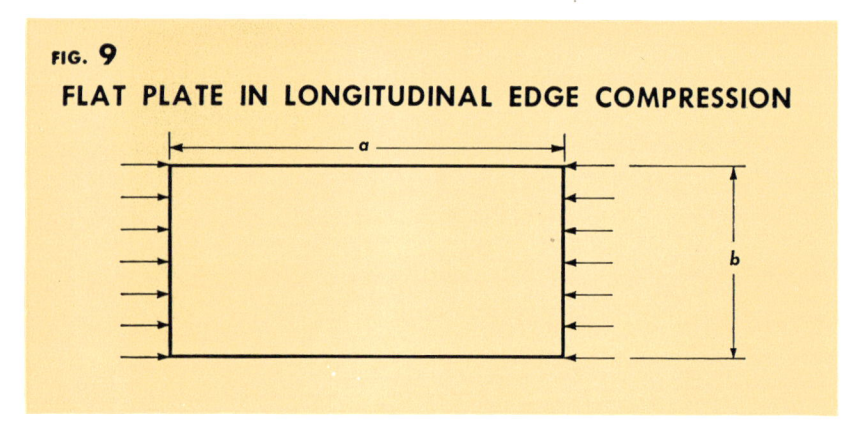

FIG. 9

FLAT PLATE IN LONGITUDINAL EDGE COMPRESSION

The critical buckling stress in a flat plate in edge compression, as shown in Fig. 9, is the stress at which buckling is imminent, and is given by the formula

$$s_{cr} = \frac{k\pi^2 E}{12(1-\mu^2)} \times \frac{t^2}{b^2}, \tag{7}$$

in which
- s_{cr} = critical unit compressive stress, psi
- E = modulus of elasticity (Young's), psi
- μ = Poisson's ratio
- b = width of plate, in.
- t = thickness of plate, in.
- k = non-dimensional plate coefficient.

The curve EF in Fig. 10 represents the value of s_{cr} in terms of $\dfrac{b/t}{\sqrt{k}}$.

Present-day analysis of buckling treats the subject according to whether the critical stress is less than the proportional limit, when the buckling is said to be elastic, or above the proportional limit, when the buckling is inelastic. In the elastic range, the value of the modulus of elasticity (Young's) of the material remains constant. In the inelastic range, it is common practice to use the tangent modulus of elasticity, which becomes increasingly less than Young's modulus as the stress increases. The yield point, s_y, is considered the limiting maximum value of the critical stress.

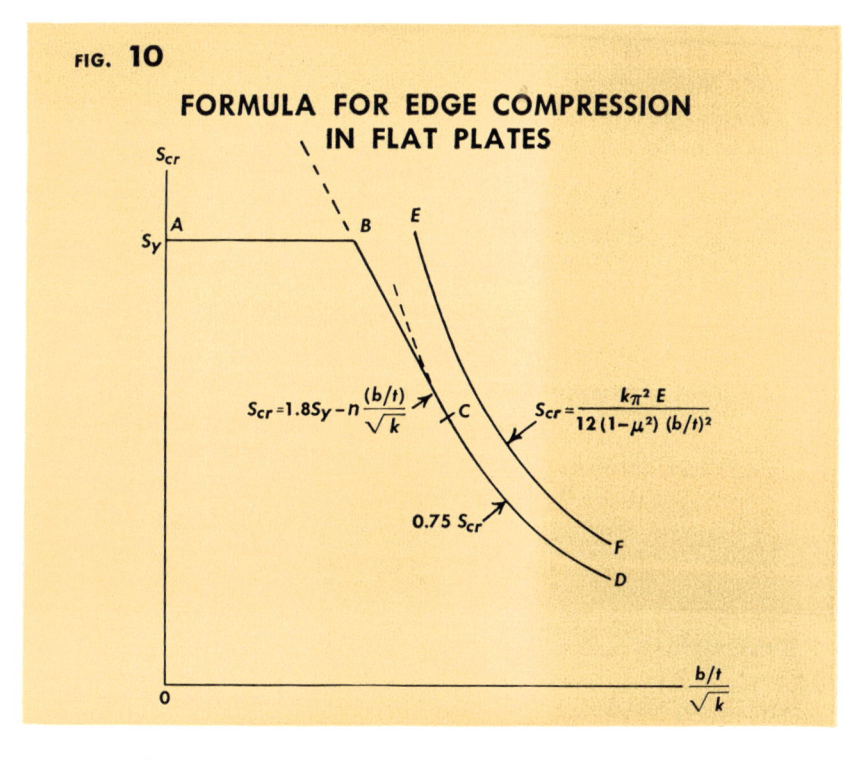

FIG. 10

FORMULA FOR EDGE COMPRESSION IN FLAT PLATES

$$S_{cr} = 1.8 S_y - n \frac{(b/t)}{\sqrt{k}}$$

$$S_{cr} = \frac{k\pi^2 E}{12(1-\mu^2)(b/t)^2}$$

$0.75\ S_{cr}$

Available test data indicate that the critical buckling stress is less than that given by the theoretical formula. The line $ABCD$ in Fig. 10 is suggested as giving values of s_{cr} in reasonable agreement with average test values. For the portion CD, s_{cr} equals 75 per cent of the theoretical value of s_{cr} given by Formula 7, while the line BC represents the expression, $s_{cr} = 1.8\ s_y - n\left(\frac{b/t}{\sqrt{k}}\right)$ and the portion AB is horizontal at $s_{cr} = s_y$.

The following tabulation gives the expressions for the three portions of the curve $ABCD$ and the limits of $\left(\frac{b/t}{\sqrt{k}}\right)$ within which each is applicable.

COMPRESSION

s_{cr} (psi)	$b/t \over \sqrt{k}$	
s_y	0 to $\dfrac{3820}{\sqrt{s_y}}$	(8a)
$1.8\,s_y - n\left(\dfrac{b/t}{\sqrt{k}}\right)$ constant $n = \dfrac{\sqrt{s_y^{\,3}}}{4770}$	$\dfrac{3820}{\sqrt{s_y}}$ to $\dfrac{5720}{\sqrt{s_y}}$	(8b)
$\dfrac{19{,}660{,}000\,k}{(b/t)^2}$	$\dfrac{5720}{\sqrt{s_y}}$ and over	(8c)

For a selected list of yield points, the values of $\dfrac{b/t}{\sqrt{k}}$ at points B and C in Fig. 10 and of n are given in Table 6.

Table 6
VALUES OF FACTORS IN FORMULA 8

s_y psi	$\dfrac{b/t}{\sqrt{k}}$ at Pt. B	$\dfrac{b/t}{\sqrt{k}}$ at Pt. C	n
33000	21.0	31.5	1260
45000	18.0	27.0	2000
50000	17.1	25.6	2340
55000	16.3	24.4	2700

A nomograph for the portion of the plot BC is given in Fig. 11. The portion AB is covered by the provision that s_{cr} shall not exceed s_y. Normally, conditions will not be encountered to warrant the use of the section CD. To guard against using the chart beyond point C, the maximum values of the ratio $\dfrac{(b/t)^2}{k}$ are indicated for various values of s_y.

The non-dimensional coefficient k depends upon the ratio a/b, Fig. 9, and the condition of the plate edge supports. It has been found, both analytically and experimentally, that when the ratio of length to width of plate is greater than 5, as is the case in most practical problems, the strength of the plate is independent of the length. For values of the ratio less than 5, the value of k increases, but it is common and conservative practice to disregard the increase. This leaves the condition of the edge supports as the controlling factor.

FIG. 11

CRITICAL COMPRESSIVE STRESS
FOR FLAT PLATES IN EDGE COMPRESSION

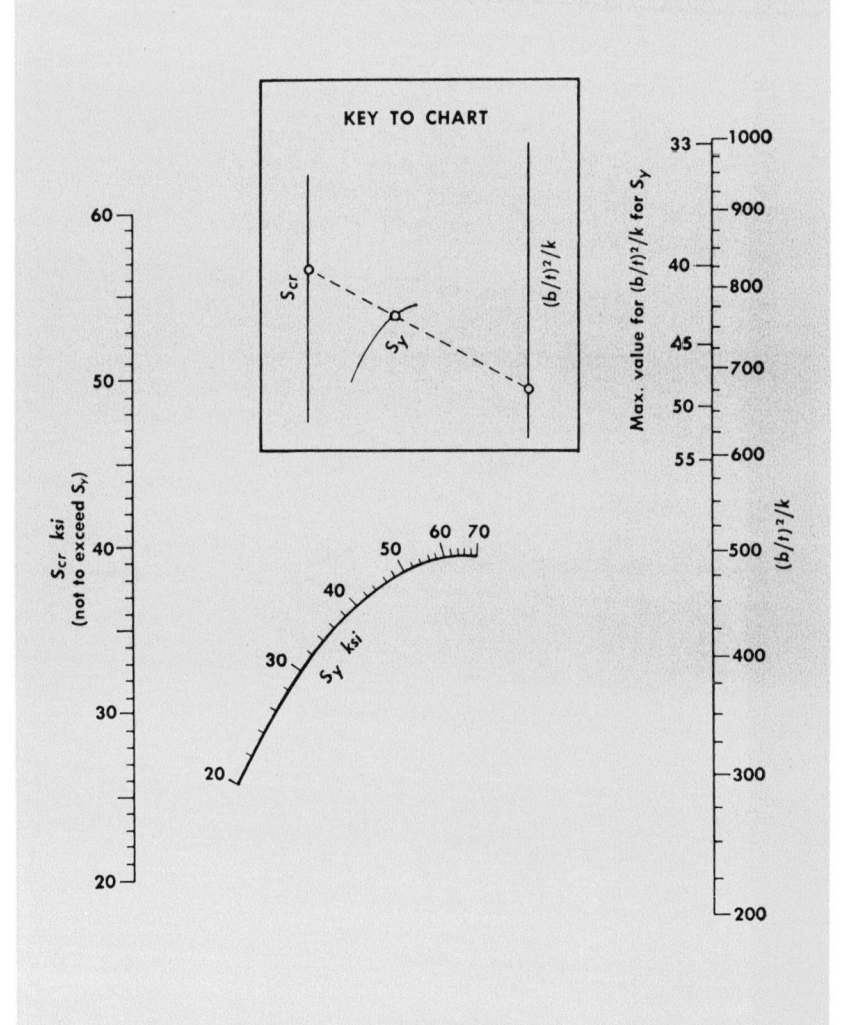

Fig. 12 illustrates several types of edge supports. Fig. 12a is representative of simply supported edges. Neither is a practical joint, but they have been used in many tests to provide freedom of rotation about the longitudinal axes of the edges, while maintaining the edges in alignment. Fig. 12b represents a fixed edge condition in which rotation is prevented. In actual practice, the edge supports of flat plates are within these two extremes, unless the edge is unsupported, or free. Fig. 12c shows several cross sections made up of flat surfaces with designations of the type of edge support commonly assumed in design. Simply supported edges are designated by S and free edges by F.

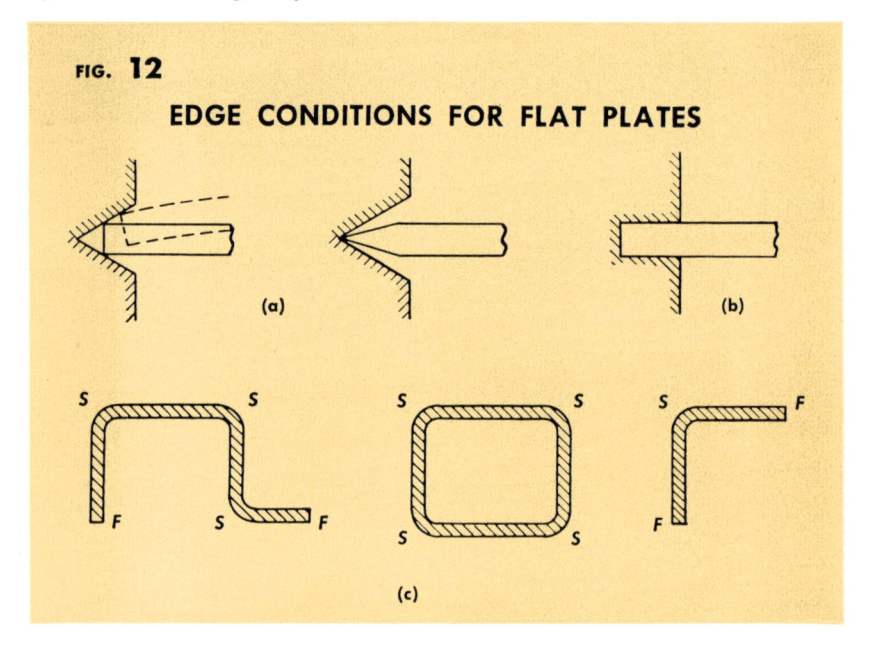

FIG. 12

EDGE CONDITIONS FOR FLAT PLATES

The values of k for various conditions of edge support, as given by Bleich,* are:

1. One edge simply supported, the other free, $k = 0.425$.
2. One edge fixed, the other free, $k = 1.277$.
3. Both edges simply supported, $k = 4.00$.
4. One edge simply supported, the other fixed, $k = 5.42$.
5. Both edges fixed, $k = 6.97$.

The choice of a value for k must depend, in large measure, upon the judgment of the designing engineer. Complete fixity of the edges is rarely achieved. Unless one is interested in securing the

---

*"Buckling Strength of Metal Structures" by F. Bleich, McGraw-Hill Book Co., New York, N. Y., 1st Ed., 1952, Table 26, p. 330.

very minimum of weight and is prepared to select the proper value of the coefficient applicable to his proposed condition, it will be simpler and more practical to assume all supported edges to be simply supported. Thus, for most structural members, the plate elements will come under either condition (1) or (3) above. When the values of k for these two cases are substituted in Formulas 8a, 8b and 8c the formulas in Table 7 are obtained for the two grades of steel shown.

Table 7

FORMULAS FOR CRITICAL UNIT STRESS IN FLAT PLATES IN EDGE COMPRESSION

Yield Point S_y psi	k	b/t	S_{cr} psi
33,000	0.425	0–13.7 13.7–20.5 Over 20.5	33,000 $59,400 - 1930(b/t)$ $\dfrac{8,360,000}{(b/t)^2}$
33,000	4.00	0–42.0 42.0–63.0 Over 63.0	33,000 $59,400 - 630(b/t)$ $\dfrac{78,640,000}{(b/t)^2}$
50,000	0.425	0–11.1 11.1–16.7 Over 16.7	50,000 $90,000 - 3600(b/t)$ $\dfrac{8,360,000}{(b/t)^2}$
50,000	4.00	0–34.2 34.2–51.2 Over 51.2	50,000 $90,000 - 1170(b/t)$ $\dfrac{78,640,000}{(b/t)^2}$

It is common practice in writing specifications, to include clauses that limit the ratio of b/t to certain maximum values, based on simply supported and free edges, at which the critical stress for the plate is equal to the yield point of the steel covered by the specifications (Point B, Fig. 10). By keeping within the maximum values given by such clauses, it is not necessary to calculate the buckling stress of the plate.

Comparisons between the limiting ratios given by a few widely used specifications and the suggestions of this Manual (Table 7) are shown in Table 8.

Table 8
SPECIFICATION REQUIREMENTS
MAXIMUM VALUES OF RATIO b/t

Edge Conditions	Yield Point	Table 7	AREA[1] Specs.	AISC[2] Specs.	AASHO[3] Specs.
Both simply supported	33,000	42.0	40	40	40
	50,000	34.2	32	..	34
One simply supported, the other free	33,000	13.7	12	12	12
	50,000	11.1	..	..	..

1. American Railway Engineering Association.
2. American Institute of Steel Construction.
3. American Association of State Highway Officials.

Practice varies with regard to the determination of the plate width, b. In riveted or welded construction, the width, b, is generally taken as the distance between rivet lines or lines of welds, as illustrated in Figs. 13a and 13b.

In rolled sections, such as beams, channels, angles, zees and cold formed and pressed sections, a common assumption for b is the distance measured from the edges of the fillets, as in Figs. 13c, 13d, and 13e. Fig. 13e is the practice used for cold formed sections in the "Specifications for the Design of Light Gage Steel Structural Members," published in April 1946, by the American Iron and Steel Institute.

A somewhat more conservative assumption is that of measuring the distance from the roots of the fillets, as in Figs. 13f, 13g, and 13h.

Still another assumption is to take the overall distance, as in Figs. 13i, 13j, and 13k.

Example 6

Determine the critical compressive stress for local buckling of the plate elements in the column section of Example 2, using the simplifying assumptions as to the plate coefficient, k, where $s_y = 50{,}000$ psi.

Outstanding Flange:

Assume one edge simply supported and the other free. $k = 0.425$

Taking $b = 3.50 - \frac{1}{2}$ web thickness $= 3.375$ in.,
$$\frac{b}{t} = \frac{3.375}{0.3125} = 10.8.$$

COMPRESSION

FIG. **13**

ASSUMED WIDTHS OF PLATE ELEMENTS

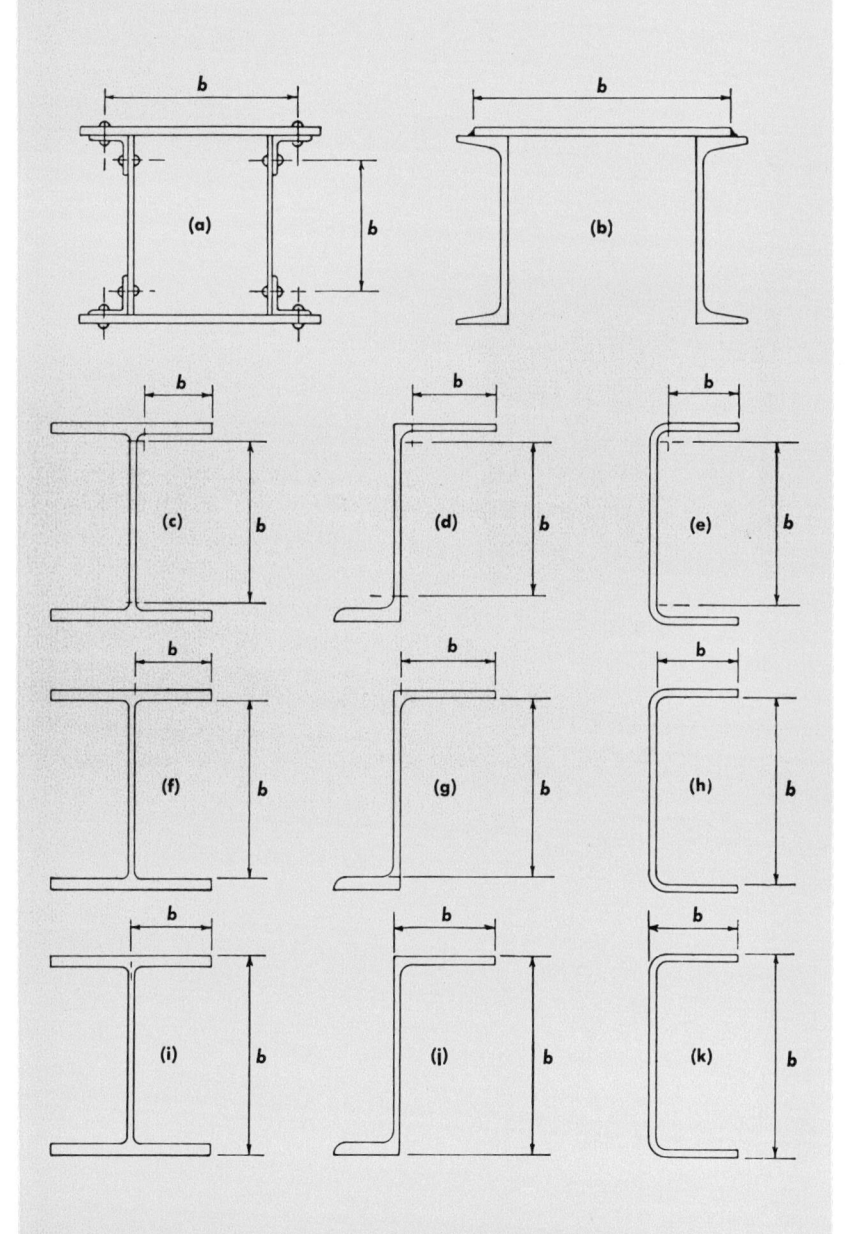

From Table 7, since $b/t = 10.8 < 11.1$, $s_{cr} = s_y = 50{,}000$ psi.

Web:

Assume both edges simply supported. $k = 4.00$

$$\frac{b}{t} = \frac{7.00}{0.25} = 28.0.$$

From Table 7, since $b/t < 34.2$, $s_{cr} = s_y = 50{,}000$ psi.

Since the critical compressive stress for the flanges and the web is equal to the yield point, the column as a whole may be designed on the basis of the yield point, as was done in Example 2.

Example 7

If the flange width of the column section in Example 2 is increased to 9 inches as shown in the sketch to the left, determine the critical compressive stress for the flange and the allowable column load with a factor of safety of 1.80.

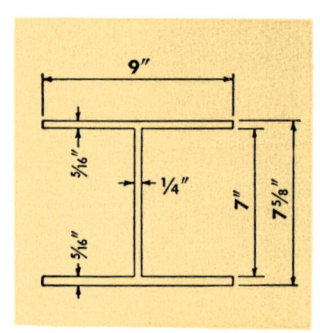

$A = 7.38$ in.²
$I_x = 82.4$ in.⁴
$r_x = 3.34$ in.

Outstanding Flange:

$$k = 0.425 \qquad \frac{b}{t} = \frac{4.375}{0.3125} = 14.0$$

From Table 7, since $b/t > 11.1$
$s_{cr} = 90{,}000 - 3600(b/t) =$
$90{,}000 - (3600 \times 14.0) = 39{,}600$ psi.

For the web, s_{cr} remains the same as in Example 6.

Since the critical stress for the flanges is 39,600 psi, the maximum stress for this section when used as a column is 39,600 psi. This stress may be thought of as an equivalent yield point and the proper column formula determined from Fig. 4.

Thus for $s_y = 39{,}600$ psi and $N = 1.80$,

$$\frac{P}{A} = 17{,}500 - 0.63 \left(\frac{L'}{r}\right)^2.$$

For pin-ended columns, $L' = 0.85L$,

$$\frac{P}{A} = 17{,}500 - 0.46 \left(\frac{L}{r}\right)^2$$

$$= 17{,}500 - 0.46 \left(\frac{12 \times 10}{3.34}\right)^2 = 16{,}910 \text{ psi.}$$

$P = 16{,}910 \times 7.38 = 125{,}000$ lb.

Comparing this column with that of Example 2, it is evident that this section is not as economical as the other.

The most economical section will result when the b/t ratio of the flange (or the web) is the maximum for which the critical compressive stress equals the yield point.

COMPRESSION

Example 8

Determine the critical compressive stresses in the plate elements of the channel cross section shown. Assume $s_y = 50,000$ psi and that all supported plate edges are simply supported.

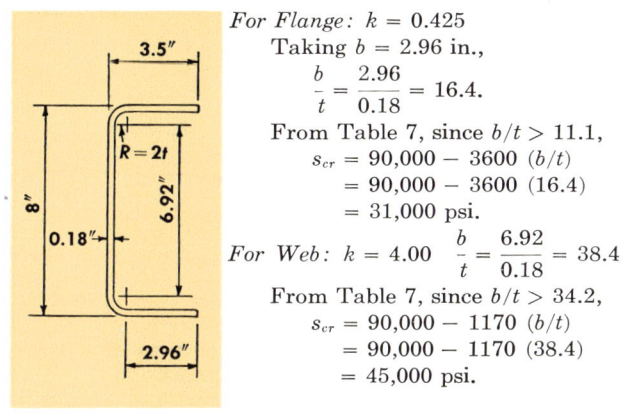

For Flange: $k = 0.425$
  Taking $b = 2.96$ in.,
  $$\frac{b}{t} = \frac{2.96}{0.18} = 16.4.$$
  From Table 7, since $b/t > 11.1$,
  $$s_{cr} = 90,000 - 3600 \ (b/t)$$
  $$= 90,000 - 3600 \ (16.4)$$
  $$= 31,000 \text{ psi.}$$

For Web: $k = 4.00 \quad \dfrac{b}{t} = \dfrac{6.92}{0.18} = 38.4$
  From Table 7, since $b/t > 34.2$,
  $$s_{cr} = 90,000 - 1170 \ (b/t)$$
  $$= 90,000 - 1170 \ (38.4)$$
  $$= 45,000 \text{ psi.}$$

This example could have been readily solved by the use of the nomograph for "Critical Stress for Flat Plates in Edge Compression" in Fig. 11.

For Flange: $\dfrac{(b/t)^2}{k} = \dfrac{(16.4)^2}{0.425} = 633$
  For $s_y = 50,000$ psi, read $s_{cr} = 31,000$ psi.

For Web: $\dfrac{(b/t)^2}{k} = \dfrac{(38.4)^2}{4.00} = 369$
  For $s_y = 50,000$ psi, read $s_{cr} = 45,000$ psi.

Example 9

Determine the critical compressive stresses in the flat plate elements of the square cross section of Example 3. Assume that $s_y = 50,000$ psi and all supported edges are simply supported.

  Flat width, $b = 6 - (6 \times 0.13) = 5.22$ in.
  $$\frac{b}{t} = \frac{5.22}{0.13} = 40.2$$
  From Table 7, since $b/t > 34.2$,
  $$s_{cr} = 90,000 - 1170 \ (b/t) = 90,000 - 1170 \ (40.2)$$
  $$= 43,000 \text{ psi.}$$

Hence the maximum compressive unit stress used in Example 3.

INTERACTION OF FLAT PLATE ELEMENTS

When several plate elements are combined or formed into one member, the action of each plate is governed by the plate or plates to which it is joined. This interaction of the plate elements offers a refinement in the determination of the plate coefficient, k.

In cases of interaction, one plate is primarily responsible for the initial local buckling. This will depend upon the relative stiffness of the several plates. The determination of the stiffness factor is readily made by rearranging the terms of Formula 7 as follows:

$$s_{cr} = \left[\frac{\pi^2 E}{12(1-\mu^2)} \right] \times \left[\frac{k}{(b/t)^2} \right]. \tag{9}$$

The terms within the second bracket comprise the stiffness factor, and it is evident that the critical buckling stress varies directly with this factor. The plate having the least stiffness factor will be the one primarily responsible for buckling. More than one plate element in a member may have the same minimum stiffness factor, in which case any one of them may be primarily responsible, but in any case, all of the plates participate in the buckling at the critical stress.

In determining the relative stiffness factors, consider those plates supported along both longitudinal edges as having a plate coefficient of 4.00, while for those with one edge free and the other simply supported k equals 0.425. With these assumptions, the plate which is primarily responsible for the instability will be the one with the smallest stiffness factor.

A few typical examples of interaction of plate elements in a compression member will illustrate the procedure for investigating the possibility of local buckling. Let us begin with the compression member of Fig. 14a, a square box section consisting of plate elements of equal thickness. Since both longitudinal edges of all four plates are supported, the value of k is the same for all and their ratios of b/t are equal. Hence, the stiffness factor, $\frac{k}{(b/t)^2}$, is the same for all four plates and any one of them can be considered as primarily responsible for local buckling.

When buckling takes place, the cross section of the member through the buckles will have the appearance shown in Fig. 14b. If the side plates buckle outward, the top and bottom plates will buckle inward, or vice versa. Since all of the plates have equal stiffness, one plate offers no restraint to another and all edges will be free to rotate about a longitudinal axis through the corners, in the manner simulated by the supports illustrated in Fig. 12a.

In the second case, illustrated in Fig. 14c, let the thickness t_1 of the top and bottom plates be greater than the thickness t of the side plates. The value of k remains 4.00 as in the first case, but the value of $(b/t)^2$ for the sides will be greater than $(b/t_1)^2$ for the top and bottom plates. Hence the smaller stiffness factor for the side plates indicates that these plates will be primarily responsible for local buckling. When these plates buckle, as shown in Fig. 14d, the action is resisted at their edges by the stiffer top and bottom plates.

COMPRESSION

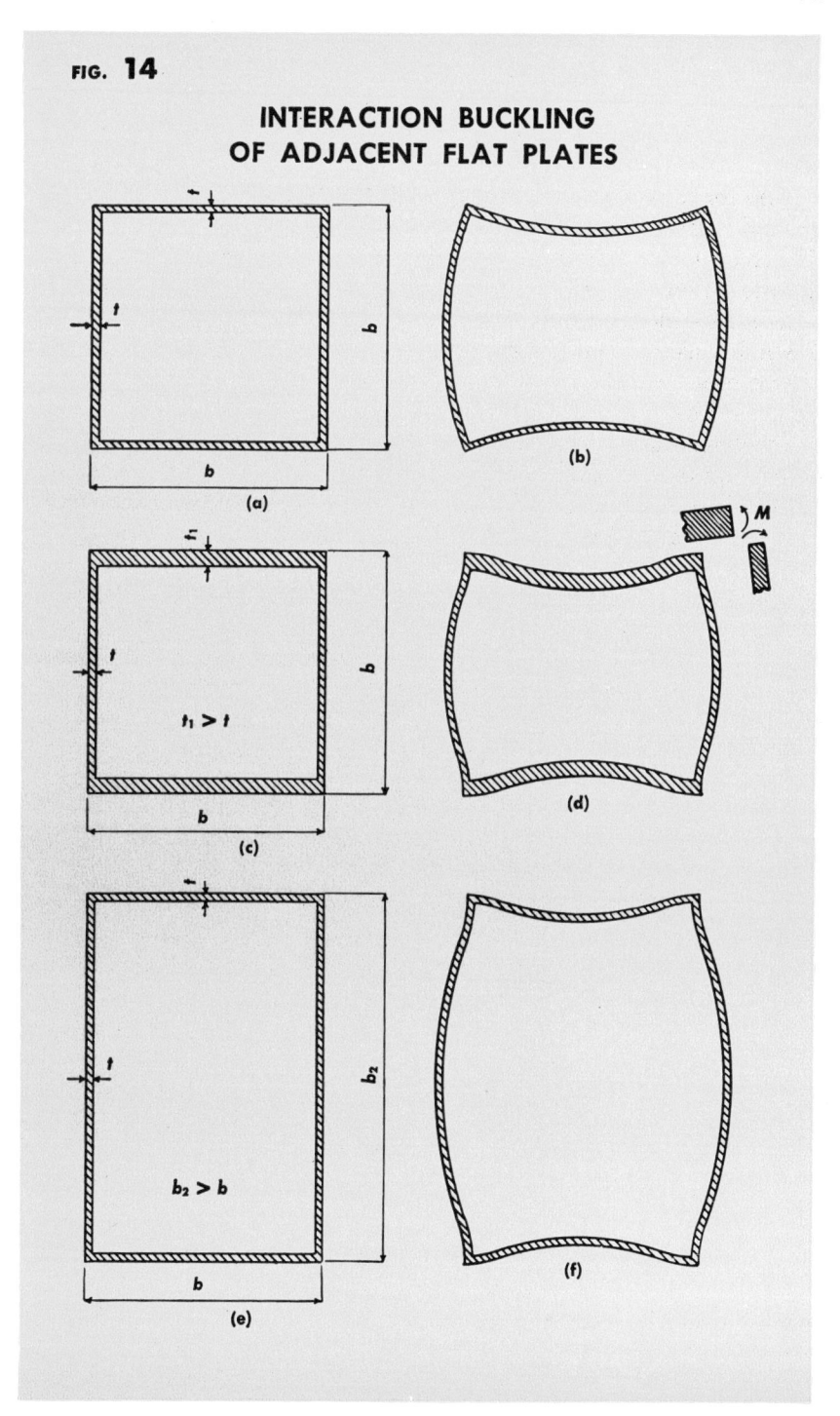

FIG. 14

INTERACTION BUCKLING
OF ADJACENT FLAT PLATES

(a) b, t

(b)

(c) $t_1 > t$, b

(d) M

(e) $b_2 > b$, b_2, b

(f)

Moments are set up at the corners which restrain the rotation of the edges of the side plates and produce a condition somewhere between simply supported and fixed. This results in an increased value of the plate coefficient, k, for the side plates, while these corner moments tend to promote buckling of the top and bottom plates and thereby reduce their value of k below that of 4.00 for simply supported edges.

In the third example, shown in Figs. 14e and 14f, with equal plate thicknesses but wider side plates, the smaller stiffness factor of the side plates would make them primarily responsible for the buckling of the section, in a manner similar to that in the second case.

In both the second and third cases, the side plates are said to be supported, or their buckling is restrained, by the top and bottom plates. What has been discussed for the box type section could also be done for other varied types of sections, such as I-sections, channels and zees.

When local buckling occurs before buckling of the member as a whole, the plate element primarily responsible for buckling is no longer able to withstand the load on it and requires the restraint of the adjoining elements until the load is such that it will cause the entire member to buckle locally. At the point of instability, the stiffness factors for all the plate elements in the column are equal. Considerable theoretical work has been done in recent years to determine the plate coefficients, taking into account the interaction of plates joined to form thin-metal columns. These coefficients have been determined for box, I, channel, zee and tee sections and can be expressed as functions of the various dimension ratios of the sections. They are given here in the form of nomographic charts, Figs. 15, 16 and 17, based on formulas given by Bleich*. To use these charts it is not necessary to know which plate element will be primarily responsible for buckling of the section.

Each chart covers one or more cases as shown at the bottom of the chart. The plate coefficient k obtained from the chart is to be used only for the particular plate element described for each case. For example, in Case II, Fig. 16, for flanges of channel sections, the value of k from the chart is used in computing the critical stress in the flange of the channel being investigated, while in Case VI, Fig. 17, k would be applied to the web of the channel.

---

*"Buckling Strength of Metal Structures" by F. Bleich, McGraw-Hill Book Co., New York, N. Y., 1st Ed., 1952, Table 29, pp. 346 and 347.

COMPRESSION

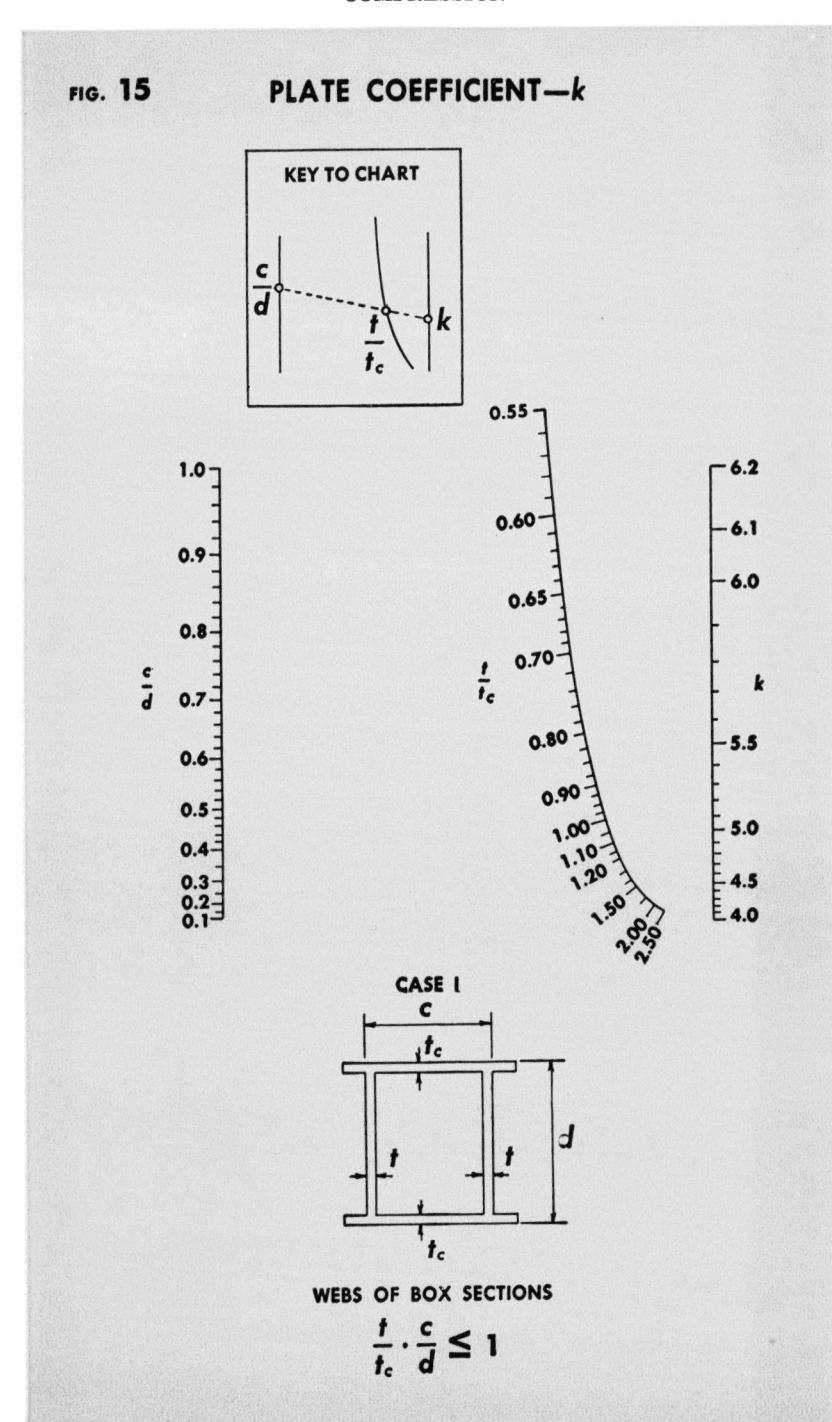

FIG. 15   **PLATE COEFFICIENT—k**

KEY TO CHART

CASE I

WEBS OF BOX SECTIONS

$$\frac{t}{t_c} \cdot \frac{c}{d} \leq 1$$

54 COMPRESSION

FIG. 16

PLATE COEFFICIENT—k

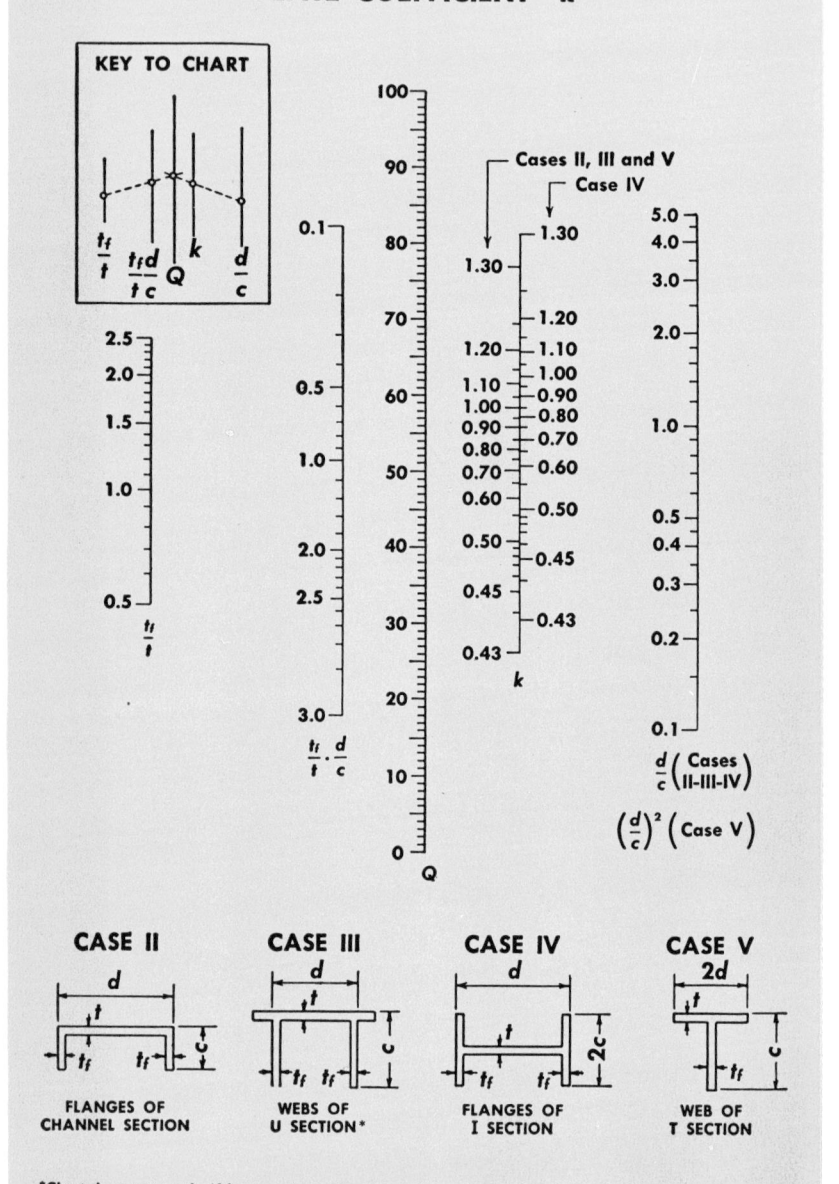

*Chart does not apply if lower edges of webs are connected by lacing bars.

COMPRESSION 55

FIG. 17   **PLATE COEFFICIENT—k**

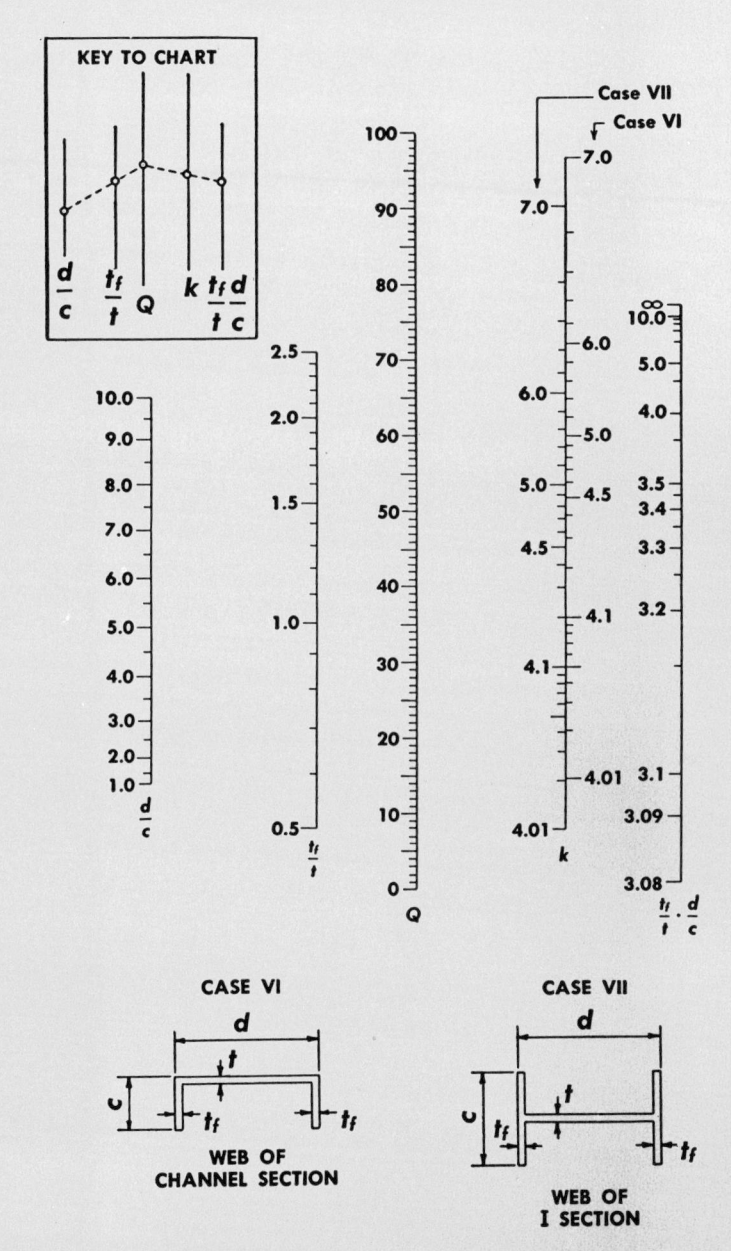

CASE VI — WEB OF CHANNEL SECTION

CASE VII — WEB OF I SECTION

The interaction of the plate elements is such that

$$\frac{k_c}{\left(\dfrac{c}{t_f}\right)^2} = \frac{k_d}{\left(\dfrac{d}{t}\right)^2} \tag{10}$$

where the subscripts c and d denote the plate coefficient for the flange and web respectively. Thus the calculated stress on the element is the critical or allowable longitudinal stress for the entire section from the standpoint of local buckling.

The use of the interaction charts will be illustrated by the following examples.

Example 10

Recalculate Example 7, using the interaction charts for plate coefficient, k

Outstanding Flange:
Use chart for Case IV in Fig. 16.

$$\frac{t_f}{t} = \frac{5/16}{1/4} = 1.25$$

$$\frac{d}{c} = \frac{7.625}{4.50} = 1.69 \qquad \frac{t_f}{t} \times \frac{d}{c} = 1.25 \times 1.69 = 2.11$$

Read $k = 0.487$ $\qquad \sqrt{k} = 0.698$

$$\frac{b}{t} = \frac{4.50}{0.3125} = 14.4$$

$$\frac{b/t}{\sqrt{k}} = \frac{14.4}{0.698} = 20.6$$

which is between the values of 17.1 and 25.6 in Table 6. Therefore, Formula 8b is applicable and gives

$$s_{cr} = (1.8 \times 50{,}000) - 2340(20.6) = 41{,}800 \text{ psi}$$

which is greater than the value of 39,600 psi in Example 7.

The critical stress in the web will also be 41,800 psi, which is less than the value of 50,000 psi obtained in Example 7. The following calculations need not be made, but illustrate the method for computing the s_{cr} for the web.

Referring to Case VII in Fig. 17, it will be seen that the chart does not apply since $\dfrac{t_f}{t} \times \dfrac{d}{c} = 2.11 < 3.08$ and is thus outside the range of applicability of the chart, indicating that the flanges are the critical elements. In this case, Equation 10 may be solved for k_d, the plate coefficient of the web:

$$k_d = \frac{(d/t)^2 \times k_c}{(c/t_f)^2} = \frac{(7/0.25)^2 \times 0.487}{(4.5/0.3125)^2} = 1.841$$

$$\frac{b/t}{\sqrt{k}} = \frac{7/0.25}{\sqrt{1.841}} = 20.6$$

which is the same as for the flange, so that again $s_{cr} = 41{,}800$ psi.

Example 11

Recalculate Example 8, using the interaction charts for plate coefficient, k.

Outstanding Flange:
Use chart for Case II, Fig. 16.
$$\frac{t_f}{t} = 1 \qquad \frac{d}{c} = \frac{8}{3.5} = 2.29 \qquad \frac{t_f}{t} \times \frac{d}{c} = 2.29$$
Read $k = 0.57$.

From Example 8, $\frac{b}{t} = 16.4$
$$\frac{(b/t)^2}{k} = \frac{(16.4)^2}{0.57} = 472.$$
From Fig. 11, for $s_y = 50,000$ psi
$s_{cr} = 39,000$ psi.

Web:
Referring to chart for Case VI, Fig. 17, it will be seen that the chart does not apply, since $\frac{t_f}{t} \times \frac{d}{c} < 3.08$.

From Formula 10, the plate coefficient for the web is
$$k_d = \frac{(d/t)^2 \times k_c}{(c/t_f)^2} = \frac{(8/0.18)^2 \times 0.57}{(3.5/0.18)^2} = 2.98.$$
From Example 8, $b/t = 38.4$
$$\frac{(b/t)^2}{k} = \frac{(38.4)^2}{2.98} = 495.$$
From Fig. 11, for $s_y = 50,000$ psi
$s_{cr} = 37,800$ psi.

From the text it is clear that the values of s_{cr} for the web and the flanges should be the same. The slight variation is due to the different plate widths taken in determining k and s_{cr}.

EFFECTIVE WIDTH OF FLAT PLATES

As was mentioned on page 40, a second method of dealing with the buckling of flat plates in edge compression is to permit local elastic buckling. This method is only applicable when the critical buckling stress, as given by Formula 8, is less than the yield point. When this condition exists, tests have shown that the plate is capable of sustaining a greater ultimate load than the load at which local buckling occurs.

This peculiarity is best understood by considering a thin rectangular plate carrying a uniformly distributed load across its width, and supported along one or both of its longitudinal edges, as in Fig. 18a. At a load slightly larger than that which produces critical stress, the portion of the plate furthest from the supports will buckle elastically, while those portions adjacent to the supports continue to develop stress. As the load is increased, the added load is carried by those portions near the supports, until the compressive yield point, s_y, is reached in the edge strips. Again, the ultimate load or maximum strength depends not only on the dimensions of the plate, but also on the stiffness of the members which form the support for the plate.

FIG. 18

EFFECTIVE WIDTH OF FLAT PLATES IN EDGE COMPRESSION

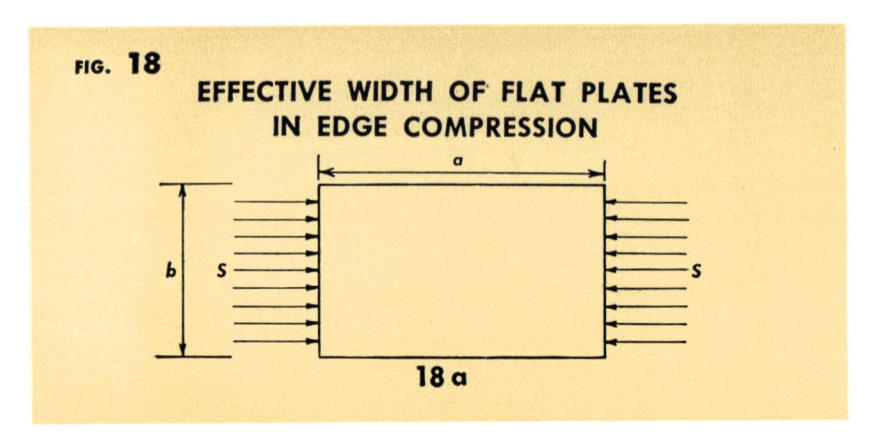

18 a

For the case where the edge strips are stressed to the yield point, the distribution of stress across the width of a thin plate supported along both longitudinal edges is shown in Fig. 18b. This condition represents the ultimate compressive load for the plate. One method of calculating this load neglects the stress s_{cr} and assumes s_y uniformly distributed on the supported edge strips, as in Fig. 18c. Thus the supported edge strips become the effective width, b_e, of the plate in resisting the ultimate load.

The load can then be written

$$P_{\text{ult.}} = b_e t s_y. \tag{11}$$

The average unit stress acting on the full plate width is

$$s_{\text{avg}} = \frac{b_e}{b} s_y.$$

FIG. 18

EFFECTIVE WIDTH OF FLAT PLATES IN EDGE COMPRESSION

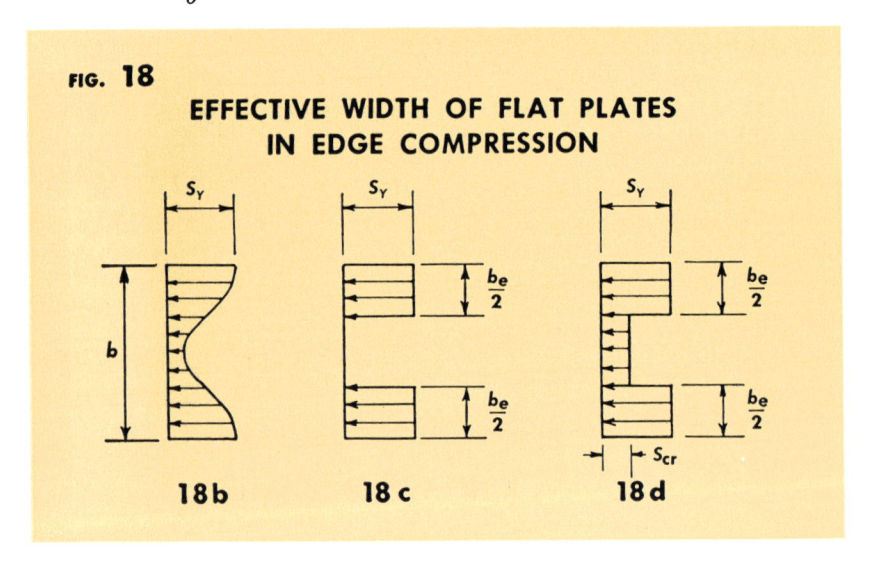

18 b   **18 c**   **18 d**

COMPRESSION

Tests indicate that this approximation is accurate for very thin plates. In more recent investigations, the same assumption as regards the effective width has been made, but with the further assumption that a stress equal to the critical stress, as determined for the entire plate, be uniformly distributed over the remaining portion of the plate, $(b - b_e)$, and included in determining the ultimate load for the plate. This condition is shown in Fig. 18d. With this modification,

$$P_{\text{ult.}} = b_e t s_y + (b - b_e) t s_{cr}. \tag{12}$$

The average unit stress on the width b at the ultimate load is

$$s_{\text{avg}} = \frac{b_e}{b} s_y + \left(1 - \frac{b_e}{b}\right) s_{cr}.$$

The ratio b_e/t may be determined for any plate by solving for b/t in Formula 8a or from the nomograph of Fig. 11 for $s_{cr} = s_y$. For the yield points, s_y, in Table 6, the ratio may be obtained from the values of $\dfrac{b/t}{\sqrt{k}}$ at point B.

The stress distribution shown in Fig. 18c is the one commonly assumed in design and only the effective width, b_e, is included in the calculation of section properties.

The following example demonstrates the method by which one may determine the ultimate compressive load on a plate by either of the above two concepts.

Example 12

Given a steel plate $14 \times \frac{3}{16}$ with both longitudinal edges simply supported. Determine the ultimate compressive load, using a steel with a yield point of 50,000 psi.

$$b/t = \frac{14}{0.1875} = 74.7$$

Method A. Using Forumla 11.
From Table 7, for $s_{cr} = s_y = 50,000$ psi
$b/t = 34.2$.
Or from Formula 8a: $\dfrac{b/t}{\sqrt{k}} = \dfrac{3820}{\sqrt{s_y}}$ and
for simply supported edges, $k = 4.0$
$$b/t = \frac{2 \times 3820}{\sqrt{50,000}} = 34.2.$$

The same value would be obtained from the nomograph of Fig. 11. Therefore,
$b_e = 34.2 \times 0.1875 = 6.41$ in.
$P_{\text{ult.}} = 6.41 \times 0.1875 \times 50,000 = 60,100$ lb.
$$s_{\text{avg}} = \frac{60,100}{14 \times 0.1875} = 22,900 \text{ psi.}$$

60 COMPRESSION

Method B. Using Formula 12.

$$\text{Calculate } \frac{(b/t)^2}{k} = \frac{(74.7)^2}{4.0} = 1395.$$

Normally, when the yield point is not one of those listed in Table 7, one would refer to Fig. 11 to obtain s_{cr}. From Fig. 11, in this case, it is seen that $(b/t)^2/k = 1395$ is beyond the limit for $s_y = 50,000$ psi, indicating that Formula 8c should be used in calculating s_{cr}.

$$s_{cr} = \frac{19,660,000}{1395} = 14,090 \text{ psi.}$$

Then

$$P_{\text{ult.}} = [6.41 \times 0.1875]\,50,000 + [(14-6.41) \times 0.1875]\,14,090$$
$$= 60,100 + 20,100 = 80,200 \text{ lb.}$$
$$s_{\text{avg}} = \frac{80,200}{14 \times 0.1875} = 30,550 \text{ psi.}$$

Note: In order to obtain the allowable working load or stress in this example, the factor of safety is applied directly to the quantities $P_{\text{ult.}}$ and s_{avg}.

The application of the effective width to a column section is illustrated in Example 13.

Example 13

Determine the working load for the column section shown, for an unbraced length of 24 feet when (A) local buckling of the flat cover plates is to be prevented and (B) local buckling of the cover plates is permitted. Assume yield point of 50,000 psi for the steel and a factor of safety of 1.80. Edges of cover plates assumed to be simply supported, $k = 4.0$.

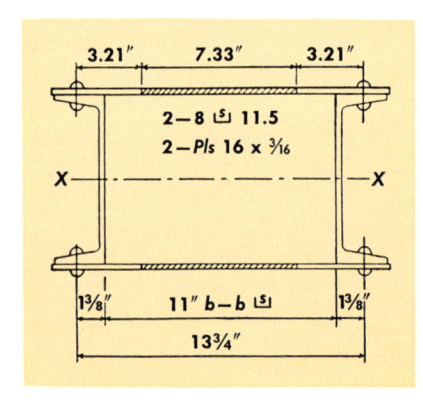

	Gross	Net
Area	12.72 in.²	9.97 in.²
I_x	165.2 in.⁴	119.1 in.⁴
r_x	3.60 in.	3.46 in.

Condition A

$$b/t = \frac{13.75}{0.1875} = 73.3 \qquad \frac{b/t}{\sqrt{k}} = \frac{73.3}{2.0} = 36.7$$

Since $(b/t)/\sqrt{k} = 36.7$ is greater than 25.6, $(b/t)/\sqrt{k}$ at point C for $s_y = 50,000$ (Table 6), Formula 8c applies.

$$s_{cr} = \frac{19,660,000 \times 4.0}{(73.3)^2} = 14,640 \text{ psi}$$

From Fig. 4, for $s_y = 14,640$ and $N = 1.80$,
$B = 6500$ $\qquad$ $C = 0.086$

For pin-ended columns,

$$\frac{P}{A} = 6500 - 0.086 \; (0.85L/r)^2$$

$$= 6500 - 0.062 \left(\frac{24 \times 12}{3.60}\right)^2 = 6100 \text{ psi}$$

$$P = 6100 \times 12.72 = 77{,}600 \text{ lb.}$$

Condition B

From Table 7, for $s_{cr} = s_y = 50{,}000$ psi and $k = 4.0$
$b/t = 34.2$,
For $t = \frac{3}{16}$ in. $b = 6.42 = b_e$ (effective width).

Assume distribution of stress as shown in Fig. 18c.
Ineffective width of cover plate $= 13.75 - 6.42 = 7.33$ in.

Properties of net section are based on omission of shaded portions of cover plates.

From Table 3, for pin-ended columns,

$$\frac{P}{A} = 22{,}500 - 0.738 \; (L/r)^2$$

$$= 22{,}500 - 0.738 \left(\frac{24 \times 12}{3.46}\right)^2 = 17{,}400 \text{ psi.}$$

Then,
$$P = 17{,}400 \times 9.97 = 173{,}000 \text{ lb.}$$

Comparing Conditions A and B, it is clear that by the latter the section may be permitted to carry a much greater load, even after the cover plate has buckled locally in its central region.

Stiffened Flat Plates It has been shown that for a rectangular plate in edge compression, with given conditions of edge support, the magnitude of the critical compressive stress is proportional to the ratio $(t/b)^2$. Obviously, the capacity of the plate can be increased by increasing the thickness of the plate. However, a more economical type of construction, with respect to weight of material used, is usually obtained by employing one or more longitudinal stiffeners which are attached to the plate. These stiffeners not only carry a portion of the compressive load but also subdivide the plate into narrower panels, thereby increasing the critical buckling stress for the plate. While solutions for the stability problem of plates with longitudinal stiffeners exist for several specific cases, the problem is generally analyzed from the standpoint of ultimate strength in a manner similar to that covered in the preceding section.

The distribution of stress in an unstiffened plate supported along its longitudinal edges, after the plate buckles, was shown in Fig. 18b. In stiffened plates, if the stiffeners are rigid enough, the plate will buckle between stiffeners and the stress distribution will be as shown in Fig. 19, with the stress in the stiffeners and adjacent plate greater than that in the buckled region.

This condition of variable stress can be replaced by effective widths of plate which cooperate with each stiffener and are subjected to the same stress as the stiffener, as determined in the previous section of this text. The combination is then treated as a column, the radius of gyration of which is that about an axis parallel to the plate.

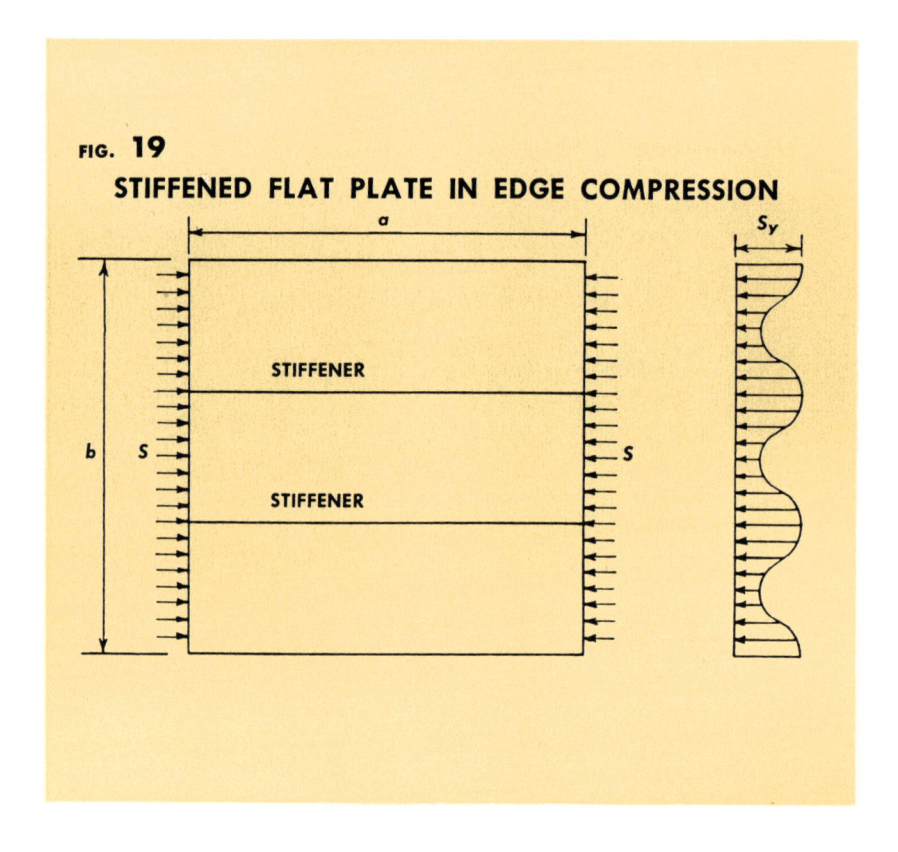

FIG. 19
STIFFENED FLAT PLATE IN EDGE COMPRESSION

Let Fig. 20 represent a flat plate in edge compression having several stiffeners of arbitrarily selected form for illustrative purposes. Dimensions b_1 and b_7 are the widths of outstanding portions of the plate, having one edge free and the other supported. Dimensions b_2 to b_6 inclusive are the widths between the supported edges of intermediate portions of the plate. The effective widths, b_{e1} to b_{e7}, shown shaded in the Figure, are determined from Formula 8a for the desired yield point and appropriate plate coefficient, k. Common design practice assumes all supported edges to be simply supported. Obviously, the effective width cannot exceed the total width of the plate under consideration.

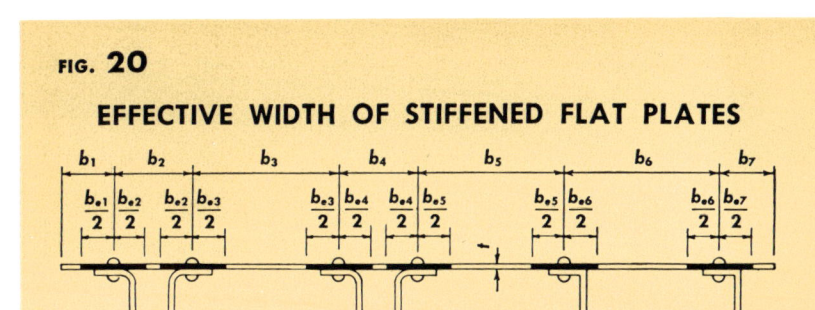

FIG. 20
EFFECTIVE WIDTH OF STIFFENED FLAT PLATES

Example 14

Given a portion of a plate in edge compression reinforced as shown in the sketch, determine the effective width of plate and the ultimate load on the combination of plate and stiffener. Assume the steel to have a yield point of 50,000 psi and the unsupported length of plate equal to 45 inches.

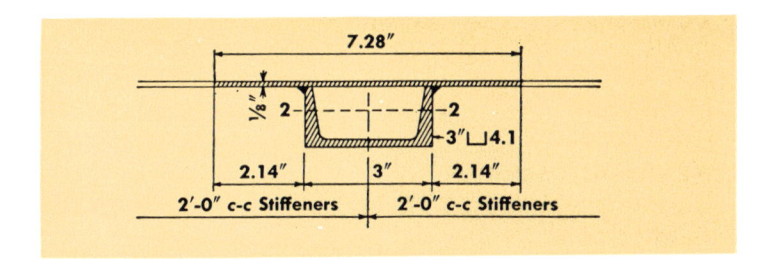

From Table 7, for $s_y = 50,000$ psi and $k = 4.0$,

$\dfrac{b_e}{t} = 34.2$. Then $b_e = 34.2 \times 0.125 = 4.28$ in.

Total effective width of plate $= 4.28 + 3.00 = 7.28$ in.
For the combination of plate and stiffener
Area $= 2.10$ sq in. $I_{2\text{-}2} = 0.75$ in.^{4} $r_{2\text{-}2} = 0.60$ in.

$L/r = \dfrac{45}{0.60} = 75$.

From Table 5, for pinned ends, $\dfrac{P}{A} = 18{,}350$ psi.

The factor of safety in this Table is 1.80
Hence, the ultimate average unit stress is $18{,}350 \times 1.80 = 33{,}000$ psi
The ultimate load is $33{,}000 \times 2.10 = 69{,}300$ lb.

Average load per inch of plate is $\dfrac{69{,}300}{24} = 2890$ lb.

Shear

IN CONTRAST to tensile and compressive stresses which act perpendicular to the plane of the cross section of a member, shearing stress is defined as the intensity of force acting in the plane of the cross section. It can be shown that if shearing stress occurs at a point on a plane, an equal shearing stress also occurs at the same point on a plane at right angles to the first. Shearing strain at a point is defined as the change in angle (expressed in radians) between two lines initially at right angles to each other. Shearing stress is directly proportional to shearing strain up to the proportional limit. This ratio of proportionality is called the modulus of elasticity in shear or the modulus of rigidity, and is usually taken as 11,000,000 psi. Working unit stresses in shear are based on either the shearing yield point or the shearing ultimate strength. To the designer, the most important problems concerning shear occur in riveted joints and in flat plates.

RIVETS

For structural purposes, rivets of structural rivet steel (ASTM Specification A 141—52T) are used in the majority of applications, even in structures of high-strength steel. In any application, the allowable stresses for rivets of this steel are the same, that is, their strength does not depend on the type of steel that is joined. The allowable shearing and bearing values for rivets vary in the various specifications depending somewhat on the basic factor of safety used in the specification. The values allowed by three widely used specifications for structural riveted joints are given in Table 9.

SHEAR

Table 9

ALLOWABLE STRESSES FOR STRUCTURAL RIVETED JOINTS
Structural Rivet Steel, ASTM Spec. A 141—52T

Specification	Shear psi	Bearing Single Shear psi	Bearing Double Shear psi
AREA	13,500	27,000	27,000
AISC	15,000	32,000	40,000
AASHO	13,500	27,000	27,000

Rivets of high-strength steel to ASTM Specification A 195—52T are commonly used with working unit stresses of 20,000 psi for shear, 30,000 psi for bearing on structural carbon steel and 40,000 psi for bearing on high-strength steels. High-strength rivets offer the possible advantage of reducing the number of rivets required in a connection and the size of the connecting gusset plates. These rivets are more expensive than structural carbon steel rivets and, within practical limits, it may be more economical to increase the size of structural carbon steel rivets before considering high-strength steel rivets.

Where corrosion and abrasion are important considerations, as in the floors and sides of railroad hopper cars, USS Cor-Ten steel rivets have been used in some applications in order to prolong the life of the rivet. In such cases, the sizes of the rivets are usually the same as those used with structural steel rivets. While the increased strength of the Cor-Ten steel rivets has not been the primary consideration in their use, where strength is a factor, it is suggested that the same working unit stresses as for high-strength rivets to ASTM Specification A 195—52T be used.

FLAT PLATES IN SHEAR

Let Fig. 21 represent a flat rectangular plate subjected to uniformly distributed shearing forces vt along the edges; v being equal to the shearing unit stress. Under the action of such shearing forces, buckling of the plate will be imminent when the shearing unit stress reaches the critical value given by the expression

$$v_{cr} = \frac{k \pi^2 E}{12(1-\mu^2)} \times \frac{t^2}{b^2}. \tag{13}$$

This expression will be recognized as being similar to the theoretical expression for the critical stress in a flat plate in edge compression,

FIG. 21

FLAT PLATE IN SHEAR

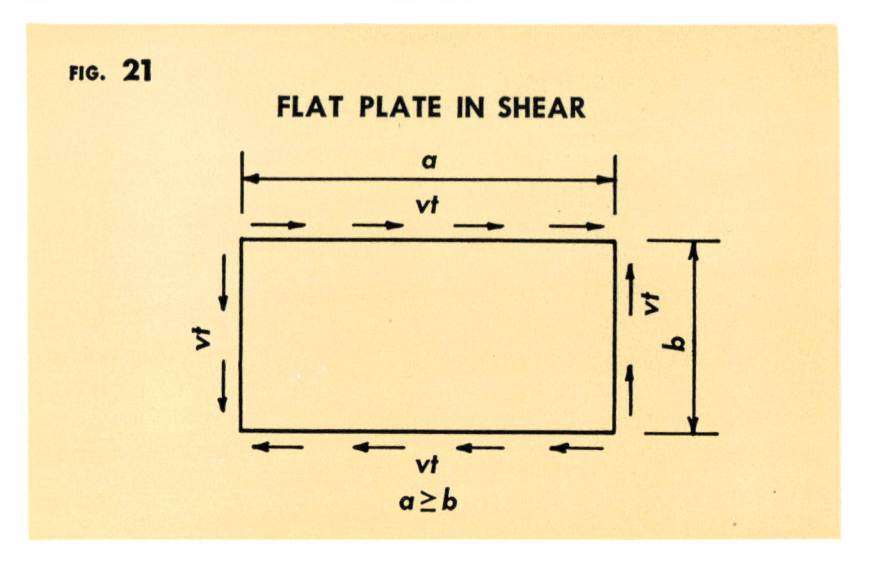

$a \geq b$

Formula 7. Again, k is a non-dimensional plate coefficient and b, the plate width.

The maximum value that the critical shearing stress may have is the value of the yield point in shear for the steel. For plates, the yield point in shear is usually taken as 58 per cent of the tensile yield point.* The yield points in shear, based on 58 per cent of the tensile yield points, are given for several grades of steel in Table 10.

Table 10
SHEARING YIELD POINT

Tensile Yield Point s_y psi	Shearing Yield Point $v_y = 0.58\, s_y$ psi
33,000	19,000
45,000	26,000
50,000	29,000
55,000	32,000

The value of k, again, depends upon the restraint at the edges of the plate and the ratio of the width to length of the plate, b/a. For simply supported edges, $k = 5.35$ for a plate of infinite length

---

*Nadai, A., *Plasticity*, Chapters 12 and 13, McGraw-Hill Book Co. (1931).

$(b/a=0)$ and $k=9.35$ for a square panel $(b/a=1)$. Intermediate values may be determined from the expression, $k=5.35+4(b/a)^2$. For most practical problems, plates in shear are usually assumed to be simply supported. For fixed edges, $k=8.98$ for a plate of infinite length and $k=14.58$ for a square panel. Intermediate values may be obtained from the expression $k=8.98+5.60(b/a)^2$. In these expressions a is always selected as the larger dimension of the rectangle.

Formulas of the type used for the critical stress in flat plates in edge compression, Fig. 10 and Formulas 8a, 8b and 8c, are again used for the critical shearing stress in flat plates. Upon substituting v_{cr} for s_{cr} and v_y (shearing yield point) for s_y in these formulas, the formulas for the critical shearing stress are:

v_{cr} psi	$\dfrac{b/t}{\sqrt{k}}$	
v_y	0 to $\dfrac{3820}{\sqrt{v_y}}$	(14a)
$1.8\,v_y - n\left(\dfrac{b/t}{\sqrt{k}}\right)$ Constant $n = \dfrac{\sqrt{v_y^3}}{4770}$	$\dfrac{3820}{\sqrt{v_y}}$ to $\dfrac{5720}{\sqrt{v_y}}$	(14b)
$\dfrac{19{,}660{,}000\,k}{(b/t)^2}$	$\dfrac{5720}{\sqrt{v_y}}$ and over	(14c)

For a selected list of shearing yield points, the values of $\dfrac{b/t}{\sqrt{k}}$ at points B and C in Fig. 10 and of n are given in Table 11.

Table II

VALUES OF FACTORS IN FORMULA 14

s_y psi	v_y psi	$\dfrac{b/t}{\sqrt{k}}$ at Pt B	$\dfrac{b/t}{\sqrt{k}}$ at Pt C	n
33,000	19,000	27.7	41.5	550
45,000	26,000	23.7	35.5	880
50,000	29,000	22.4	33.6	1040
55,000	32,000	21.4	32.0	1200

In order to obtain the allowable shearing stress in a panel, a factor of safety must be applied to v_{cr}, such that the allowable shearing stress, v, equals v_{cr}/N.

The critical shearing stress in a long flat plate can be substantially increased by the addition of transverse stiffeners which subdivide the plate into smaller panels, each of which may be considered separately as a simply supported rectangular plate in computing the buckling stress.

The majority of problems involving flat plates in shear arise in considering the webs of beams and girders. This specific problem is treated in a later section of this Manual entitled "Web Buckling Due to Shear."

Example 15

Assuming in Fig. 21 that $b = 28$ in., $a = 40$ in. and that the thickness of the plate is $\frac{1}{8}$ in., determine the allowable shearing stress on the edges of the plate—for a factor of safety of 1.80, and a steel having a shearing yield point of 32,000 psi. Assume plate edges to be simply supported.

$$\frac{b}{a} = \frac{28}{40} = 0.70$$

$$k = 5.35 + 4(0.70)^2 = 7.31$$

$$\frac{b}{t} = \frac{28}{0.125} = 224$$

$$\frac{b/t}{\sqrt{k}} = \frac{224}{\sqrt{7.31}} = 82.8$$

From Table 11, since $\dfrac{b/t}{\sqrt{k}} > 32.0$ (Point C), use Formula 14c.

$$v_{cr} = \frac{19,660,000 \times 7.31}{(224)^2} = 2860 \text{ psi.}$$

For $N = 1.80$,

$$\text{allowable shearing stress} = \frac{2860}{1.80} = 1590 \text{ psi.}$$

Stresses in Beams

A BEAM is a structural member whose primary function is to support transverse loads. These loads produce bending in the beam. Internal stresses due to bending are of two kinds: fiber stresses (variously referred to as normal, bending, longitudinal, or flexural stresses) which act perpendicular to a transverse cross section of the beam, and shearing stresses which act in both the transverse and longitudinal directions.

The fiber stress due to bending is given by the formula

$$s = \frac{My}{I}, \tag{15}$$

where

s = fiber stress, psi
M = external bending moment, in.-lb
y = distance to fiber, measured from neutral axis, in.
I = moment of inertia of beam cross section about the neutral axis, in.[4]

The maximum fiber stress occurs at the fibers furthest from the neutral axis and, since one is most interested in these maximums, Formula 15 is more often written

$$s = \frac{Mc}{I}, \tag{16}$$

where c is the distance to the extreme fiber. In this expression, the quantity I/c is called the section modulus and is usually denoted by S. Most handbooks on structural design list the values of S for the various rolled structural shapes and commonly used built-up sections. Formula 16 expressed in terms of the section modulus becomes

$$s = \frac{M}{S}. \tag{17}$$

For beam cross sections which are symmetrical about the neutral axis, the section modulus to either of the extreme fibers is the same, whereas for unsymmetrical sections, the section modulus to each extreme fiber is different.

In design, the basic allowable unit stress for extreme fibers in tension, due to bending, is the same as that allowed in axially loaded bars in tension. When calculating the moment of inertia of the net cross-sectional area of the beam, the areas through holes on the tension side are usually deducted.

In regard to the allowable compressive unit stress to be used in design, several types of buckling phenomena must be considered in each particular problem. For beams with relatively compact compression flanges, and for which the laterally unsupported length of the beam is not excessive, the working compressive unit stress to be used is the basic allowable compressive unit stress, $s = s_y/N$, which is also equal to the allowable tensile unit stress. The questions as to whether the beam section is compact and whether the beam is adequately supported laterally, are discussed in sections to follow.

The shearing stress at any point in a beam is given by the formula

$$v = \frac{VQ}{It}, \tag{18}$$

where
v = shearing stress, psi
V = vertical shear, lb
Q = moment with respect to the neutral axis of the portion of the cross-sectional area which is above (or below) the point in the beam depth at which the shearing stress is desired, in.[3]
I = moment of inertia of beam cross section, in.[4]
t = width of material measured parallel to the neutral axis at the point where the shearing stress is desired, in.

Ordinarily, the shearing stress is a maximum at the neutral axis and zero at the extreme fibers.

In the design of channel and I-shaped beams, it is customary to assume that all of the vertical shear is resisted by the web and that the maximum shearing stress in the beam or girder is equal to the average shearing stress over the web only. In order to simplify calculations, it is further assumed that the web extends the entire depth of the beam. Thus, the shearing stress in the webs of channel and I-shaped beams is

$$v = \frac{V}{dt} \quad (19)$$

where t is the thickness of the web and d, the depth of the beam.

In regard to the allowable shearing stress in the webs of beams, it is necessary to consider the possibility of buckling of the web due to shear. This aspect in the design of web plates is covered in a later section, on page 79. When web buckling, due to shear, does not govern the design, the allowable shearing stress is the shearing yield point, divided by the factor of safety. Allowable shearing stresses for various grades of steel, designated by their tensile yield points, are given in Table 12. These stresses are based on a factor of safety of 1.80 on the shearing yield point, $v_y = 0.58\ s_y$.

Table 12

ALLOWABLE SHEARING STRESSES

Tensile Yield Point psi	Allowable Shearing Stress psi
33,000	10,500
45,000	14,500
50,000	16,000
55,000	17,500

LOCAL BUCKLING OF COMPRESSION FLANGES

Due to the longitudinal compressive fiber stress in beams, relatively thin material used as component parts of compression flanges may fail by local buckling.

The variation of normal stress through the thickness of the thin flanges of beams is negligible and therefore the stress distribution may be considered as uniform. Since these flanges are flat and usually long compared to the dimensions of the cross section of the flanges, the problem is again the buckling of flat plates in edge compression. The allowable compressive stress in beams may therefore be limited by the allowable stress that the compression flange may withstand, when it is considered as a plate.

The subject of flat plates under the action of a uniform compressive stress has been discussed in a previous section of this Manual, page 40. The reader is referred to this section for the determination of the limiting stress or limiting proportions for the compression flanges of beams. Any of the concepts, such as the assumed or calculated coefficient of plate edge restraint, critical buckling stress, effective plate width or ultimate average stress may be used.

LATERAL BUCKLING OF BEAMS

In the absence of adequate lateral support, I-shaped beams loaded in the plane of the web may be unstable in the lateral direction. Such beams when stressed beyond certain critical limits buckle sideways. Theoretical formulas have been developed for the critical buckling stress at which lateral buckling is imminent. These formulas take into account the type of load, (concentrated, uniform, or pure bending), and where the load is applied, (at top flange, centroid, or bottom flange). For the case of a beam subjected to pure bending, a theoretical expression[*] for the buckling stress is

$$s_{cr} = \frac{\pi^2 E}{2\left(\frac{L}{d}\right)^2} \sqrt{\left(\frac{I_y}{2I_x}\right)^2 + \frac{KI_y}{2(1+\mu)I_x^2}\left(\frac{L}{\pi d}\right)^2} \qquad (20)$$

where

s_{cr} = critical buckling stress, psi

E = modulus of elasticity, psi

L = length of span, laterally unsupported, in.

d = depth of beam, in.

I_x = moment of inertia about neutral axis for bending in plane of web, in.[4]

I_y = moment of inertia about neutral axis for bending in the lateral direction, in.[4]

K = torsional constant, in.[4]

μ = Poisson's ratio.

It has been shown that this formula can be used satisfactorily for beams carrying transverse loads.

In cases where I_x is several times I_y, the first term under the radical becomes negligible as compared to the second term. Such is the case for most rolled and built-up I-shaped members used as beams. For beams of this type, the first term is neglected and in view of the usual shape of I-shaped beams, certain approximations

---

[*]"Strength of Slender Beams," by George Winters, Transactions ASCE Vol. 109, 1944, p. 1321. "Strength of Beams as Determined by Lateral Buckling," by Karl de Vries, Transactions ASCE Vol. 112, 1947, p. 1245 and discussion by George Winters.

can be made for the quantities I_x, I_y and K. Formula 20, then becomes

$$s_{cr} = \frac{18.83 \times 10^6}{\dfrac{Ld}{bt}}, \tag{21}$$

in which b is the total width of the compression flange and t its thickness.

For beams with wide, thin flanges, $(b/t > 20)$, the assumptions made to obtain Formula 21 are not valid, since the second term of Formula 20 approaches the order of magnitude of the first. Some of the lighter rolled sections fall into this category.

The use of I-shaped sections formed from light gage sheet or strip and then spot-welded has been increasing in recent years. See Fig. 22. For beams of this type, which have very thin, wide flanges, the second term of Formula 20 becomes small compared to the first. Again, by making an approximation, the expression for the critical stress becomes

$$s_{cr} = \frac{447.2 \times 10^6}{\left(\dfrac{L}{r_y}\right)^2}, \tag{22}$$

in which L, as previously, is the laterally unsupported span length and r_y the radius of gyration about the centroidal axis parallel to the web.

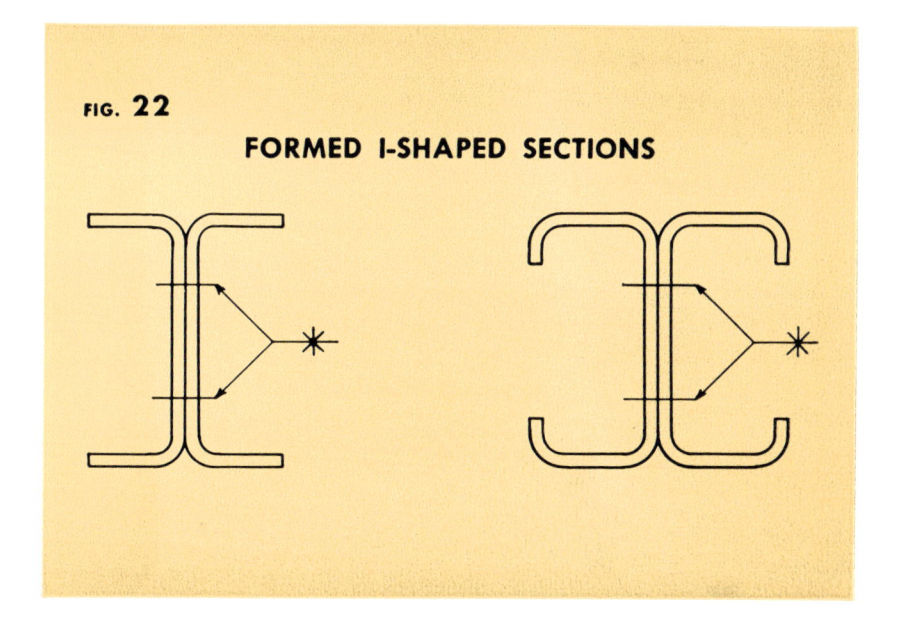

FIG. 22

FORMED I-SHAPED SECTIONS

74   STRESSES IN BEAMS

Formulas 21 and 22 plot as Euler type curves, as shown in Fig. 23. The results of actual tests seem to indicate that these theoretical formulas, without modification, give values of the critical buckling stress which are practical. Therefore, the curves for the critical buckling stress are formed by the horizontal lines $s_{cr} = s_y$ and either Formula 21 or 22 as in Fig. 23.

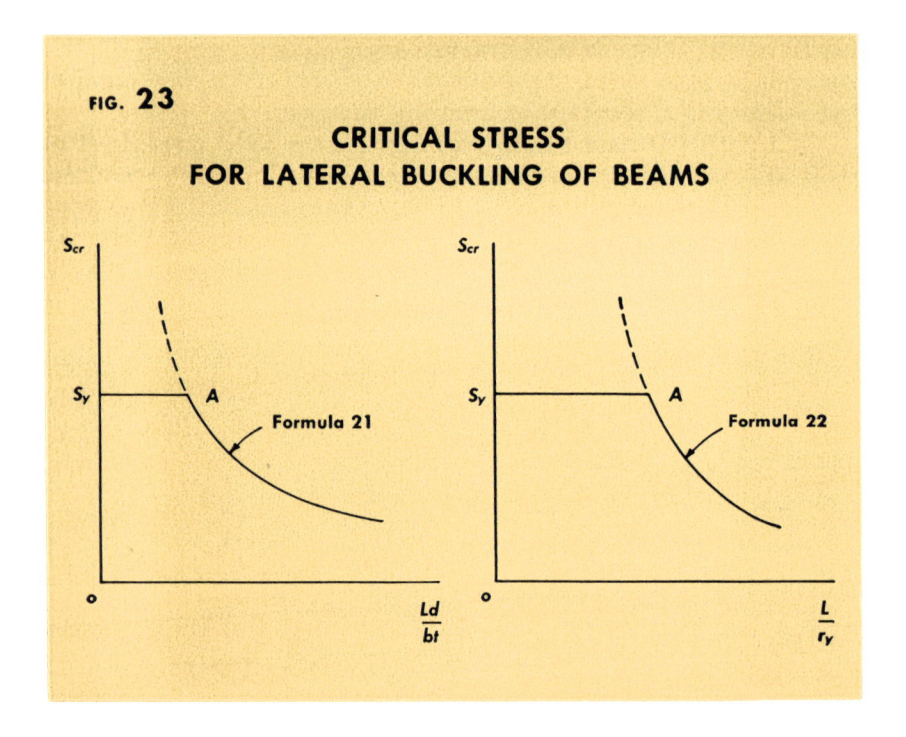

FIG. 23

CRITICAL STRESS FOR LATERAL BUCKLING OF BEAMS

In order to obtain the allowable compressive unit stress to be used in the design of beams, a factor of safety must be applied to s_{cr} such that the allowable stress, s, equals s_{cr}/N. Using a factor of safety, $N = 1.80$, Formula 21 becomes

$$s = \frac{10.46 \times 10^6}{\dfrac{Ld}{bt}}, \qquad (23)$$

and Formula 22 becomes

$$s = \frac{248.5 \times 10^6}{\left(\dfrac{L}{r_y}\right)^2}. \qquad (24)$$

The limiting values of Ld/bt and L/r_y up to which $Ns = s_{cr} = s_y$ (points A in Fig. 23), are given in Table 13 for a few of the more common yield points.

Table 13

MAXIMUM VALUES OF $\dfrac{Ld}{bt}$ and $\dfrac{L}{r_y}$

s_y psi	$\dfrac{Ld}{bt} = \dfrac{18.83 \times 10^6}{s_y}$	$\dfrac{L}{r_y} = \sqrt{\dfrac{447.2 \times 10^6}{s_y}}$
33,000	571	116
45,000	418	100
50,000	377	95
55,000	342	90

Thus, when these ratios are not exceeded in a particular beam, the working, or allowable, compressive unit stress again is the basic allowable compressive unit stress, s_y/N. In cases where the ratios are exceeded, the allowable working unit stress is that obtained from either Formula 21 or 22 with a suitable factor of safety. Values of the ratio d/bt, used in Formula 21, are given for the rolled sections used as beams in the Steel Construction Manual of the American Institute of Steel Construction.

Having two formulas, the question now arises as to which formula is the correct one to use. There are no simple rules other than those in the discussion leading up to each formula. Where there is doubt, it is safe practice to compute the buckling stress by both formulas and to use the larger of the two values. A close approximation to the value which would be obtained from Formula 20 may be had by taking the square root of the sum of the squares of the values from Formulas 21 and 22.

All of the formulas given in this discussion are applicable to I-shaped members only. In predicting failure by local buckling, it is assumed that no eccentric moment or torque is produced by the loads or reactions. Eccentrically loaded columns of I-shaped section, which have I_x several times greater than I_y, should also be investigated to insure against lateral instability.

Example 16

The 12 WF 45 beam is loaded by the framing members as shown in the figure. If the yield point of the steel in the beam is 50,000 psi, determine the allowable fiber stress for the beam using a factor of safety of 1.80.

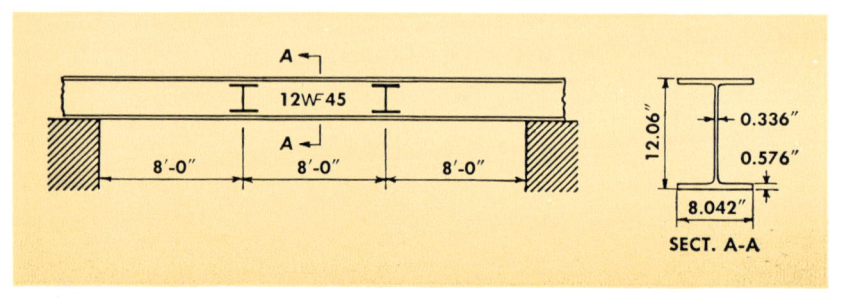

For the 8 ft-0 in. laterally unsupported span,
$$\frac{Ld}{bt} = \frac{8 \times 12 \times 12.06}{8.042 \times 0.576} = 250.$$

From Formula 23, the allowable compressive unit stress is,
$$s = \frac{10.46 \times 10^6}{\dfrac{Ld}{bt}} = \frac{10.46 \times 10^6}{250} = 41{,}840 \text{ psi}.$$

Since this stress is greater than $50{,}000/1.80 = 27{,}800$ psi, the fiber stress is not limited due to lateral buckling, and the allowable fiber stress for the beam is 27,800 psi.

Example 17

Determine the maximum distance between lateral supports such that the compressive fiber stress of a beam whose cross section is shown will not be limited by lateral buckling. The steel has a yield point of 45,000 psi.

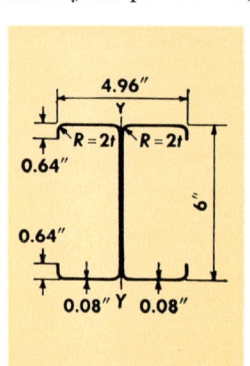

Since this is a formed section for which $\dfrac{b}{t} = \dfrac{4.96}{0.08} = 62$ (greater than 20), use Formula 22. For this section, $r_y = 1.17$ in.

$$s_{cr} = \frac{447.2 \times 10^6}{\left(\dfrac{L}{r_y}\right)^2} = 45{,}000 \text{ psi}$$

$$L = r_y \sqrt{\frac{447.2 \times 10^6}{s_{cr}}}$$

$$= 1.17 \sqrt{\frac{447.2 \times 10^6}{45{,}000}}$$

$$= 116.6 \text{ in.} = 9'-8\tfrac{1}{2}''$$

From Formula 21, the value obtained for L is 27.7 in. $= 2'-3\tfrac{3}{4}''$. Using the larger value, derived from Formula 22, the maximum distance between lateral supports is $9'-8\tfrac{1}{2}''$. The value of L obtained from Formula 20 is 119.2 in. which indicates that Formula 22 is a close approximation.

WEB BUCKLING

The stresses produced in the web of a beam by bending may cause instability of the web. In discussing buckling of the web, two cases are important to consider: (1) At points of maximum bending moment, usually near mid-span, the shear can be neglected and the part of the web between two stiffeners may be considered as a rectangular plate in pure bending due to the normal stresses as shown in Fig. 24a. (2) Near the beam supports, the shearing stresses are most significant and the portion of the web between two stiffeners may be considered as a rectangular plate subjected to uniform shear along its edges as shown in Fig. 24b. The intermediate condition of a section of beam web between two stiffeners under the action of combined shear and bending usually will not be critical if the beam is proportioned and stiffened to satisfy the above two conditions.

Web Buckling Due to Compression As shown in Fig. 24a, the webs of beams are subjected to horizontal compressive stresses which vary from zero at the neutral axis to a maximum at the extreme top edge. This condition of stress may produce buckling of thin webs similar to that produced in plates subjected to uniform edge compression. The rational design of web plates starts with the determination of the required thickness of the web at the point of maximum bending moment, where these stresses are great-

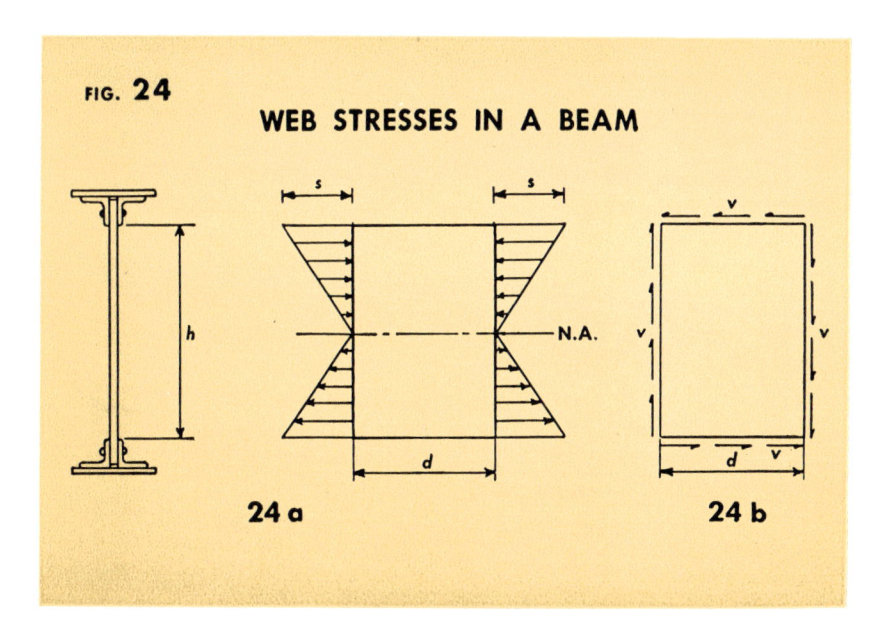

FIG. 24

WEB STRESSES IN A BEAM

24 a   24 b

est. This may be done by means of the following expression for plate buckling, similar to that given by Formula 8b:

$$s_{cr} = 1.8 \, s_y - \frac{\sqrt{s_y^3}}{4770}\left(\frac{h/t}{\sqrt{k}}\right) \tag{25}$$

where in this case, the clear distance between flanges, h, is the plate width and s_{cr} the critical stress at the edge of the web at which buckling is imminent. Neglecting the restraint of the stiffeners and of the flanges, web plates subjected to pure bending may be considered as simply supported, long plates, for which the plate coefficient, k, is 24.*

Since the maximum normal stress occurs at the extreme fiber of the flange, the greatest stress in the web will be somewhat less than the maximum stress in the beam. The extreme fiber stress at the section of maximum bending moment is approximately s_y/N, or the limiting stress due to some other compressive buckling phenomenon, divided by the factor of safety. After examining many types of beams, both rolled and built-up, it has been found that on the average, the maximum stress in the web may be taken as 70 per cent of the extreme fiber stress. The stress at the edge of the clear web then is $0.70 \, s_y/N$. Buckling of the web, due to compression, does not necessarily constitute failure of the entire beam, and, since the restraining effect of the flanges is neglected, the factor of safety against this type of buckling need not be as high as that used against other types of failures. Letting the factor of safety against failure of webs due to pure bending be 70 per cent of the normal factor, the critical stress becomes

$$s_{cr} = \frac{0.70N \times 0.70 \, s_y}{N} = 0.49 \, s_y.$$

Substituting this value for s_{cr} in Formula 25, the maximum value of the ratio of the thickness of the web to its depth is

$$\frac{h}{t} = \frac{30{,}600}{\sqrt{s_y}}. \tag{26}$$

Limiting ratios of h/t for steels with different yield points are shown in Table 14.

Thus a girder or beam of high-strength steel with a yield point of 50,000 psi should have a web thickness of not less than 1/137 of the distance between flanges or side plates. Obviously high-strength steels have lower limiting values of the ratio, h/t, than that for structural carbon steel.

---

*"Buckling Strength of Metal Structures" by F. Bleich, McGraw-Hill Book Co., New York, N. Y., 1st Ed., 1952, Table 36, p. 411.

Table 14
MAXIMUM VALUES h/t

s_y psi	h/t
33,000	168
45,000	144
50,000	137
55,000	130

When necessary, the web may be greatly strengthened by means of horizontal stiffeners, but the less costly way may be that of increasing the web thickness to meet the requirements of Formula 26 or Table 14.

Web Buckling Due to Shear Having determined the minimum allowable thickness of web, the next step in design is to find the ratio of h/t at which vertical web stiffeners will not be necessary, except of course, at points of load concentration. This may be done by considering the web under the action of shears as shown in Fig. 24b. When stiffeners are not present, the length of the web plate is large in comparison to its width, h, the web depth. The critical shearing stress may be obtained from Formula 14b upon substituting h for b.

The plate coefficient for a rectangular plate assumed to be simply supported has been given in the previous section, "Flat Plates in Shear," and applied to this case $k=5.35+4(h/d)^2$. Since the ratio h/d for a plate without stiffeners is small, k approaches 5.35. The limiting value of the ratio h/t at which stiffeners are not required, is obtained when the critical shearing stress is equal to the yield point in shear. Substituting $k = 5.35$ and $v_{cr} = v_y$ in Formula 14b,

$$\frac{h}{t} = \frac{8800}{\sqrt{v_y}}. \tag{27}$$

Taking the shearing yield point for the web plates of beams as 58 per cent of the tensile yield point, Formula 27 becomes

$$\frac{h}{t} = \frac{11600}{\sqrt{s_y}}. \tag{28}$$

Limiting ratios of h/t for various yield points of steel are given in Table 15. When the ratio h/t exceeds that given by Formula 28 or in Table 15, stiffeners are required.

Table 15
LIMITING VALUES OF h/t WITHOUT STIFFENERS

Tensile Yield Point s_y psi	Shearing Yield Point $v_y = 0.58\,s_y$ psi	h/t
33,000	19,000	64
45,000	26,000	55
50,000	29,000	52
55,000	32,000	49

The proper spacing of stiffeners may be determined by considering the critical shearing stress in a plate. Referring to Fig. 24b, it is now assumed that the distance between stiffeners, d, is less than the height of the web, h, so that d now becomes the plate width. The plate coefficient then is $k = 5.35 + 4\,(d/h)^2$, again assuming the plate to be simply supported. Since buckling of a stiffened web does not necessarily mean complete failure of the beam or girder and since the restraint offered to the web panel by the flanges and stiffeners is not considered in the plate coefficient, the theoretical expression for the critical shearing stress in a plate is used without modification up to the yield point. The expression for the critical shearing stress as obtained from Formula 13 upon substituting d for b is

$$v_{cr} = \frac{k\,\pi^2\,E}{12(1-\mu^2)} \times \frac{t^2}{d^2}. \tag{29}$$

Again the factor of safety is applied to the critical stress such that $v_{cr} = Nv$, where v is the maximum shearing stress in the web panel. Substituting the expressions for k and v_{cr} in Formula 29 and solving for the ratio of stiffener spacing to web thickness, we have

$$\frac{d}{t} = \frac{116}{\sqrt{\dfrac{Nv}{10500} - \left(\dfrac{100}{h/t}\right)^2}}. \tag{30}$$

Applying a factor of safety of 1.80 to Formula 30 we then have

$$\frac{d}{t} = \frac{116}{\sqrt{\dfrac{v}{5800} - \left(\dfrac{100}{h/t}\right)^2}}. \tag{31}$$

The limiting value of v in the above expressions is the allowable shearing stress for webs of beams and plate girders. When stiffeners

STRESSES IN BEAMS

are required, they should be placed at intervals not greater than the depth of the web or the distance given by Formula 30.

Table 16
SPACING OF STIFFENERS

SPECIFICATIONS		
AREA	AISC	AASHO
Clear depth 72 in. max $d = \dfrac{10{,}500t}{\sqrt{v}}$	.... 84 in. max $d = \dfrac{11{,}000t}{\sqrt{v}}$	Clear depth 72 in. max $d = \dfrac{9000t}{\sqrt{v}}$

Should buckling of thin webs of stiffened girders occur, diagonal tensile stresses are set up in the web which put the vertical stiffeners in compression. The action is analagous to that of a Pratt truss and is the basis of design in extremely light weight construction.

Specifications usually stipulate the maximum stiffener spacing in several ways—the least value is to be used. The requirements of three well-known specifications are given in Table 16.

Example 18

A simply supported girder having a cross section as shown, carries a uniformly distributed load of 5600 lb per ft on a span of 50 ft. If the steel in the girder has a yield point of 50,000 psi, check the web for buckling due to compression and locate stiffeners to prevent buckling due to shear. Use a safety factor of 1.85.

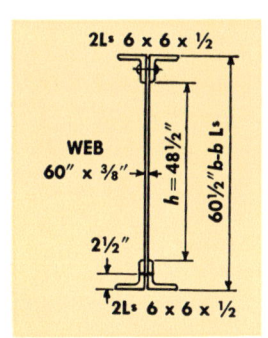

Compression buckling:

$$\frac{h}{t} = \frac{48.5}{0.375} = 129$$

From Table 14, the maximum value of h/t for $s_y = 50{,}000$ psi is 137. Since $h/t = 129 < 137$, the web is safe against compression buckling.

Shear buckling:

From Table 15, the limiting h/t for $s_y = 50{,}000$ psi is 52.

Since $h/t = 129 > 52$, stiffeners are required to prevent shear buckling.

Maximum vertical shear,

$$V = \frac{wL}{2} = \frac{5600 \times 50}{2} = 140{,}000 \text{ lb.}$$

Shear stress in web,

$$v = \frac{V}{A_w} = \frac{140{,}000}{60 \times 0.375} = 6220 \text{ psi (where } A_w = \text{area of web).}$$

Using Formula 30,
$$\frac{d}{t} = \frac{116}{\sqrt{\dfrac{1.85 \times 6220}{10{,}500} - \left(\dfrac{100}{129}\right)^2}} = 165.$$

Therefore
$d = 165 \times 0.375 = 61.9$ in.,
or using the AREA Specifications (see Table 16),
$$d = \frac{10500 \times 0.375}{\sqrt{6220}} = 49.9 \text{ in.}$$

Since d is greater than the clear height of the web, stiffeners should be spaced at not more than $d = h = 48.5$ in.

COMBINED COMPRESSION AND TRANSVERSE LOADS

For the most part, the preceding sections have covered stresses in members caused by loads of one type only, that is, tension, compression or shear. Many structural members and machine parts, however, are simultaneously subjected to loads of two or more types. This section will concern itself only with members which are subjected to direct compressive forces and lateral loads. Taken individually, members which withstand axial compressive loads are called columns, whereas members which support transverse loads or end moments are called beams. Thus, the combination of the two types of loads to a single member commonly classifies the member as a beam-column.

Members are very often subjected to such a combination of loads in practice; for example, structural compression members subjected to wind loadings or other types of side loads, and the very common case of a beam whose loads act at an angle to the transverse direction.

Let us consider the simple case of a member of length, L, subjected to a single transverse concentrated load, W, at mid-span, and a compressive axial load, P, at the ends of the member as shown in Fig. 25. Let it be required to find the maximum normal unit stress on a transverse section of the beam.

As a first approximation, the resulting maximum stress, which occurs at the mid-section, is

$$s_{\max} = \frac{P}{A} + \left(\frac{WL}{4}\right)\frac{c}{I}, \tag{32}$$

where A is the gross cross-sectional area of the member, c, the distance to the outermost fiber and $WL/4$ the bending moment at the center of the span due to the load, W. (See Beam Formulas, Case 18 in the appendix.)

STRESSES IN BEAMS

This first approximation neglects the bending moment produced by the end load acting eccentrically to the neutral axis of the beam, which eccentricity is caused by the deflection of the beam under the concentrated load, W. (See Fig. 25.) As a second approximation, the maximum fiber stress is

$$s_{\max} = \frac{P}{A} + \left(\frac{WL}{4} + P\Delta\right)\frac{c}{I}, \tag{33}$$

where $\Delta = WL^3/48EI$ given in Case 18, Beam Formulas.

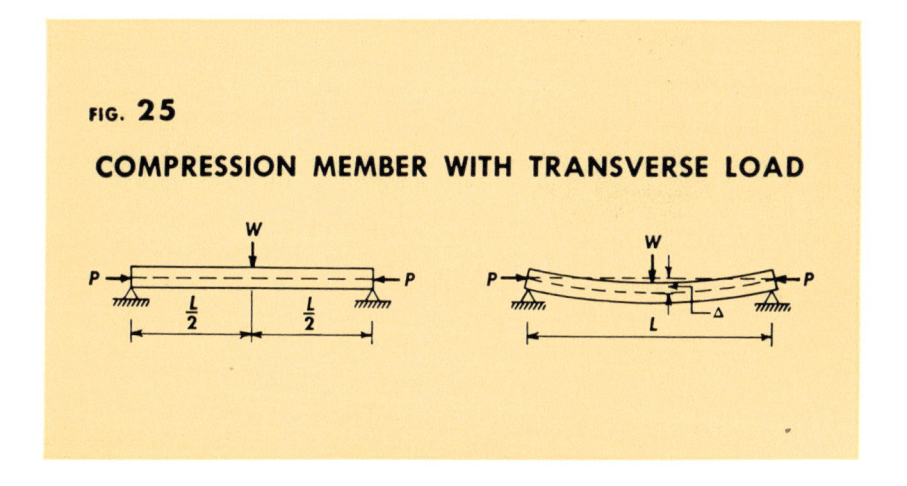

FIG. 25

COMPRESSION MEMBER WITH TRANSVERSE LOAD

Since the true value of Δ depends not only on the transverse load, but also on the total bending moment $(WL/4 + P\Delta)$, and the value of the bending moment depends in turn on the value of Δ, one is led to a method of approximation in solving Formula 33. Thus, the value of the deflection caused by the bending moment produced by the transverse load alone is first found. This deflection is then used in determining a new total bending moment, from which a closer approximation to the true value of Δ is obtained. The more times this step is repeated, the closer one approaches the true maximum stress in the beam.

The number of approximations necessary to determine the true stress depends on the stiffness or moment of inertia of the member with regard to the end load. When the magnitude of the axial compressive load approaches the value of the critical load at which the member fails by buckling as a column, the deflections become very sensitive to slight changes in the eccentricity of the compressive load. The method of approximations may be used to determine the maximum stress in many members subjected to the simultaneous action of lateral and longitudinal forces.

84   STRESSES IN BEAMS

The exact solution for the maximum bending moment that occurs in the member shown in Fig. 25 is

$$M_{max} = \frac{WL}{4} \times \frac{\tan\frac{L}{2}\sqrt{\frac{P}{EI}}}{\frac{L}{2}\sqrt{\frac{P}{EI}}}. \tag{34}$$

The first factor in the above expression represents the maximum bending moment produced by the load, W, acting alone, while the second factor is a magnification factor, due to the action of the axial force, P, on the bending moment. The true maximum stress

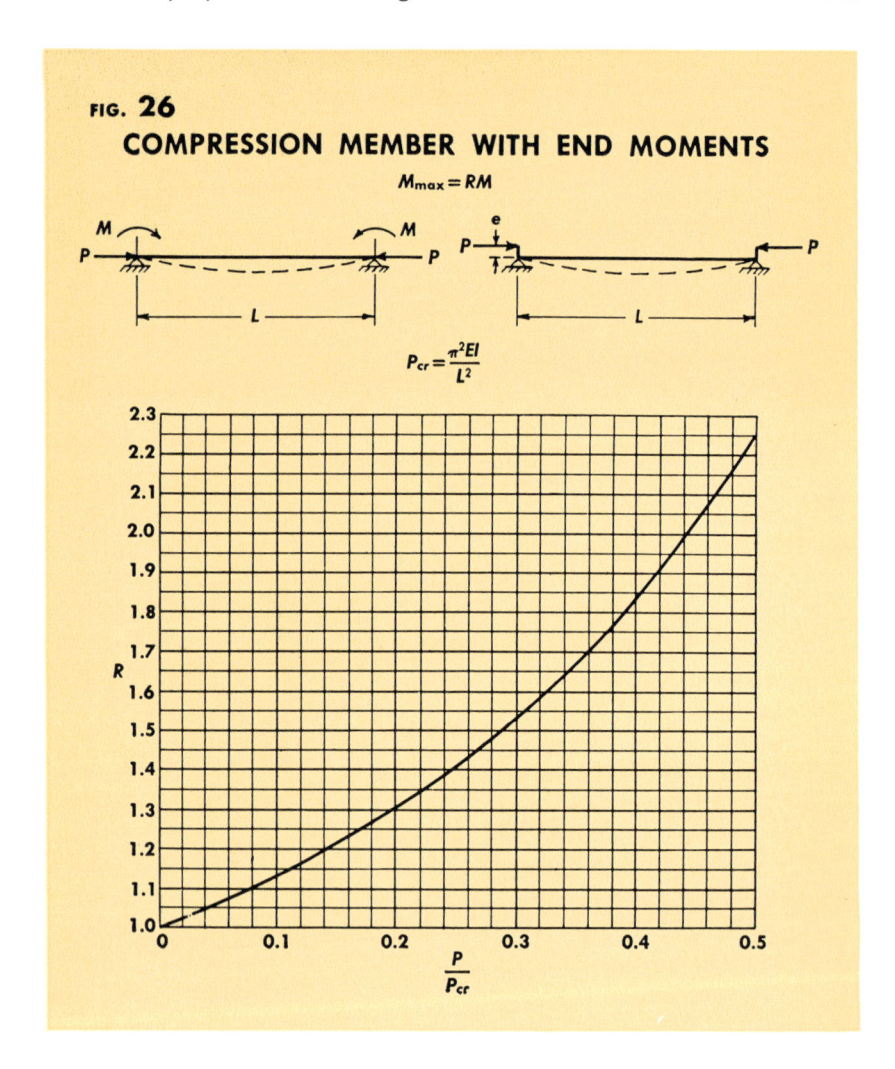

FIG. 26
COMPRESSION MEMBER WITH END MOMENTS
$M_{max} = RM$

$P_{cr} = \frac{\pi^2 EI}{L^2}$

$\frac{P}{P_{cr}}$

is then

$$s_{max} = \frac{P}{A} + \frac{M_{max}\,c}{I}. \tag{35}$$

The exact solutions for the maximum bending moment in members subjected to the simultaneous action of both longitudinal and transverse forces have been obtained for numerous loading conditions. To cover these would be beyond the scope of the Manual, and therefore only three cases are given here. These are shown in chart form in Figs. 26, 27, and 28. In each case the maximum fiber stress would be found as in Formula 35. The ratio P/P_{cr}, which is a factor in each case, determines the effect of the end load on the maximum bending moment. In this ratio, the critical load, P_{cr}, is the Euler critical column load and its use here is as a constant for

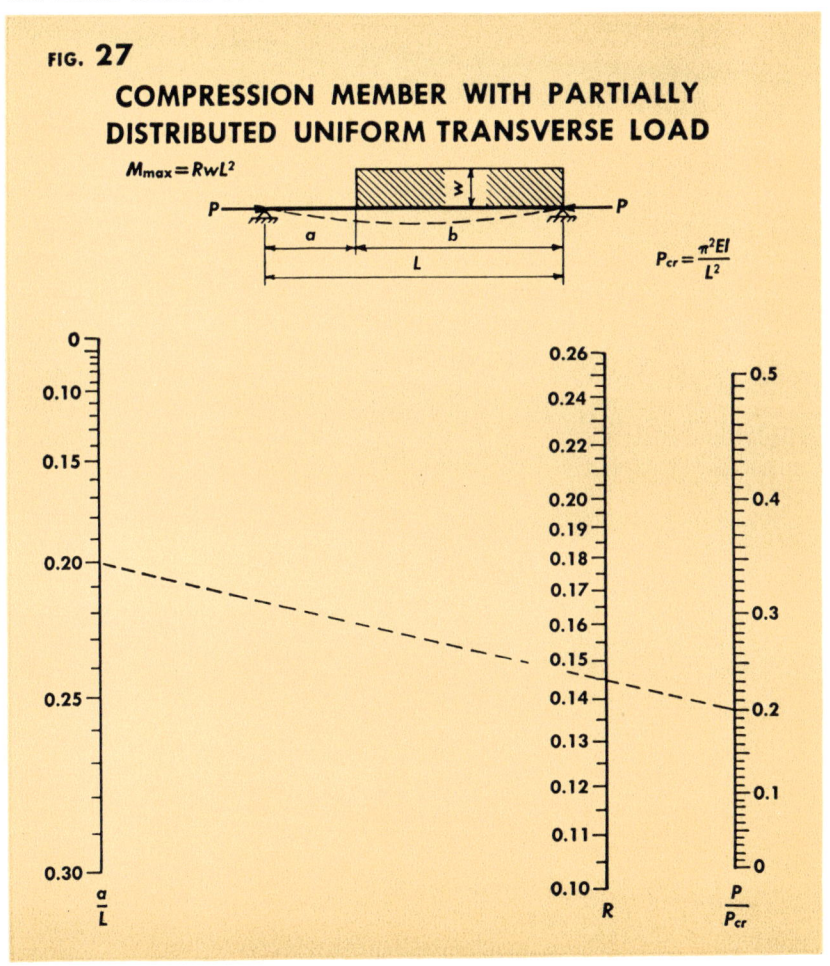

FIG. 27

COMPRESSION MEMBER WITH PARTIALLY DISTRIBUTED UNIFORM TRANSVERSE LOAD

$M_{max} = RwL^2$

$P_{cr} = \dfrac{\pi^2 EI}{L^2}$

the member, without regard to the stress it produces. The design of members of this type is a trial procedure until a section is found which satisfies Formula 35.

Figs. 26, 27 and 28 may also be used for loading conditions which comprise combinations of these cases, such as a compression member with both a uniformly distributed load and a uniformly varying load. In doing so it is suggested that the maximum bending moments be added to obtain the total maximum bending moment. An error is introduced in doing this, since the maximum bending moment does not occur at the same position in the member for each load combination. For the loading cases given, the positions

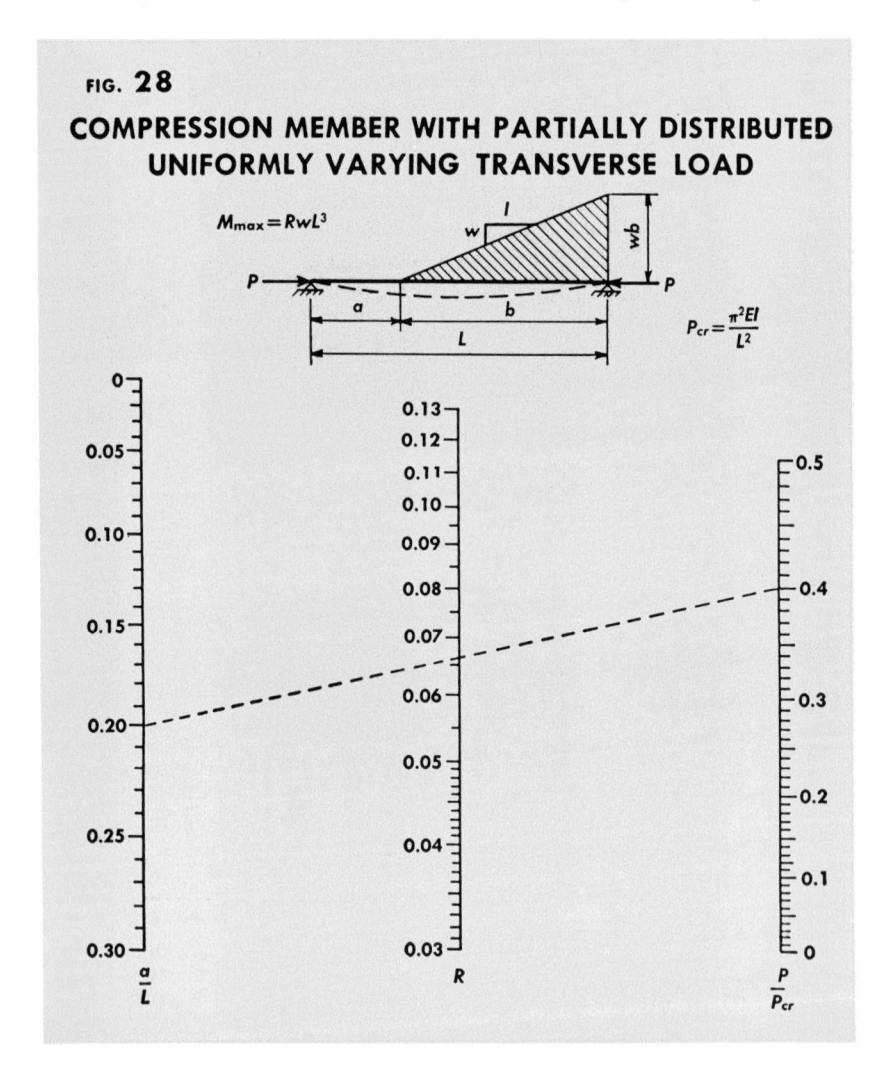

FIG. 28

COMPRESSION MEMBER WITH PARTIALLY DISTRIBUTED UNIFORMLY VARYING TRANSVERSE LOAD

$M_{max} = RwL^3$

$P_{cr} = \dfrac{\pi^2 EI}{L^2}$

STRESSES IN BEAMS 87

of maximum bending moments vary slightly from the center of the span and therefore the error is small, and for most practical purposes, negligible.

The procedure in allowing for a factor of safety in problems of this type is, in most applications, similar to that used in eccentrically loaded columns. Where the designer is interested in providing a safety factor for both the compressive and transverse loads, both should be multiplied by the factor of safety and then these loads used to determine the maximum bending moment. The maximum stress is then obtained from Formula 35. This stress should not exceed the yield point or any limiting stress in the member due to some form of compression buckling. In cases where the end load is known with certainty, such as a preloaded member, the stress obtained by using the working loads in Formula 35 should not exceed the allowable working stress, s_y/N.

Example 19

Check the member loaded as shown to see if it is safe for a steel with a yield point of 50,000 psi, using a factor of safety of 1.80.

Properties of cross section.

Using the effective area method, assume that the maximum compressive stress in the top fiber, due to the given loads multiplied by the factor of safety, is 50,000 psi.

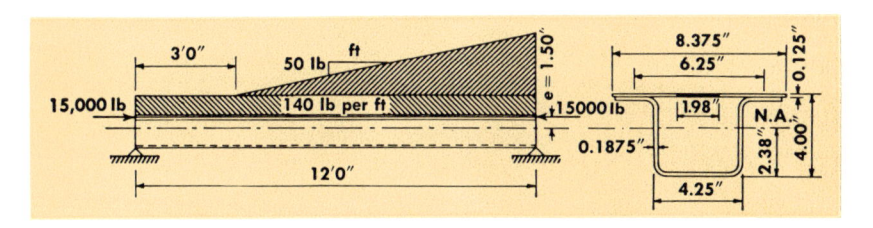

From Table 7, the maximum value of b/t, assuming the plate is simply supported, is 34.2. The maximum effective width between welds is

$b_e = 34.2 \times \frac{1}{8}'' = 4.275$ in.

Therefore, the ineffective length of the plate is $6.25'' - 4.275''$ = 1.975 in. (shown shaded).

As a first approximation, the properties of the section are:
$A = 3.53$ in.², $I_x = 8.64$ in.⁴,
Top $S_x = 5.33$ in.³, Bottom $S_x = 3.63$ in.³

Maximum bending moment.

Multiplying the given loads by $N = 1.80$, they become,
End load = 27,000 lb
Uniform load = 252 lb/ft
Varying load = 90 lb/ft per ft of length

For the section as a column,
$$P_{cr} = \frac{\pi^2 EI}{L^2} = \frac{\pi^2 \times 29 \times 10^6 \times 8.64}{(12 \times 12)^2} = 119{,}300 \text{ lb}$$
and
$$\frac{P}{P_{cr}} = \frac{27{,}000}{119{,}300} = 0.226.$$

Moment due to end load. From Fig. 26, with $P/P_{cr} = 0.226$, $R = 1.36$.
$$M_{max} = RM = 1.36 \times 27{,}000 \times 1.50/12 = 4590 \text{ ft-lb.}$$

Moment due to uniform load. From Fig. 27, with $P/P_{cr} = 0.226$ and $a/L = 0$, $R = 0.162$.
$$M_{max} = RwL^2 = 0.162 \times 252 \times 12^2 = 5880 \text{ ft-lb.}$$

Moment due to uniformly varying distributed load. From Fig. 28, with $P/P_{cr} = 0.226$ and $a/L = 3/12 = 0.25$, $R = 0.0446$.
$$M_{max} = RwL^3 = 0.0446 \times 90 \times 12^3 = 6940 \text{ ft-lb.}$$

Assuming the total maximum bending moment occurs at mid-span,
$$\Sigma M_{max} = 4590 + 5880 + 6940 = 17{,}410 \text{ ft-lb.}$$

Maximum fiber stresses, $s_{max} = \dfrac{P}{A} + \dfrac{M_{max}}{S}$

Top fiber,
$$s_{max} = -\frac{27{,}000}{3.53} - \frac{17{,}410 \times 12}{5.33} = 46{,}850 \text{ psi (comp.).}$$

Bottom fiber,
$$s_{max} = -\frac{27{,}000}{3.53} + \frac{17{,}410 \times 12}{3.63} = 49{,}900 \text{ psi (tension).}$$

When the calculated stress in the compression flange does not equal the stress which was assumed in calculating the properties of the cross section by the effective area method, the problem should be reworked until the assumed and calculated stresses are equal. In this example, the difference between the calculated and the assumed stresses is small and further calculations may not be considered necessary. Additional calculations indicate that the assumed and calculated stresses in the top flange are equal at 46,300 psi, resulting in a stress of 50,600 psi in the bottom flange. For practical purposes, the member may be considered safe for the loading shown in the sketch.

Deformation and Deflection

EXTERNAL loads acting on a body produce changes in the shape and size of the body called deformations or strains. The amount of deformation under a given load is governed by the mechanical properties of the material and the geometrical form of the body. At times, deformations become important to the designer and may govern the design itself. Such would be the case when two materials of different mechanical properties act together in a composite member, or when, for special reasons, the deformation must remain within specified maximum limits.

Members subjected to axial tension or compression, such that the stress does not exceed the proportional limit, deform so that the total change in length in a length L is

$$e = \frac{PL}{AE}, \tag{36}$$

where
  P = total axial load, lb
  L = length of member, in.
  A = cross-sectional area, in.^{2}
  E = modulus of elasticity, psi.

When dealing with compression members, Formula 36 applies only to short members not subject to buckling. Formula 36 can also be written

$$e = s\frac{L}{E}, \tag{37}$$

where
  s = average stress in member, psi.

Since the modulus of elasticity for all grades of steel is essentially constant, within the elastic region, two members of equal length but with different average stresses, due to axial loads, will deform in the same ratio as the average stresses. Thus high-strength steels, which are usually employed at higher stresses than those for structural carbon steel, will naturally have the greater deformation.

The vertical displacement of a beam under load is called deflection. The expression for the deflection of any beam under a given load is in the form of

$$\Delta = \text{Constant} \times \frac{WL^3}{EI}, \tag{38}$$

where
- W = given load on beam, lb
- L = span length, in.
- E = modulus of elasticity, psi
- I = moment of inertia, in.[4]

The given load may be a concentrated, uniformly distributed, or uniformly varying load. Each type must be treated separately and when more than one type of loading occurs on the same beam, the separate deflections at any given point in the span may be combined to obtain the total deflection.

By a simple transformation, Formula 38 may be expressed in the following terms:

$$\Delta = \text{Constant} \times \frac{sL^2}{Ed} \tag{39}$$

in which
- s = unit stress in bending, psi
- d = depth of beam or girder, in.

From Formula 39 it is evident that, other factors remaining the same, an increase in the allowable stress, as would be the case when substituting a high-strength steel for structural carbon steel, will result in an increase in the deflection in proportion to the working stresses of the two steels.

An examination of Formulas 38 and 39 shows that the deflection under a given total load may be decreased by any or all of the following methods.
 1. Decrease the bending moment by:
    a. Changing the distribution of the load.
    b. Introducing restraining moments at the ends of the span.
 2. Decrease the span length.
 3. Increase the depth of the beam.

In general, stress and not deformation or deflection is the criterion for design.

BEAM FORMULAS

The calculation of the reactions, shears, moments and deflections of beams for various loads and conditions of end supports will be greatly facilitated by the tables of "Beam Formulas" in the appendix.

Combinations of loads may be treated by superposition, that is, calculating each loading condition separately and adding the results together. The deflection at the center of the span, for most conditions, in which the loads are reasonably well distributed over the span, will give a very close approximation to the actual maximum deflection.

In using these formulas, care must be exercised to use the following sign conventions.

Loads   Loads acting downward are positive.

Bending Moment   The bending moment at any section of a horizontal beam is considered to be positive when it produces compressive stress in the top fibers of the beam at the section and tensile stress in the bottom fibers.

Deflection   Deflections downward are negative and upward are positive.

Angle of Rotation   The slope, or angle of rotation of the tangent to the elastic curve is positive when in a counter-clockwise direction.

End Reactions   The vertical component of any reaction is positive when it acts upward. The restraining moment produced in beams with one or both ends fixed is positive when the direction of the moment is clockwise at the left end, and counter-clockwise at the right end. Fig. 29 illustrates the end reactions and moments in their positive sense.

FIG. **29**

SIGN CONVENTIONS

92   DEFORMATION AND DEFLECTION

Substitutions in Formulas   All of the formulas listed will give answers with the correct sign when the substitutions are made correctly. When reactions and moments already calculated are factors in subsequent portions of the calculations, these factors should be used with the signs originally obtained. The units of measure must be consistent.

Example 20

Using the tables of Beam Formulas, select a W℉ beam to support the load shown, if the allowable fiber unit stress is 24,000 psi. For the beam selected, calculate the deflection at the center of the span.

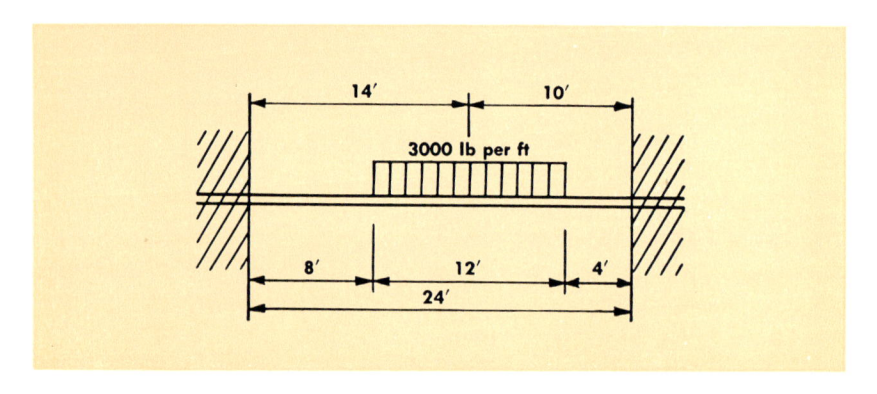

Referring to Case 1, Beam Formulas,

$$R_1 = \frac{3000 \times 12}{4 \times 24^3}[4 \times 10^2(24 + 2 \times 14) - 12^2(4-8)]$$
$$= 13{,}917 \text{ lb},$$
$$R_2 = 3000 \times 12 - 13{,}917 = 22{,}083 \text{ lb},$$
$$M_1 = \frac{3000 \times 12}{24 \times 24^2}\left\{12^2[24 + 3(4-8)] - 24 \times 10^2 \times 14\right\}$$
$$= -83{,}000 \text{ ft-lb},$$
$$M_2 = (13{,}917 \times 24) - (3000 \times 12 \times 10) + (-83{,}000)$$
$$= -109{,}000 \text{ ft-lb, and at } x = 8 + \frac{13{,}917}{3000} = 12.639 \text{ ft}$$
$$M_{\max \text{ pos}} = -83{,}000 + (13{,}917 \times 10.320) = 60{,}600 \text{ ft-lb}.$$

Therefore, M_2 is a maximum. The required section modulus is

$$S = \frac{M_2}{s} = \frac{109{,}000 \times 12}{24{,}000} = 54.5 \text{ in.}^3$$

Use a 16 W℉ 36. $S_x = 56.3$ in.^{3} and $I_x = 446.3$ in.^{4}

The deflection at the center of the span, $x = 12$ ft, is

$$\Delta_x = \frac{1}{24EI}[12(-83{,}000)12^2 + 4 \times 13{,}917 \times 12^3 - 3000 \times 4^4]$$
$$= -\frac{2.000 \times 10^6}{EI} = -\frac{2.000 \times 10^6 \times 12^3}{29 \times 10^6 \times 446.3} = -0.267 \text{ in.}$$

Formed Sections

A WIDE variety of formed sections are used in many industries as structural members, and are made from plate, sheet, and strip by means of brake presses, draw-benches, dies, cold roll-forming machines, or other equipment used for forming purposes.

The use of formed sections made from high-strength steels has been found especially advantageous in many instances where rolled sections are not available in the desired size or form, or in the reduced thickness needed to obtain the full benefit of the higher strength.

It is common shop parlance to speak of high-strength steels as being stiffer than structural carbon steel. Elastically one steel is no stiffer than another, so that what is meant is that a greater force in cold forming is required to produce a given amount of permanent deformation in high-strength steel than in structural carbon steel of the same thickness. The total forming pressure required, however, is often no greater because the high-strength steel is frequently used in thinner sections.

The technique of cold forming high-strength steels consists principally in making provision for a more liberal radius of bend, slightly increased die clearance, and more spring back. These features produce no serious difficulties when the shop personnel understand how the steel should be worked. The recommended practices for cold forming the USS High-Strength Steels are given in Table 17.

Certain operations require the forming of members of such thickness or shape that cold pressing is impracticable, and in these cases hot forming is recommended. When hot forming is employed, the inside radius of bend may be reduced in many instances from those recommended above for cold forming. Most satisfactory results in forming high-strength steels have been obtained by forming at temperatures between 1500 F and 1650 F at the dies.

Table 17

MINIMUM INSIDE RADIUS OF BEND FOR COLD FORMING

Thickness of Material—t	Brand Names of USS Steel	
	COR-TEN *TRI-TEN *TRI-TEN "E"	MAN-TEN
1/16 in. and under	1 t	2 t
Over 1/16 in. to 1/8 in. incl.	2 t	2 t
Over 1/8 in. to 1/4 in. incl.	2 t	2½ t
Over 1/4 in. to 1/2 in. incl.	3 t	3½ t
Over 1/2 in.	Hot forming is recommended	

*Not available in thicknesses less than 0.180 inch.

Formed sections offer the designer an almost unlimited variety of sections to fit the particular type of construction. Since such sections are usually fabricated from relatively thin material, the proportions of these sections are frequently limited by the consideration of local buckling of their component elements.

The basic formed section used in many structural applications is the channel used by itself, or used back-to-back to form an I-shaped section, or used toe-to-toe to form a box section. The problem often arises of improving the stability of the outstanding flanges. This may be done by the addition of stiffening lips at the outer edges of the flanges, as shown in Fig. 22.

In effect, these stiffening lips increase the stiffness of the flange when considered as a plate in edge compression and make possible the use of considerably wider flanges. When the stiffener consists of a simple lip bent at right angles to the flange and with a depth of at least $8t$, the flange may be considered as adequately stiffened, for which condition the coefficient of plate buckling, k, for the flange may be taken as 1.65. The plate buckling coefficient for the unstiffened flange, a plate simply supported along one edge, is 0.425. Referring to Table 6, the allowable ratio of b/t for stiffened

continued on page 103

FORMED SECTIONS

TABLE 18
PROPERTIES OF ELEMENTS

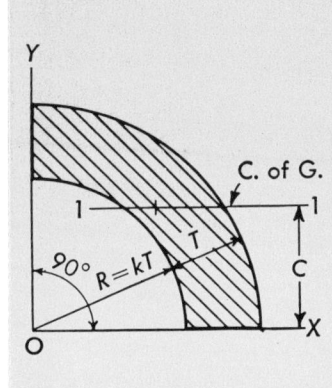

FILLET

Thickness (inch) T
Radius of fillet $R = kT$
Length (inch) $L = \dfrac{\pi}{4}(2k+1)T$
Area (sq. in.) $A = \dfrac{\pi}{4}(2k+1)T^2$
Moment $M_x = \left(\dfrac{3k^2+3k+1}{3}\right)T^3$
Distance $C = \dfrac{M_x}{A} = \dfrac{4}{3\pi}\left(\dfrac{3k^2+3k+1}{2k+1}\right)T$
Moment of inertia $I_x = \dfrac{\pi}{16}(4k^3+6k^2+4k+1)T^4$
Moment of inertia $I_{1\text{-}1} = I_x - \dfrac{4}{9\pi}\left[\dfrac{(3k^2+3k+1)^2}{2k+1}\right]T^4$

$\dfrac{\pi}{4} = 0.78540 \quad \dfrac{4}{9\pi} = 0.14147$

$\dfrac{\pi}{16} = 0.19635 \quad \dfrac{4}{3\pi} = 0.42441$

Item	Values of k					
	1.0	1.5	2.0	2.5	3.0	3.5
L	2.3562T	3.1416T	3.9270T	4.7124T	5.4978T	6.2832T
A	2.3562T²	3.1416T²	3.9270T²	4.7124T²	5.4978T²	6.2832T²
C	0.9903T	1.2998T	1.6128T	1.9275T	2.2433T	2.5596T
M_x	2.3333T³	4.0833T³	6.3333T³	9.0833T³	12.3333T³	16.0833T³
I_x	2.9452T⁴	6.6759T⁴	12.7627T⁴	21.7948T⁴	34.3612T⁴	51.0509T⁴
$I_{1\text{-}1}$	0.6345T⁴	1.3685T⁴	2.5485T⁴	4.2863T⁴	6.6935T⁴	9.8818T⁴

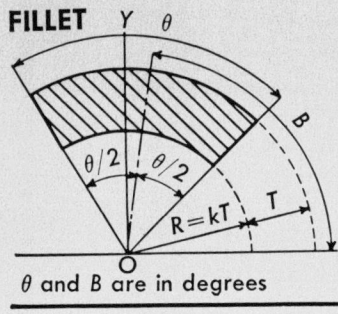

FILLET

θ and B are in degrees

$A = \dfrac{\theta}{57.30}(k+\tfrac{1}{2})T^2$

$M_x = \dfrac{(k+1)^3 - k^3}{3}\left(2\sin\dfrac{\theta}{2}\sin B\right)T^3$

$I_x = \dfrac{(k+1)^4 - k^4}{8}\left(\dfrac{\theta}{57.30} - \cos 2B \sin \theta\right)T^4$

Attention should be paid to the signs of the sines and cosines.

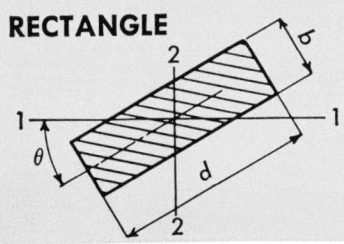

RECTANGLE

$I_{1\text{-}1} = \dfrac{bd^3\sin^2\theta}{12} + \dfrac{b^3 d\cos^2\theta}{12}$

$I_{2\text{-}2} = \dfrac{bd^3\cos^2\theta}{12} + \dfrac{b^3 d\sin^2\theta}{12}$

TABLE 19
POWERS OF t

t	t^2	t^3	t^4	$t^3/12$
0.01	0.00010	0.00000	0.00000	0.00000
0.02	0.00040	0.00001	0.00000	0.00000
0.03	0.00090	0.00003	0.00000	0.00000
0.04	0.00160	0.00006	0.00000	0.00001
0.05	0.00250	0.00013	0.00001	0.00001
0.06	0.00360	0.00022	0.00001	0.00002
0.07	0.00490	0.00034	0.00002	0.00003
0.08	0.00640	0.00051	0.00004	0.00004
0.09	0.00810	0.00073	0.00007	0.00006
0.10	0.01000	0.00100	0.00010	0.00008
0.11	0.01210	0.00133	0.00015	0.00011
0.12	0.01440	0.00173	0.00021	0.00014
0.13	0.01690	0.00220	0.00029	0.00018
0.14	0.01960	0.00274	0.00038	0.00023
0.15	0.02250	0.00338	0.00051	0.00028
0.16	0.02560	0.00410	0.00066	0.00034
0.17	0.02890	0.00491	0.00084	0.00041
0.18	0.03240	0.00583	0.00105	0.00049
0.19	0.03610	0.00686	0.00130	0.00057
0.20	0.04000	0.00800	0.00160	0.00067
0.21	0.04410	0.00926	0.00194	0.00077
0.22	0.04840	0.01065	0.00234	0.00089
0.23	0.05290	0.01217	0.00280	0.00101
0.24	0.05760	0.01382	0.00332	0.00115
1/4	0.06250	0.01563	0.00391	0.00130
9/32	0.07910	0.02225	0.00626	0.00185
5/16	0.09766	0.03052	0.00964	0.00254
11/32	0.11816	0.04062	0.01396	0.00338
3/8	0.14063	0.05273	0.01978	0.00439
13/32	0.16504	0.06705	0.02724	0.00559
7/16	0.19141	0.08374	0.03664	0.00698
15/32	0.21973	0.10300	0.04828	0.00858
1/2	0.25000	0.12500	0.06250	0.01042

TABLE 19—Continued
POWERS OF t

t	t^2	t^3	t^4	$t^3/12$
17/32	0.28223	0.14993	0.07965	0.01249
9/16	0.31641	0.17798	0.10011	0.01483
19/32	0.35254	0.20932	0.12428	0.01744
5/8	0.39063	0.24414	0.15259	0.02035
21/32	0.43066	0.28262	0.18547	0.02355
11/16	0.47266	0.32495	0.22340	0.02708
23/32	0.51660	0.37131	0.26688	0.03094
3/4	0.56250	0.42188	0.31641	0.03516
25/32	0.61035	0.47684	0.37253	0.03974
13/16	0.66016	0.53638	0.43581	0.04470
27/32	0.71191	0.60068	0.50682	0.05006
7/8	0.76563	0.66992	0.58618	0.05583
29/32	0.82129	0.74429	0.67452	0.06202
15/16	0.87891	0.82397	0.77248	0.06866
31/32	0.93848	0.90915	0.88074	0.07576
1	1.00000	1.00000	1.00000	0.08333
1- 1/32	1.06348	1.09671	1.13098	0.09139
1- 1/16	1.12891	1.19946	1.27443	0.09996
1- 3/32	1.19629	1.30844	1.43111	0.10904
1- 1/8	1.26563	1.42383	1.60181	0.11865
1- 5/32	1.33691	1.54581	1.78734	0.12882
1- 3/16	1.41016	1.67456	1.98854	0.13955
1- 7/32	1.48535	1.81027	2.20627	0.15086
1- 1/4	1.56250	1.95312	2.44141	0.16276
1- 9/32	1.64160	2.10330	2.69486	0.17528
1- 5/16	1.72266	2.26099	2.96754	0.18842
1-11/32	1.80566	2.42636	3.26042	0.20220
1- 3/8	1.89063	2.59961	3.57446	0.21663
1-13/32	1.97754	2.78091	3.91066	0.23174
1- 7/16	2.06641	2.97046	4.27003	0.24754
1-15/32	2.15723	3.16843	4.65363	0.26404
1- 1/2	2.25000	3.37500	5.06250	0.28125

TABLE 20

$R = 1.0t$ **PROPERTIES OF FILLETS**

t	L	A	C	M_x	I_x	I_{1-1}
0.01	0.0236	0.0002	0.0099	0.0000	0.0000	0.0000
0.02	0.0471	0.0009	0.0198	0.0000	0.0000	0.0000
0.03	0.0707	0.0021	0.0297	0.0001	0.0000	0.0000
0.04	0.0942	0.0038	0.0396	0.0001	0.0000	0.0000
0.05	0.1178	0.0059	0.0495	0.0003	0.0000	0.0000
0.06	0.1414	0.0085	0.0594	0.0005	0.0000	0.0000
0.07	0.1649	0.0115	0.0693	0.0008	0.0001	0.0000
0.08	0.1885	0.0151	0.0792	0.0012	0.0001	0.0000
0.09	0.2121	0.0191	0.0891	0.0017	0.0002	0.0000
0.10	0.2356	0.0236	0.0990	0.0023	0.0003	0.0001
0.11	0.2592	0.0285	0.1089	0.0031	0.0004	0.0001
0.12	0.2827	0.0339	0.1188	0.0040	0.0006	0.0001
0.13	0.3063	0.0398	0.1287	0.0051	0.0009	0.0002
0.14	0.3299	0.0462	0.1386	0.0064	0.0011	0.0002
0.15	0.3534	0.0530	0.1485	0.0079	0.0015	0.0003
0.16	0.3770	0.0603	0.1584	0.0096	0.0019	0.0004
0.17	0.4006	0.0681	0.1684	0.0115	0.0025	0.0005
0.18	0.4241	0.0763	0.1783	0.0136	0.0031	0.0007
0.19	0.4477	0.0851	0.1882	0.0160	0.0038	0.0008
0.20	0.4712	0.0942	0.1981	0.0187	0.0047	0.0010
0.21	0.4948	0.1039	0.2080	0.0216	0.0057	0.0012
0.22	0.5184	0.1140	0.2179	0.0248	0.0069	0.0015
0.23	0.5419	0.1246	0.2278	0.0284	0.0082	0.0018
0.24	0.5655	0.1357	0.2377	0.0322	0.0098	0.0021
1/4	0.5890	0.1473	0.2476	0.0365	0.0115	0.0025
9/32	0.6627	0.1864	0.2785	0.0519	0.0184	0.0040
5/16	0.7363	0.2301	0.3095	0.0712	0.0281	0.0061
11/32	0.8099	0.2784	0.3404	0.0948	0.0411	0.0089
3/8	0.8836	0.3314	0.3714	0.1230	0.0583	0.0126
13/32	0.9572	0.3889	0.4023	0.1564	0.0802	0.0173
7/16	1.0308	0.4510	0.4333	0.1954	0.1079	0.0232
15/32	1.1045	0.5177	0.4642	0.2403	0.1422	0.0306
1/2	1.1781	0.5890	0.4952	0.2917	0.1841	0.0397

TABLE 21

$R = 2.0t$

PROPERTIES OF FILLETS

t	L	A	C	M_x	I_x	I_{1-1}
0.01	0.0393	0.0004	0.0161	0.0000	0.0000	0.0000
0.02	0.0785	0.0016	0.0323	0.0001	0.0000	0.0000
0.03	0.1178	0.0035	0.0484	0.0002	0.0000	0.0000
0.04	0.1571	0.0063	0.0645	0.0004	0.0000	0.0000
0.05	0.1963	0.0098	0.0806	0.0008	0.0001	0.0000
0.06	0.2356	0.0141	0.0968	0.0014	0.0001	0.0000
0.07	0.2749	0.0192	0.1129	0.0022	0.0003	0.0001
0.08	0.3142	0.0251	0.1290	0.0032	0.0005	0.0001
0.09	0.3534	0.0318	0.1451	0.0046	0.0009	0.0002
0.10	0.3927	0.0393	0.1613	0.0063	0.0013	0.0003
0.11	0.4320	0.0475	0.1774	0.0084	0.0019	0.0004
0.12	0.4712	0.0565	0.1935	0.0110	0.0027	0.0005
0.13	0.5105	0.0664	0.2097	0.0139	0.0037	0.0007
0.14	0.5498	0.0770	0.2258	0.0174	0.0048	0.0010
0.15	0.5890	0.0884	0.2419	0.0214	0.0065	0.0013
0.16	0.6283	0.1005	0.2580	0.0260	0.0084	0.0017
0.17	0.6676	0.1135	0.2742	0.0311	0.0107	0.0021
0.18	0.7069	0.1272	0.2903	0.0369	0.0134	0.0027
0.19	0.7461	0.1418	0.3064	0.0434	0.0166	0.0033
0.20	0.7854	0.1571	0.3226	0.0507	0.0204	0.0041
0.21	0.8247	0.1732	0.3387	0.0586	0.0248	0.0049
0.22	0.8639	0.1901	0.3548	0.0674	0.0299	0.0060
0.23	0.9032	0.2077	0.3709	0.0771	0.0357	0.0071
0.24	0.9425	0.2262	0.3871	0.0875	0.0424	0.0085
1/4	0.9817	0.2454	0.4032	0.0990	0.0499	0.0100
9/32	1.1045	0.3106	0.4536	0.1409	0.0799	0.0160
5/16	1.2272	0.3835	0.5040	0.1933	0.1218	0.0243
11/32	1.3499	0.4640	0.5544	0.2573	0.1782	0.0356
3/8	1.4726	0.5523	0.6048	0.3340	0.2524	0.0504
13/32	1.5953	0.6481	0.6552	0.4246	0.3477	0.0694
7/16	1.7181	0.7517	0.7056	0.5304	0.4676	0.0934
15/32	1.8408	0.8629	0.7560	0.6523	0.6162	0.1230
1/2	1.9635	0.9817	0.8064	0.7917	0.7977	0.1593

TABLE 22

$R = 2.5t$ **PROPERTIES OF FILLETS**

t	L	A	C	M_x	I_x	$I_{1\text{-}1}$
0.01	0.0471	0.0005	0.0193	0.0000	0.0000	0.0000
0.02	0.0942	0.0019	0.0386	0.0001	0.0000	0.0000
0.03	0.1414	0.0042	0.0578	0.0003	0.0000	0.0000
0.04	0.1885	0.0075	0.0771	0.0005	0.0001	0.0000
0.05	0.2356	0.0118	0.0964	0.0012	0.0001	0.0000
0.06	0.2827	0.0170	0.1157	0.0020	0.0002	0.0000
0.07	0.3299	0.0231	0.1349	0.0031	0.0004	0.0001
0.08	0.3770	0.0302	0.1542	0.0046	0.0009	0.0002
0.09	0.4241	0.0382	0.1735	0.0066	0.0015	0.0003
0.10	0.4712	0.0471	0.1928	0.0091	0.0022	0.0004
0.11	0.5184	0.0570	0.2120	0.0121	0.0033	0.0006
0.12	0.5655	0.0679	0.2313	0.0157	0.0046	0.0009
0.13	0.6126	0.0796	0.2506	0.0200	0.0063	0.0012
0.14	0.6597	0.0924	0.2699	0.0249	0.0083	0.0016
0.15	0.7069	0.1060	0.2891	0.0307	0.0111	0.0022
0.16	0.7540	0.1206	0.3084	0.0372	0.0144	0.0028
0.17	0.8011	0.1362	0.3277	0.0446	0.0183	0.0036
0.18	0.8482	0.1527	0.3470	0.0530	0.0229	0.0045
0.19	0.8954	0.1701	0.3662	0.0623	0.0283	0.0056
0.20	0.9425	0.1885	0.3855	0.0727	0.0349	0.0069
0.21	0.9896	0.2078	0.4048	0.0841	0.0423	0.0083
0.22	1.0367	0.2281	0.4241	0.0967	0.0510	0.0100
0.23	1.0838	0.2493	0.4433	0.1105	0.0610	0.0120
0.24	1.1310	0.2714	0.4626	0.1255	0.0724	0.0142
1/4	1.1781	0.2945	0.4819	0.1420	0.0852	0.0168
9/32	1.3254	0.3728	0.5421	0.2021	0.1364	0.0268
5/16	1.4726	0.4602	0.6024	0.2772	0.2079	0.0409
11/32	1.6199	0.5568	0.6626	0.3690	0.3043	0.0598
3/8	1.7671	0.6627	0.7228	0.4790	0.4311	0.0848
13/32	1.9144	0.7777	0.7831	0.6090	0.5937	0.1168
7/16	2.0617	0.9020	0.8433	0.7606	0.7986	0.1570
15/32	2.2089	1.0355	0.9035	0.9356	1.0523	0.2069
1/2	2.3562	1.1781	0.9638	1.1354	1.3622	0.2679

TABLE 23
PROPERTIES OF FILLETS

$R = 3.0t$

t	L	A	C	M_x	I_x	$I_{1\text{-}1}$
0.01	0.0550	0.0005	0.0224	0.0000	0.0000	0.0000
0.02	0.1100	0.0022	0.0449	0.0001	0.0000	0.0000
0.03	0.1649	0.0049	0.0673	0.0004	0.0000	0.0000
0.04	0.2199	0.0088	0.0897	0.0007	0.0001	0.0000
0.05	0.2749	0.0137	0.1122	0.0016	0.0002	0.0000
0.06	0.3299	0.0198	0.1346	0.0027	0.0003	0.0001
0.07	0.3848	0.0269	0.1570	0.0042	0.0007	0.0001
0.08	0.4398	0.0352	0.1795	0.0063	0.0014	0.0003
0.09	0.4948	0.0445	0.2019	0.0090	0.0024	0.0005
0.10	0.5498	0.0550	0.2243	0.0123	0.0034	0.0007
0.11	0.6048	0.0665	0.2468	0.0164	0.0052	0.0010
0.12	0.6597	0.0792	0.2692	0.0213	0.0072	0.0014
0.13	0.7147	0.0929	0.2917	0.0271	0.0100	0.0019
0.14	0.7697	0.1078	0.3141	0.0338	0.0131	0.0025
0.15	0.8247	0.1237	0.3365	0.0417	0.0175	0.0034
0.16	0.8796	0.1407	0.3589	0.0506	0.0227	0.0044
0.17	0.9346	0.1589	0.3814	0.0606	0.0289	0.0056
0.18	0.9896	0.1781	0.4038	0.0719	0.0361	0.0070
0.19	1.0446	0.1985	0.4262	0.0846	0.0447	0.0087
0.20	1.0996	0.2199	0.4487	0.0987	0.0550	0.0107
0.21	1.1545	0.2425	0.4711	0.1142	0.0667	0.0130
0.22	1.2095	0.2661	0.4935	0.1313	0.0804	0.0157
0.23	1.2645	0.2908	0.5160	0.1501	0.0962	0.0187
0.24	1.3195	0.3167	0.5384	0.1704	0.1141	0.0222
1/4	1.3744	0.3436	0.5608	0.1928	0.1344	0.0262
9/32	1.5463	0.4349	0.6309	0.2744	0.2151	0.0419
5/16	1.7181	0.5369	0.7010	0.3764	0.3278	0.0639
11/32	1.8899	0.6496	0.7711	0.5010	0.4797	0.0934
3/8	2.0617	0.7732	0.8412	0.6503	0.6797	0.1324
13/32	2.2335	0.9074	0.9114	0.8269	0.9360	0.1823
7/16	2.4053	1.0523	0.9815	1.0328	1.2590	0.2452
15/32	2.5771	1.2080	1.0516	1.2703	1.6590	0.3232
1/2	2.7489	1.3744	1.1217	1.5417	2.1476	0.4183

TABLE 24
PROPERTIES OF FILLETS

$R = 3.5t$

t	L	A	c	M_x	I_x	I_{1-1}
0.01	0.0628	0.0006	0.0256	0.0000	0.0000	0.0000
0.02	0.1257	0.0025	0.0512	0.0001	0.0000	0.0000
0.03	0.1885	0.0057	0.0768	0.0005	0.0000	0.0000
0.04	0.2513	0.0101	0.1024	0.0010	0.0001	0.0000
0.05	0.3142	0.0157	0.1280	0.0021	0.0003	0.0001
0.06	0.3770	0.0226	0.1536	0.0035	0.0005	0.0001
0.07	0.4398	0.0308	0.1792	0.0055	0.0010	0.0002
0.08	0.5027	0.0402	0.2048	0.0082	0.0020	0.0004
0.09	0.5655	0.0509	0.2304	0.0117	0.0036	0.0007
0.10	0.6283	0.0628	0.2560	0.0161	0.0051	0.0010
0.11	0.6911	0.0760	0.2816	0.0214	0.0077	0.0015
0.12	0.7540	0.0905	0.3072	0.0278	0.0107	0.0021
0.13	0.8168	0.1062	0.3328	0.0354	0.0148	0.0029
0.14	0.8796	0.1232	0.3584	0.0441	0.0194	0.0038
0.15	0.9425	0.1414	0.3840	0.0544	0.0260	0.0050
0.16	1.0053	0.1608	0.4096	0.0659	0.0337	0.0065
0.17	1.0681	0.1816	0.4352	0.0790	0.0429	0.0083
0.18	1.1310	0.2036	0.4608	0.0938	0.0536	0.0104
0.19	1.1938	0.2268	0.4864	0.1103	0.0664	0.0128
0.20	1.2566	0.2513	0.5119	0.1287	0.0817	0.0158
0.21	1.3195	0.2771	0.5375	0.1489	0.0990	0.0192
0.22	1.3823	0.3041	0.5631	0.1713	0.1195	0.0231
0.23	1.4451	0.3324	0.5887	0.1957	0.1429	0.0277
0.24	1.5080	0.3619	0.6143	0.2223	0.1695	0.0328
1/4	1.5708	0.3927	0.6399	0.2514	0.1996	0.0386
9/32	1.7671	0.4970	0.7199	0.3579	0.3196	0.0619
5/16	1.9635	0.6136	0.7999	0.4909	0.4870	0.0943
11/32	2.1598	0.7424	0.8799	0.6533	0.7127	0.1379
3/8	2.3562	0.8836	0.9599	0.8481	1.0098	0.1955
13/32	2.5525	1.0370	1.0399	1.0784	1.3906	0.2692
7/16	2.7489	1.2027	1.1199	1.3468	1.8705	0.3621
15/32	2.9452	1.3806	1.1999	1.6566	2.4647	0.4772
1/2	3.1416	1.5708	1.2799	2.0104	3.1907	0.6176

flange at which s_{cr} is equal to s_y (Point B in Fig. 10) for structural carbon steel ($s_y = 33{,}000$ psi) would be $21.0 \times \sqrt{1.65} = 27.0$. Similarly, for a high-strength steel ($s_y = 50{,}000$ psi), $b/t = 17.1 \times \sqrt{1.65} = 22.0$.

Although the structural designer has a wide choice of sections formed from flat material, he is handicapped by the lack of tables of design properties. In the absence of such tables each new selection requires a new calculation of the design properties. For the purposes of calculating design properties, the cross-sectional area of any formed section may be considered as being made up of thin rectangular elements joined together by fillets, or rounded corners. The properties of fillet elements may be determined from the formulas in Table 18. The first part of this table covers 90-degree fillets and the second part, fillets of any angle. Expressions for determining the moment of inertia of a rectangular element about either of two rectangular axes passing through the centroid are also given in the Table. The use of this Table will be facilitated by the tabulated values of the powers of t to be found in Table 19. As a further aid to the designer, the properties of fillets for radii of bend equal to $1.0\,t$, $2.0\,t$, $2.5\,t$, $3.0\,t$ and $3.5\,t$ for various thicknesses up to $\tfrac{1}{2}$ in. are given in Tables 20 to 24.

In proportioning structural sections formed from light gage material, design engineers should be familiar with the "Specifications for the Design of Light Gage Structural Steel Members" and the "Light Gage Steel Manual" issued by the American Iron and Steel Institute.

Designing Against Corrosion

The material in this section, with a few minor changes and omissions, was presented by H. Malcolm Priest as a paper under the title "Designing Against Corrosion of Steel in Railroad Rolling Stock" at the Railroad Corrosion Conference sponsored by the International Nickel Company, Inc. at Wrightsville Beach, North Carolina, May 1-3, 1951. The paper was subsequently published in Railway Mechanical and Electrical Engineer, June 1951, under the title, "Rust— How to Combat It by Proper Design."

MANY people are keenly aware of the fact that corrosion is the source of serious economic loss and waste of natural resources. Others are actively concerned with the reduction of these losses and much research has been devoted to the fundamental aspects of the problem. Enlightened design can make an effective contribution, although it can seldom be expected to eliminate the deleterious effects of corrosion. Nevertheless, design should always seek to control or minimize these effects.

The steel industry has sought one approach to the corrosion problem through the chemical composition of the steel. Beginning with structural carbon steel, it has developed other grades, with increasing resistance to corrosion, that progress through copper steel, high-strength low-alloy steels, to the stainless steels.

The increased corrosion resistance is obtained by the addition to the steel of alloying elements which at the same time increase the cost. Consequently, the final selection of a steel depends upon a balance between the desired corrosion resistance and willingness to pay the extra cost involved. Until recent years, copper steel had been used almost exclusively in railroad car construction when added corrosion resistance was essential. A further advance was provided by some of the high-strength steels whose superior corrosion resisting properties, accompanied by the added advantage of greater strength with only a moderate cost premium, have given these steels an increasing acceptance in the railroad, as well as in many other fields.

Various familiar means have long been utilized for protecting steel against the ravages of corrosion. The most common are painting, galvanizing, tinplating, or the application of asphaltic and other compounds. The function of these methods is to interpose essentially neutral substances between the steel and the corroding media. At best, they but delay the inevitable attack unless an unbroken protective coating can be continuously maintained.

Designing engineers have often endeavored to obtain longer life from structures by adding an arbitrary amount to the thickness of material to allow for corrosion, or by specifying some minimum thickness regardless of strength requirements. In other cases, where strength is a secondary factor, the thickness has been determined on the basis of the rate of corrosion as found from experience with the type of structure under consideration. Such methods as these are not without merit but they do not go to the real root of the trouble. They are an acceptance of existing conditions rather than a remedy such as may be obtained through improved design. There is greater warrant for them when the possibilities of design have been exhausted.

There is a wider realization today that construction details play a role in corrosion, whenever they provide conditions that accelerate the action. The control of these details lies very largely in the realm of design, which is the specific subject of this discussion. Design is concerned more with the fact than with the theory of corrosion.

Corrosion is defined as the destruction of a metal by chemical or electro-chemical reaction with its environment. The amount of corrosion depends on the composition of the metal and the environment. The effects on various grades of steel corroded on test racks in an industrial atmosphere are plotted in Fig. 1.

It is noticeable that after three years of exposure the steels corroded at essentially linear rates. During the first three years the protective rusts are being developed and the corrosion rates are non-linear and relatively high. It is also noteworthy that the better grades of steel acquire a uniform protective rust film earlier than does structural carbon steel. The rust films on steel are much more protective when they are developed under alternate wet and dry conditions than under continuously moist conditions.

On test racks, specimens wet by dew and rain become periodically dry and may remain so for a considerable percentage of the time. According to the generally accepted electrochemical theory of corrosion, steel can corrode only when there is at least a film of moisture on the metal surface. Therefore, it behooves us to so design our steel structures that the surface remains wet for minimum lengths of time.

Whenever the protective rust coating is removed by erosion or cracked by bending, a fresh metal surface is exposed to corrosion. The rate of loss is again the same as indicated at the left-hand end of the chart in Fig. 1. Thus it is readily seen why mechanical action is often conducive to accelerated corrosion.

Most technological advances have been made through the careful and painstaking accumulation and study of data obtained from observations and tests. Not the least of these advances have been contributed by failures. There is a curious reluctance at times to discuss failures, as though they were like skeletons in a closet. In reality, they have been the source of some of the most valuable information and have contributed immeasurably to the progress of science and the improvement of many arts.

An excellent way to approach the subject of designing against corrosion is to observe actual conditions and to seek explanations of any unusual rates of corrosion. Inevitably, we shall deal with

FIG. 30   Corrosion loss in side sheets of hopper cars

failures—normal failures, they might be called—and shall examine them only with a view to extending the time before they occur in future construction.

Let us begin with the ordinary hopper car*—a type of car in which problems of corrosion are numerous. Railroad mechanical people are all too familiar with the condition illustrated in the photograph of Fig. 30. The first question that comes to mind is: Why did this failure occur?—and before any answer can be given, we must gather more facts about conditions.

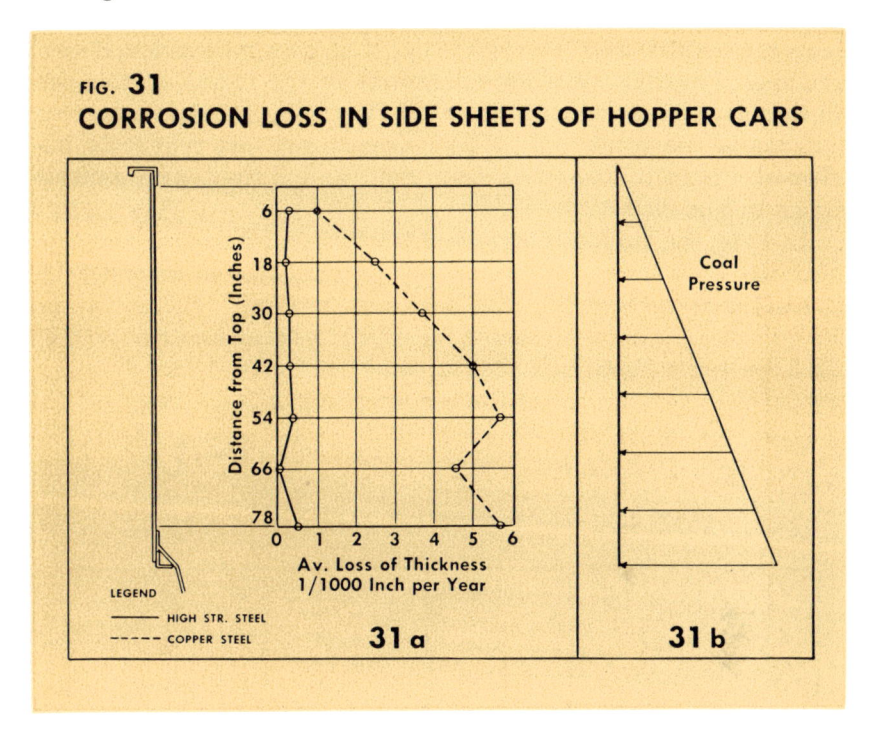

FIG. 31
CORROSION LOSS IN SIDE SHEETS OF HOPPER CARS

31 a

31 b

Av. Loss of Thickness 1/1000 Inch per Year

Distance from Top (Inches)

Coal Pressure

LEGEND
— HIGH STR. STEEL
--- COPPER STEEL

At the conclusion of an investigation of the service life of various steels in hopper cars, the side sheets from several cars were removed, cleaned and gaged for thickness, with the results depicted in Fig. 31a. From the top bulb angle to the side sill there was an increasing loss which parallels, in a general manner, the increase in horizontal

---

*While this article was written for railroad mechanical engineers and car designers, the principles of designing against corrosion are so clearly evident that their application to other types of structures should not be difficult. The hopper car (perhaps more popularly known as a coal car) is a common sight on every railroad and the interested reader may readily examine one to observe the various construction features mentioned.

pressure of the lading of coal, shown in Fig. 31b. The outward pressure creates bending stresses in the side sheet and also augments the frictional or erosive action of the lading during the unloading operation. Both of these mechanical actions vary directly with the pressure, and their effect might be expected to be more pronounced toward the side sill.

We need to look closely at the detail arrangement of the structure at the side sill where the most common construction is that shown in Fig. 32a. The significant feature to note is the ledge or shelf formed by the top edges of the sill angle and the hopper sheet. This ledge retains dirt and powdered coal that trap moisture and coal leachings. Clearly, there are conditions in the region of the side sill that can and do contribute to the failure locally although other portions of the sheet, only a few inches away, are relatively unaffected. Hence it is not surprising that we find the typical failures shown in Fig. 30.

In 1944, the United States Steel Corporation designed, and subsequently built early in 1946, an experimental car to demonstrate several ideas for meeting the corrosion problem. There was no thought that the car represented the ultimate in construction, rather the hope was entertained that it would stimulate wider thinking toward the development of further improvements.

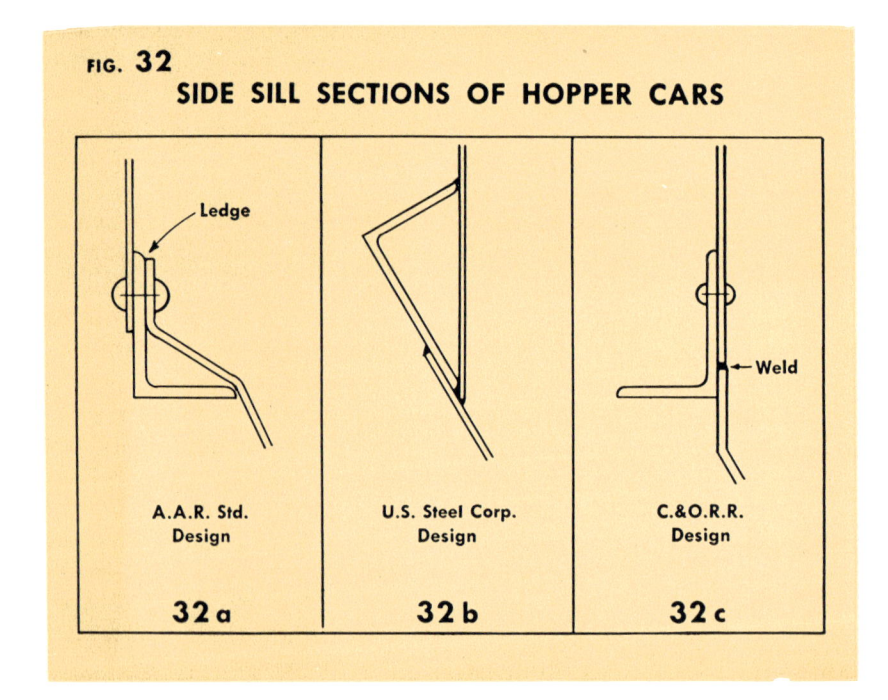

FIG. 32
SIDE SILL SECTIONS OF HOPPER CARS

A.A.R. Std. Design	U.S. Steel Corp. Design	C.&O.R.R. Design
32a (Ledge)	32b	32c (Weld)

Among the ideas was the side sill arrangement shown in Fig. 32b. By way of comparison the standard construction is given in Fig. 32a. Through redesigning, it became possible to eliminate the ledge, thereby removing one source of trouble. The new hopper cars of the Chesapeake & Ohio have the side sill detail shown in Fig. 32c and again the ledge has been effectively eliminated. In both cars, a corrosion resisting, high-strength steel was used to obtain added margin of life expectancy.

Vibration is undoubtedly a contributing factor to the failures of side sheets along the edges of supporting members. There are many opportunities for investigation of problems arising from vibration in railroad rolling stock, but the subject is a very complicated one. Flat sheets, as in hopper car sides, are particularly susceptible to vibration—the effect of which is to bend the sheets most severely at the supporting edges. Every object has a natural frequency of vibration and when the exciting force is applied with the same frequency, there is a pronounced and often violent increase in the amplitude of vibration. This phenomenon is known as "resonance."

The consequences of vibration are accelerated corrosion and loss of strength from reduced sections of the sheets at the supports, where stresses are at a maximum. Wherever resonance is encountered, it is imperative to change the natural frequency, and the problem can be met in several ways. The size of the flat panels may be changed by decreasing the spacing between side stakes or by adding stiffeners or corrugations to break up the panels into smaller flat areas. Increasing the thickness of the sheet will increase the frequency but decrease the amplitude of vibration and decrease the induced bending stress. No set rules can be laid down—the solution is perforce a matter of trial.

Car shakeouts for unloading hopper cars have been on the market since the latter part of 1946 and their operation depends upon the vibratory action set up by revolving eccentric weights. The action is so severe as to shake the whole car body and to set the side sheets into pronounced vibration. The rust scale is not only loosened at the supported edges but over the entire area as well. As will be shown presently, the most damaging effect of the vibration arises from the bending moments at the supports. The stresses resulting from these moments are increased by the presence of a reduced thickness of material or of corrosion pits which act as stress raisers.

In 1934 the Pressed Steel Car Company brought out a 50-ton hopper car of high-strength steel, weighing only 30,000 lb. The side sheets were only $3/32$-inch thick as compared to standard construction with $3/16$-inch sheets of copper steel. After 100 of these cars had been in service about 11 or 12 years, the typical failures along the side sill angles began to appear just above the usual ledge. This length of time to failure did not differ greatly from that in sides of $3/16$-inch copper steel. The added corrosion resistance of the high-strength steel could hardly account for all of the performance of the $3/32$-inch sheet. Again, we look for a possible reason and find it in the design. Each of the side panels was dished outward in a buckled form. Vibration could not flex the buckled sheets in the manner common to flat sheets, and there seems little doubt that this particular feature of the design accounts in part for the relatively superior performance of the thin sheets.

The relative merits of inside and outside stakes are worth careful consideration. From the standpoint of corrosion, inside stakes have very little in their favor. It should always be remembered that steel surfaces on the inside of a hopper car are not painted and are fully exposed to corrosive action. Inside stakes also impede the smooth flow of lading and the construction affords numerous opportunities for local corrosion.

Fig. 33 illustrates the side construction of the AAR* standard hopper cars with inside stakes and two other designs with outside

---

*Association of American Railroads

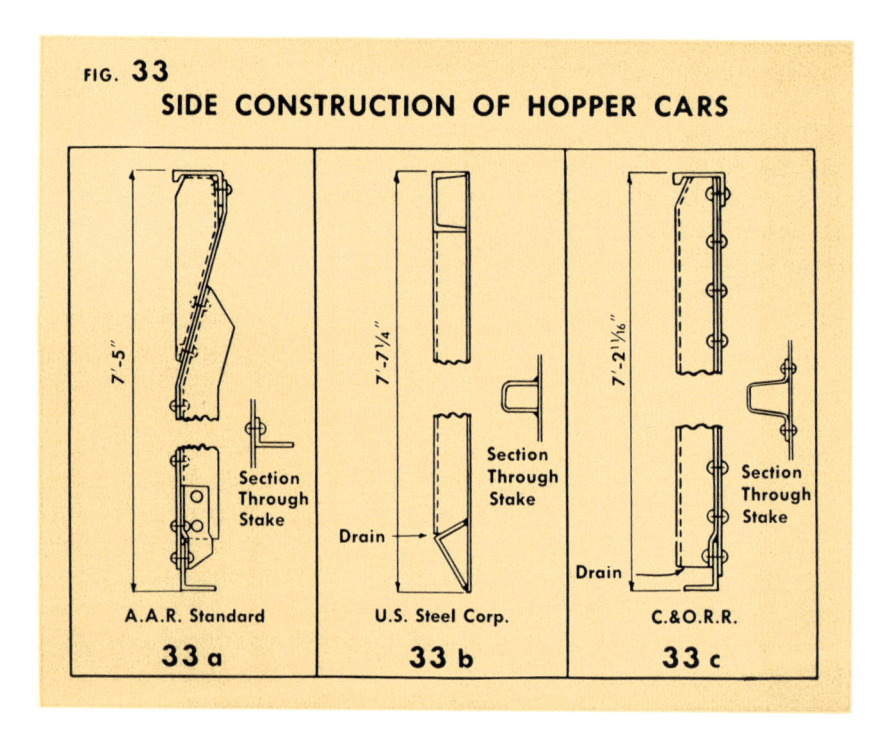

FIG. 33
SIDE CONSTRUCTION OF HOPPER CARS

33 a — A.A.R. Standard — Section Through Stake — 7'-5"

33 b — U.S. Steel Corp. — Section Through Stake — Drain — 7'-7¼"

33 c — C.&O.R.R. — Section Through Stake — Drain — 7'-2 1/16"

stakes. It is evident that the construction for inside stakes is more elaborate—requiring the forming of the side sheets, the trimming and forming of stakes and outside extensions. By contrast, the other types of construction require no forming of the sheets and the stakes are of simple form. Furthermore, the stakes can be kept painted since they are not exposed to the lading.

The smooth interiors of the U. S. Steel and C. & O. designs reduce the chances for local corrosion. Contrast these types of construction with the standard design in the photograph of Fig. 34 showing an inside stake and the accumulation of dirt on ledges and in crevices.

An important point in design of stakes is to provide for drainage of any moisture from the inside. Water will seep between the faying surfaces of the stakes and sheets and collect inside unless drainage can take place. The stake in Fig. 34 apparently has no such provision. The outside stakes in Fig. 33 have outlets as indicated. In the case of the U. S. Steel car, the opening was inadvertently closed by welding. When the welds were chipped out, some of the stakes were found to have as much as two quarts of water entrapped. It had seeped in between intermittent welds connecting the stakes to the sheet.

FIG. 34 Accumulation of dirt on ledges at inside stake

The life of floor sheets in hopper cars is not entirely determined by corrosion. Present-day methods of unloading with clam shell buckets, building fires under cars to thaw frozen lading, and the impact of lading falling from considerable heights subject the floor to very severe abuse of a destructive character. This mechanical damage has the effect of loosening rust scale, distorting the sheets, opening joints and thereby clearing the way for fresh corrosion attack. Design must meet these conditions by providing adequate stiffness in the floor supports.

As in the previous discussion of side sheets, it is well to examine the nature and location of failures that commonly occur in the floors. Fig. 35 shows the losses in thickness as found in the investigation of service life of various grades of steel. One readily recognizes the increasing rate of loss from the upper end of the floor to the door opening. Here again is a case where erosion plays a part. The loss is related to the depth and weight of lading and the quantity that slides over the surface of the steel. It is becoming more common practice to recognize this condition by increasing the thicknesses of the floor from the ends to the hopper chutes.

One of the striking facts about floor failures is their proximity to the supporting members. There must be a reason for this, and

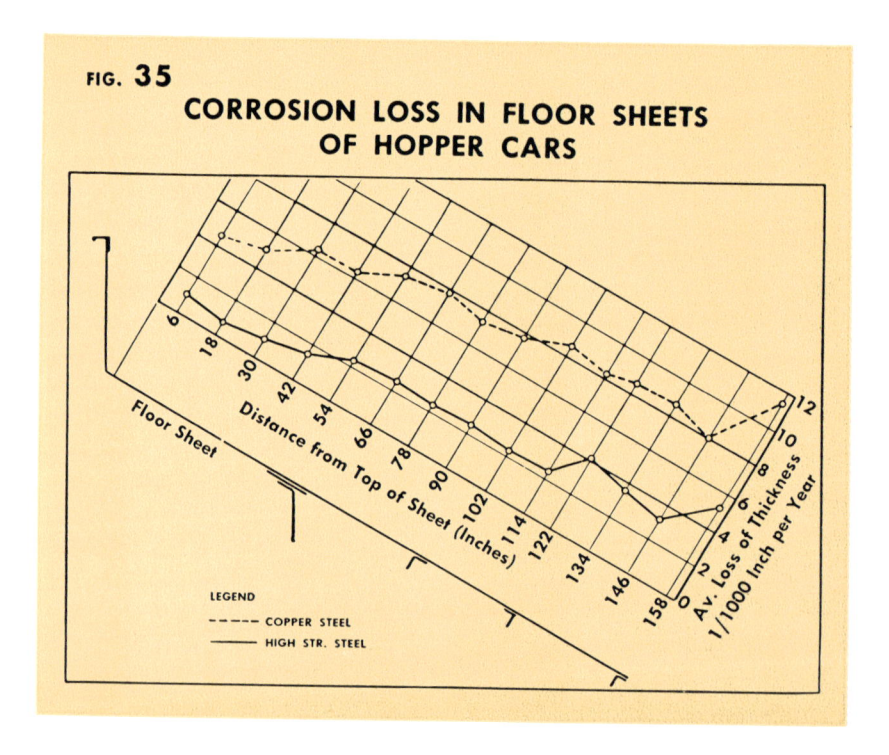

FIG. 35

CORROSION LOSS IN FLOOR SHEETS OF HOPPER CARS

LEGEND
- - - - COPPER STEEL
——— HIGH STR. STEEL

FIG. 36   Failures in floor sheets of hopper cars

again it is a case where bending or flexure enters into the situation. The condition is aggravated when the flexure is accompanied by excessive deflection of the sheets, as may occur when the floor stiffeners are not adequate. This is shown in the photograph of Fig. 36.

Fig. 37 shows a failure in a floor sheet just above an inside stake at the body bolster. The collection of dirt behind this stake, even with a small deflecting plate welded in the corner, undoubtedly contributed to the acceleration of corrosion. Then too, the flexure added its contribution with the inevitable consequences. In this particular case, the condition was further complicated by the failure of the upper floor stiffeners to function effectively—resulting in excessive deflections.

The failure of these floor stiffeners is an interesting case. They were zees extending from the end of the car to the bolster. Being of an unsymmetrical section, they eventually twisted in a manner to lose much of their strength and permitted the upper floor to sag several inches. As a part of the major repairs to these cars, the zee stiffeners have been replaced with pressed channels, back to back, which form symmetrical members that provide better support.

It has been noted that failures of floor sheets are more numerous

FIG. 37 Failure of floor at bolster stake

at the edges of supporting members. A contributing reason for this tendency may be found from a consideration of the two cases of bending illustrated in Fig. 38a. The plates are assumed to be fixed at the supports in both examples. The upper sketch shows a plate being bent downward over a rigid support and it should be noted that the bending effect is concentrated at the supporting edge, A. In the lower sketch an intermediate plate is introduced which participates in the bending at the support and acts as a cushion to the top plate, as well as serving to distribute the bending effect over a greater distance. This construction is often followed where it is desired to reduce the stress concentration at points of rigid support.

Some examples of the construction around the top flanges of body bolsters may be examined in the light of the foregoing discussion. These are depicted in Figs. 38b to 38f. The floor sheet in Fig. 38b has an intermediate support at edge B and also at edge A, but at the latter location the lower floor sheet is in the joint and adds extra stiffness or rigidity. Hence the condition at A should be less satisfactory from the standpoint of concentration of flexure in the upper floor sheet at the edge of the supporting member. Fig. 38c show a rather common type of beam bolster with the top flange bent to the 30-deg. slope of the floor. At both edges A and B the floor is supported on a thick and comparatively rigid beam flange and will be bent more sharply at the edges.

The construction shown in Fig. 38d is similar to that shown in the car in Fig. 36 where it will be seen that the failure was at the lower edge of the bolster flange plate. While the floor sheet at edge B has an intermediate support, the cantilever portion of the flange plate may have been short enough to have had considerable rigidity.

An improved detail is illustrated in Fig. 38e, in which all the lapping of the floor sheets is over the bolster flange, concentrating the rigidity there and giving intermediate support to the floor at edges A and B.

Another attempt to provide flexibility at the bolster is shown in Sketch f and is the construction used in the U. S. Steel experimental hopper car. Bending of the flange of the beam bolster was avoided in favor of press-brake forming of what might be called a bolster extension. The vertical leg and flanges of this extension were intended to relieve the stress concentration.

In all of these sketches, the reader should keep in mind the erosion to which floors are subjected and relate it to the bending of the

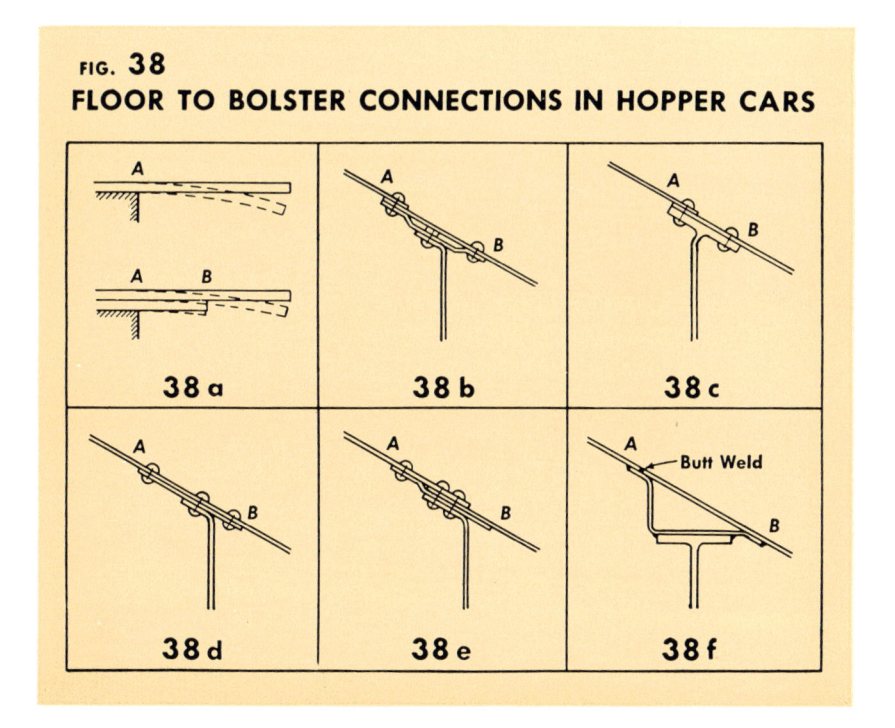

FIG. 38
FLOOR TO BOLSTER CONNECTIONS IN HOPPER CARS

FIG. 39

DETAIL AT DOOR FRAME

Detail at Door Frame — Floor Sheet, Door, A

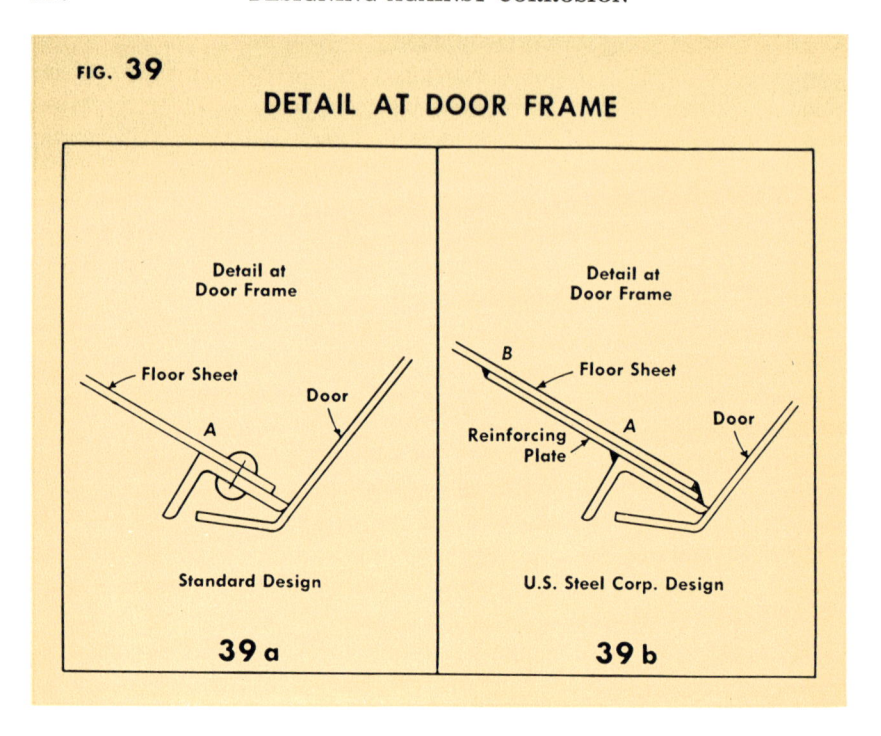

Standard Design

39 a

Detail at Door Frame — B, Floor Sheet, Reinforcing Plate, A, Door

U.S. Steel Corp. Design

39 b

sheets. The evidence is ample to connect the combination of these two factors to the concentration of premature corrosion failures at the edges of rigid supports.

The lower edge of the hopper sheet over the door angle is often a point of early failure. A combination of the heaviest load and the greatest amount of erosion occurs here. Fig. 39a shows the details of the construction to be found in most cars. Failure usually occurs at edge A where the leg of the door angle normal to the floor sheet furnishes a stiff support for the sheet. An endeavor to meet this condition was made in the U. S. Steel experimental car and is depicted in Fig. 39b. A reinforcing plate, 12 inches wide, was added to distribute the flexure away from the edge A. Of course the erosive action during unloading will inevitably reduce the thickness of the floor sheet and when failure occurs the reinforcing plate is in position to support the lading. In effect, the ultimate patching operation was performed in advance and the beneficial support from the plate was obtained from the outset.

The lower flange of the door itself serves to catch coal leachings which run over the lip and along the bottom surface before dropping to the ground. Thus the flange can be attacked on both surfaces—a condition that is not good from the standpoint of corrosion.

DESIGNING AGAINST CORROSION

The design of joints should not be overlooked as a factor having a bearing on corrosion. The riveted lap joint of Fig. 40a has an inherent possibility of moisture seepage between the faying surfaces. Rusting is likely to follow and often the corrosion product, since it occupies a much greater volume than the original steel, will force the surfaces apart. This is particularly true of thin material and actually happened in some side stakes (Fig. 40b). The flanges were buckled between rivets—which be it said, were spaced further apart than the thickness of material warranted. Corrosion did excessive damage, resulting in the replacement of the stakes at the time of the first major repair.

Specifications generally contain limitations on the spacing of rivets in compression members to assure the strength against buckling and to obtain a tight joint.

It is well to remember that the expansion of rivets during driving sets up compressive stresses in the surrounding materials which can cause wrinkling or buckling between rivets. In an early application of high-strength steel side sheets to box cars a lesser thickness than the usual 0.10 in. in copper steel was used. Smaller rivets on closer spacing were thought desirable for a watertight joint. A trial indicated, however, that the usual size of rivet and spacing were better.

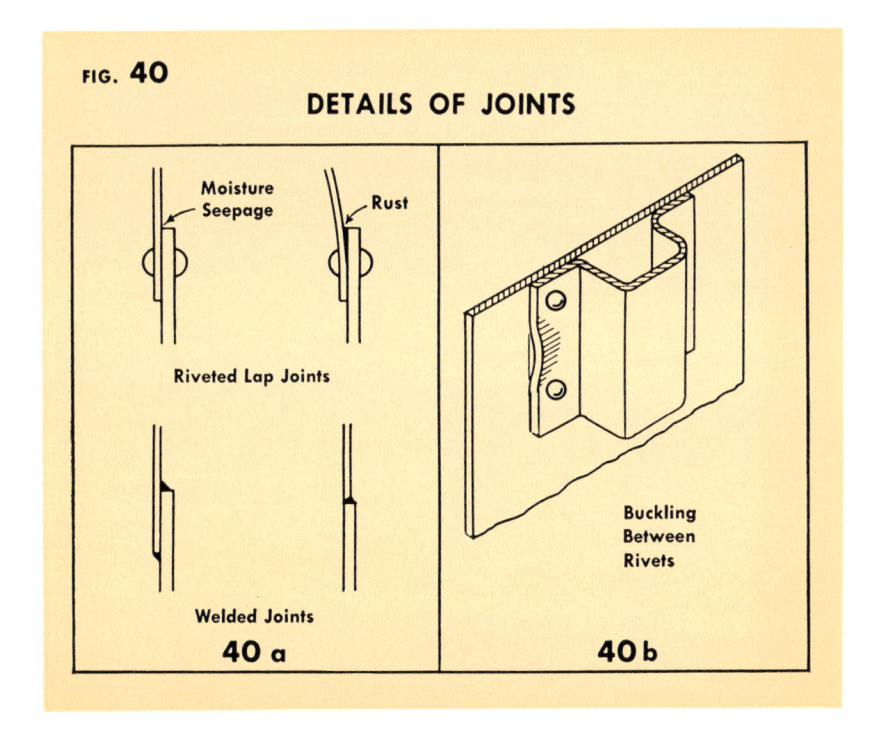

FIG. 40 DETAILS OF JOINTS

Riveted Lap Joints — Moisture Seepage, Rust

Welded Joints

40 a

Buckling Between Rivets

40 b

Welding has presented engineers with a broad field in which to devise and develop new designs and to make a fresh and often novel approach to old procedures. In its relation to corrosion, welding has opened new possibilities for sealing joints against moisture, as is readily apparent from the sketch in Fig. 40a. It has offered opportunities for eliminating lap joints in favor of butt joints. A study of the sketches in Fig. 32 will quite clearly reveal the part played by welding in achieving conditions effective in reducing corrosion damage. Fig. 38f illustrates the use of a butt weld to eliminate the usual lap joint in the floor.

The discussion, so far, has centered around the hopper car because it is believed that most of the corrosion problems are typified in this car. Corrosion in all cases is basically the same process and only the environment varies. The presence of moisture, certain chemicals or mechanical action will produce similar effects in any type of car or structure.

Box and refrigerator cars have special conditions arising from condensation of moisture, which collects in low spots and pockets. Obviously, effort should be made to eliminate such places, wherever possible. A good example of changes for the better is evident in the progressive development of details in the region of the side sill.

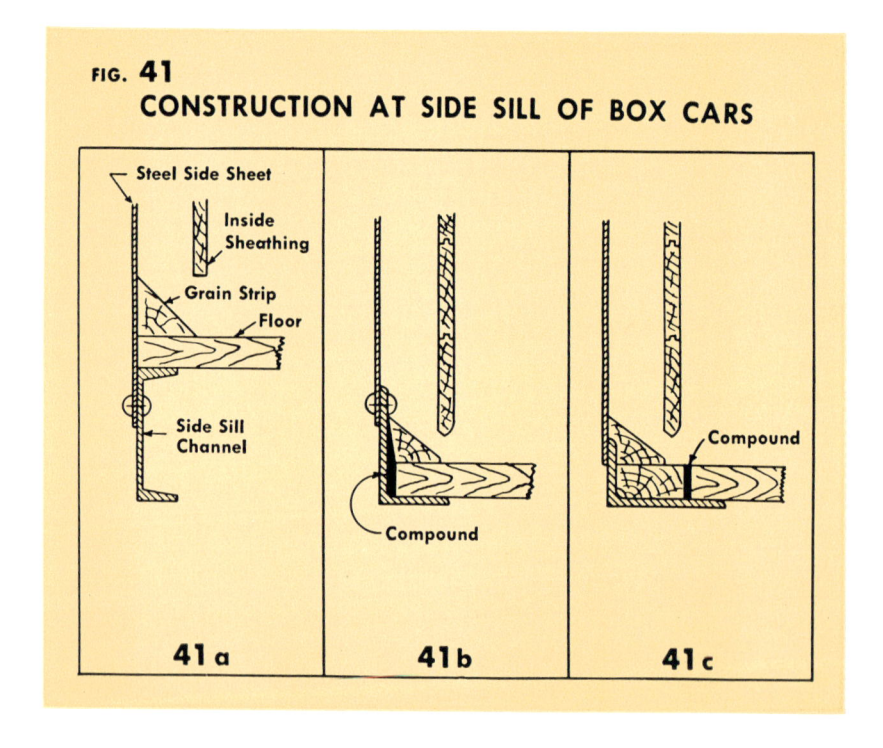

FIG. 41
CONSTRUCTION AT SIDE SILL OF BOX CARS

41a — Steel Side Sheet, Inside Sheathing, Grain Strip, Floor, Side Sill Channel

41b — Compound

41c — Compound

Figs. 41a and 41b show two stages in the evolution.

Fig. 41a illustrates the construction that was quite common practice 20-25 years ago. Condensed moisture, running down the inside surface of the side sheet could find its way rather easily between the grain strip and floor plank and the steel sheet, where it would be retained for a considerable period. This is not a favorable condition with respect to corrosion. A later AAR design, which is still standard, shown in Fig. 41b, used a 6 in. x $3\frac{1}{2}$ in. x $\frac{5}{16}$ in. angle with the long leg vertical, thus removing the thin steel side sheet from the region where moisture collects. It is true that there is a small ledge formed by the top toe of the angle, but this point is exposed to the air so that the moisture that does collect can more readily evaporate than in the case where it is trapped between surfaces. However, this small ledge is a good place to apply some protective compound to reduce the possibility of corrosion.

Fig. 41c is illustrative of the construction proposed for a design in high-strength steel. In view of the above discussion it would seem as though the conditions with respect to corrosion are more like those in Fig. 41a and therefore less favorable for retarding corrosion.

In a lot of 97 box cars the lower corners of the end side sheets began to corrode through after only ten years and have had to be patched. The repair has been made on many of the cars and as any of the remainder return to the home line the same condition is found to exist. Otherwise, the side sheets are in good condition. A flanged gusset between the side sills and the end posts of these cars was found to be a contributing cause. The gusset and side sheet were in close proximity and the space between them served to collect dirt and moisture.

Refrigerator cars are a special case since salt brine is almost always present. Drippings are a serious problem not alone to the under frame of the cars but to the track and bridge structures. The AAR is giving much study to this whole matter.

Galvanizing of all steel in contact with ice and salt brine is the common method for protection against corrosion. It is essential to prevent access of brine to those parts of the steel structure which are not protected by galvanizing. One particular case is known where brine from overhead bunkers splashed over the edges and ran down the side sheets, causing serious damage to the sheets and side posts.

Gondolas and flat cars with wood floors are subject to corrosion where the wood rests on the steel and retains moisture in the joint. During the repairs to a lot of gondolas it was noted that the center sill covers were badly corroded along the center line. This rather singular occurrence led to an investigation of the buckling resistance of this cover plate in compression. Because the ratio of its unsupported width to thickness was large, it had a small margin against buckling. It seemed quite probable that buckling took place along the central portion of the plate, loosening the rust film, exposing the underlying steel to fresh attack and eventually leading to the failure that took place. Here was a case where design could help to correct a difficulty arising from corrosion.

Passenger and dining cars have contributed a generous share of corrosion problems. Great quantities of moisture must be handled in these cars and ventilation disposes of most of it. However, it is difficult to deal with the condensation on cold sheets and the penetration of moisture into cracks and crevices. No detail of construction is too insignificant to warrant a study of its corrosion potentialities.

The possibility of corrosive leachings from insulation should not be overlooked. In one instance, a hair insulation had been fireproofed with magnesium chloride which caused very serious corrosion of stainless steel and would have produced an even more severe attack on plain steel.

Car washing compounds containing acids, such as oxalic acid, can be troublesome, particularly if the joints are not tight. Vibration and working of a structure increase the difficulty of maintaining tight joints, but it is the function of design to endeavor to prevent the access of moisture to the interior parts of a structure. A case in point is a corrosion attack that occurred in the sheets adjacent to the curved corners of some windows. The flexibility of the sheet at these points appeared to be the most likely cause, and it is possible that a small stiffening element across the corners would have prevented the trouble.

The widespread use of various metals in passenger cars places the designing engineer under the necessity of giving attention to the possible contact of two metals that may cause galvanic corrosion if moisture is present. For example, contact between stainless steel and plain steel may cause an accelerated corrosion of the plain steel.

The construction details of passenger cars are so varied that no attempt has been made to deal with them specifically. Either the elimination of pockets where moisture can be retained or added protection are two general principles to be followed in reducing corrosion.

Some of the high-strength low-alloy steels on the market today are much more resistant to corrosion than structural carbon steel. With such steels available, the remedies for excessive corrosion have not been exhausted by the designer who has given consideration only to the methods so far discussed.

Reference again to Fig. 1 will afford a comparison over a period of nearly 12 years among these steels when exposed in an industrial atmosphere. L is a structural steel with low residual copper content, K is a structural copper steel and the remainder are high-strength steels. It should be noted that not all high-strength steels possess equal corrosion resistance, although most of them are as good as, if not superior to, copper steel.

At the end of the test period the relative rates of resistance to corrosion, with steel L as the base, were $L:K:A$ as $1.0:2.5:6.3$. It is commonly stated that the atmospheric corrosion resistance ratios of these three steels are as follows: Carbon steel $= 1.0$; copper steel $= 2.0$; high-strength steel (most corrosion resistant composition) $= 4$ to 6.

The actual service experience will naturally vary considerably from the above ratios, depending upon the environment and conditions of operation. The charts of Fig. 31a and Fig. 35 afford a direct comparison in hopper car service between copper steel and a corrosion resistant high-strength steel. These curves are an integration of all the factors affecting the life of side and floor sheets.

Long experience with copper steel indicates that its life expectancy is about $1\frac{1}{2}$ times that of structural carbon steel in hopper car service. Service experience in hopper cars, extending over the past seventeen years, is now affording evidence that the more corrosion-resistant grades of high-strength steels last about $1\frac{1}{2}$ times longer than copper steel.

These high-strength steels can be utilized in several ways. Because of their greater strength, they can be used in reduced thicknesses without impairment of the strength of the structure. With proper reduction in thickness a life equal to that of copper steel can be expected. This was the most general approach to the design of cars with high-strength steels during the period immediately following the introduction of these steels in 1934.

Weight savings up to $3\frac{1}{2}$ and even 5 tons per car were obtained with the high-strength steels, making available a corresponding increase in pay load capacity. The extra cost of material was largely offset by the reduction in weight of steel required, so that the first cost of a car was nearly equalized.

In recent years the trend in the use of high-strength steels has been quite definitely toward their utilization in the same and even greater thicknesses than have been common practice with copper steel.

The cost of major repairs has risen so high that it has become of vital importance to extend the time between shoppings. It is here that the corrosion-resistant high-strength steels can make a substantial contribution by providing extra life, the extension depending upon the thickness used.

The aim of this discussion has not been to propose specific designs, but rather to suggest a method of approach to corrosion problems through a knowledge of how corrosion occurs in different environments. One can always learn much from examining structures with a critical eye and mind to determine, if possible, the underlying causes of whatever corrosion is found.

Corrosion protection costs money, but neglect to take it into account will often prove still more costly. When first cost is made the deciding factor, there is no assurance that, in the long run, the total cost will be a minimum. So long a time elapses before the costs of corrosion are developed that the temptation to procrastinate is always present.

Corrosion is still a challenge to everyone concerned with the problem it creates and fully warrants all the study and research that is being devoted to its reduction. As a summary of the ways in which a designer should endeavor to minimize corrosion, the following suggestions should prove helpful.

1. Eliminate all ledges, pockets and crevices where dirt and moisture can collect.
2. Provide for drainage of moisture, especially from enclosed portions of the structure.
3. Avoid construction in which excessive flexure can constantly loosen the rust film.
4. Give consideration to the possible effects of vibration.
5. Utilize the enhanced corrosion-resisting properties of a high-strength steel such as USS Cor-Ten steel.

APPENDIX

Beam Formulas

*Characteristics of
USS High-Strength Steels*

Bibliography

BEAM FIXED AT BOTH ENDS
UNIFORM LOAD PARTIALLY DISTRIBUTED

BEAM FORMULAS Case 1

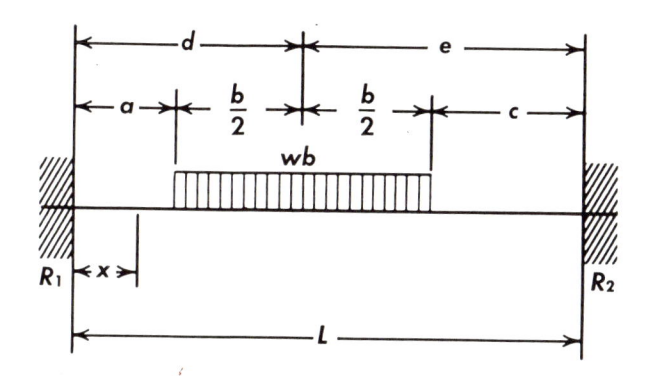

$$R_1 = \frac{wb}{4L^3}[4e^2(L+2d) - b^2(c-a)]$$

$$R_2 = wb - R_1$$

$$M_1 = \frac{wb}{24L^2}\{b^2[L+3(c-a)] - 24e^2d\}$$

$$M_2 = R_1 L - wbe + M_1$$

at $x = a + \dfrac{R_1}{w}$

$$M_{\text{max. positive}} = M_1 + R_1\left(a + \frac{R_1}{2w}\right)$$

when $0 < x < a$

$$M_x = M_1 + R_1 x$$

$$\triangle_x = \frac{1}{6EI}(3M_1 x^2 + R_1 x^3)$$

when $a < x < (a+b)$

$$M_x = M_1 + R_1 x - \frac{w}{2}(x-a)^2$$

$$\triangle_x = \frac{1}{24EI}[12M_1 x^2 + 4R_1 x^3 - w(x-a)^4]$$

BEAM FORMULAS
Case 2

**BEAM FIXED AT BOTH ENDS
UNIFORMLY DISTRIBUTED LOAD**

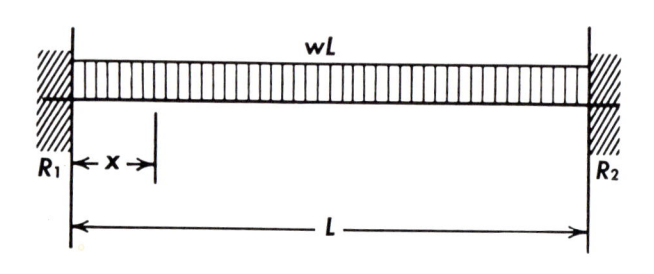

$$R_1 = R_2 = \frac{wL}{2}$$

$$M_1 = M_2 = M_{max.\ negative} = -\frac{wL^2}{12}$$

at $x = \dfrac{L}{2}$

$$M_{max.\ positive} = \frac{wL^2}{24}$$

$$\triangle_{max.} = -\frac{wL^4}{384EI}$$

when $0 < x < L$

$$M_x = \frac{w}{12}(6Lx - 6x^2 - L^2)$$

$$\triangle_x = -\frac{wx^2}{24EI}(L-x)^2$$

**BEAM FIXED AT BOTH ENDS
CONCENTRATED LOAD AT ANY POINT**

BEAM FORMULAS Case 3

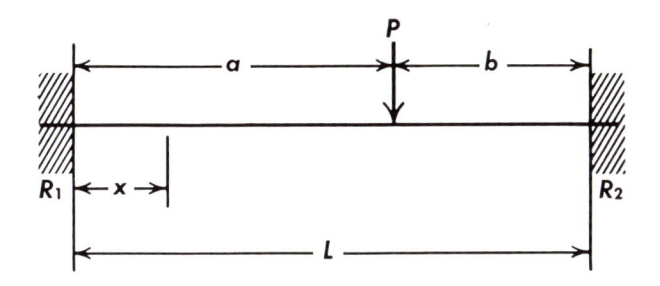

$$R_1 = \frac{Pb^2}{L^3}(L+2a)$$

$$R_2 = \frac{Pa^2}{L^3}(L+2b)$$

$$M_1 = M_{\text{max. negative if } a<b} = -\frac{Pab^2}{L^2}$$

$$M_2 = M_{\text{max. negative if } a>b} = -\frac{Pa^2b}{L^2}$$

at $x = a$

$$M_{\text{max. positive}} = \frac{2P}{L}\left(\frac{ab}{L}\right)^2$$

$$\triangle_a = -\frac{P}{3EI}\left(\frac{ab}{L}\right)^3$$

at $x = \dfrac{2aL}{L+2a}$ when $a > b$

$$\triangle_{\text{max.}} = -\frac{2Pa}{3EI}\left(\frac{ab}{L+2a}\right)^2$$

when $0 < x < a$

$$M_x = M_1 + R_1 x$$

$$\triangle_x = \frac{Pb^2 x^2}{6EIL^3}(3ax + bx - 3aL)$$

BEAM FORMULAS
Case 4

**BEAM FIXED AT BOTH ENDS
CONCENTRATED LOAD AT CENTER**

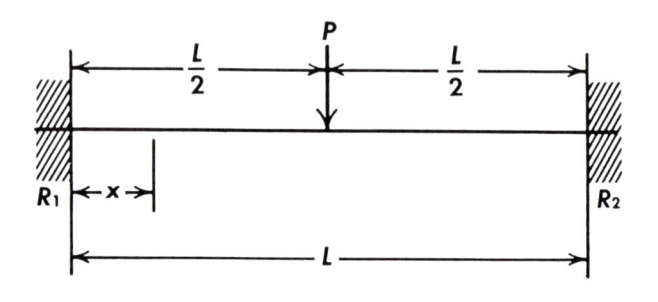

$$R_1 = R_2 = \frac{P}{2}$$

$$M_1 = M_2 = M_{max.\ negative} = -\frac{PL}{8}$$

at $x = \frac{L}{2}$

$$M_{max.\ positive} = \frac{PL}{8}$$

$$\triangle_{max.} = -\frac{PL^3}{192EI}$$

when $0 < x < \frac{L}{2}$

$$M_x = \frac{P}{8}(4x - L)$$

$$\triangle_x = \frac{Px^2}{48EI}(4x - 3L)$$

BEAM FIXED AT BOTH ENDS—UNIFORMLY VARYING LOAD PARTIALLY DISTRIBUTED

BEAM FORMULAS Case 5

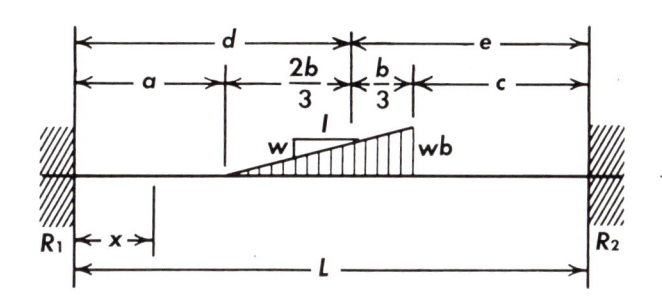

$$R_1 = \frac{wb^2}{540L^3}[56b^3 - 45b^2(L-2a) + 270e^2(L+2d)]$$

$$R_2 = \frac{wb^2}{2} - R_1$$

$$M_1 = \frac{wb^2}{540L^2}[b^2(30L - 45a - 28b) - 270de^2]$$

$$M_2 = M_1 + R_1 L - \frac{wb^2 e}{2}$$

at $x = a + \sqrt{\frac{2R_1}{w}}$

$$M_{max.\ positive} = M_1 + R_1\left[a + \frac{2}{3}\sqrt{\frac{2R_1}{w}}\right]$$

when $0 < x < a$

$$M_x = M_1 + R_1 x$$

$$\triangle_x = \frac{1}{6EI}(3M_1 x^2 + R_1 x^3)$$

when $a < x < (a+b)$

$$M_x = M_1 + R_1 x - \frac{w}{6}(x-a)^3$$

$$\triangle_x = \frac{1}{120EI}[60M_1 x^2 + 20R_1 x^3 - w(x-a)^5]$$

when $(a+b) < x < L$

$$M_x = M_1 + R_1 x - \frac{wb^2}{2}(x-d)$$

$$\triangle_x = \frac{1}{6EI}[3M_2(L-x)^2 + R_2(L-x)^3]$$

BEAM FORMULAS
Case 6

**BEAM FIXED AT BOTH ENDS
UNIFORMLY VARYING LOAD**

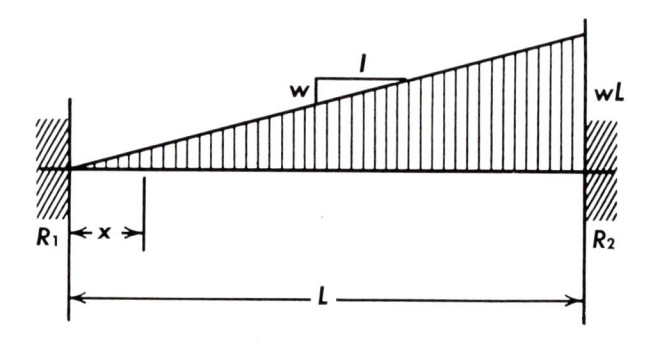

$$R_1 = \frac{3wL^2}{20}$$

$$R_2 = \frac{7wL^2}{20}$$

$$M_1 = -\frac{wL^3}{30}$$

$$M_2 = M_{\text{max. negative}} = -\frac{wL^3}{20}$$

at $x = 0.5477L$

$$M_{\text{max. positive}} = 0.02144wL^3$$

at $x = 0.5247L$

$$\triangle_{\text{max.}} = -0.0013085\frac{wL^5}{EI}$$

when $0 < x < L$

$$M_x = \frac{w}{60}(9L^2x - 10x^3 - 2L^3)$$

$$\triangle_x = \frac{wx^2}{120EI}(3L^2x - x^3 - 2L^3)$$

BEAM FIXED AT ONE END, SUPPORTED AT OTHER
UNIFORM LOAD PARTIALLY DISTRIBUTED

BEAM FORMULAS Case 7

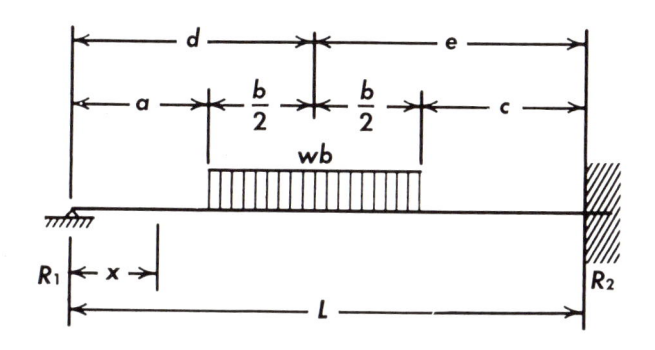

$$R_1 = \frac{wb}{8L^3}(12e^2L - 4e^3 + b^2d)$$

$$R_2 = wb - R_1$$

$$M_2 = M_{max.\ negative} = \frac{wb}{8L^2}(12e^2L - 4e^3 + b^2d - 8eL^2)$$

at $x = a + \frac{R_1}{w}$

$$M_{max.\ positive} = R_1\left(a + \frac{R_1}{2w}\right)$$

when $0 < x < a$

$$M_x = R_1 x$$

$$\triangle_x = \frac{x}{24EI}[4R_1(x^2 - 3L^2) + wb(b^2 + 12e^2)]$$

when $a < x < (a+b)$

$$M_x = R_1 x - \frac{w}{2}(x-a)^2$$

$$\triangle_x = \frac{1}{24EI}[4R_1 x(x^2 - 3L^2) + wbx(b^2 + 12e^2) - w(x-a)^4]$$

when $(a+b) < x < L$

$$M_x = R_1 x - wb(x-d)$$

$$\triangle_x = \frac{1}{6EI}[3M_2(L-x)^2 + R_2(L-x)^3].$$

BEAM FORMULAS
Case 8
BEAM FIXED AT ONE END, SUPPORTED AT OTHER UNIFORMLY DISTRIBUTED LOAD

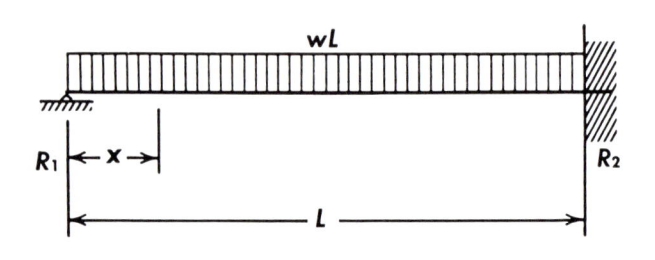

$$R_1 = \frac{3wL}{8}$$

$$R_2 = \frac{5wL}{8}$$

$$M_2 = M_{max\ negative} = -\frac{wL^2}{8}$$

at $x = \frac{3L}{8}$

$$M_{max.\ positive} = \frac{9wL^2}{128}$$

at $x = 0.4215L$

$$\triangle_{max.}\ (approx.) = -\frac{41wL^4}{7570EI}$$

when $0 < x < L$

$$M_x = R_1 x - \frac{wx^2}{2}$$

$$\triangle_x = \frac{wx}{48EI}(3Lx^2 - 2x^3 - L^3)$$

BEAM FIXED AT ONE END, SUPPORTED AT OTHER
CONCENTRATED LOAD AT ANY POINT

BEAM FORMULAS
Case 9

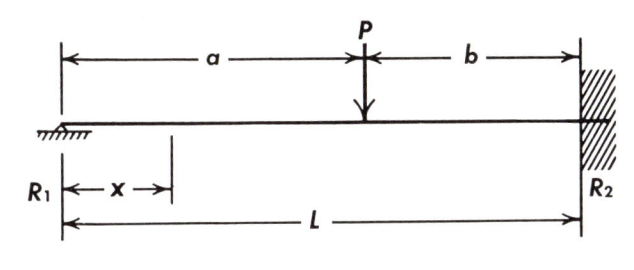

$$R_1 = \frac{Pb^2}{2L^3}(2L+a)$$

$$R_2 = \frac{Pa}{2L^3}(3L^2 - a^2)$$

$$M_2 = M_{\text{max. negative}} = -\frac{Pab}{2L^2}(L+a)$$

at $x = a$

$$M_{\text{max. positive}} = R_1 a$$

$$\triangle_a = -\frac{Pa^2b^3}{12EIL^3}(3L+a)$$

at $x = L\left(\dfrac{L^2+a^2}{3L^2-a^2}\right)$ where $a < (\sqrt{2}-1)L$

$$\triangle_{\text{max.}} = -\frac{Pa(L^2-a^2)^3}{3EI(3L^2-a^2)^2}$$

at $x = L\sqrt{\dfrac{a}{2L+a}}$ where $a > (\sqrt{2}-1)L$

$$\triangle_{\text{max.}} = -\frac{Pab^2}{6EI}\sqrt{\frac{a}{2L+a}}$$

when $0 < x < a$

$$M_x = R_1 x$$

$$\triangle_x = \frac{Pb^2 x}{12EIL^3}[(2L+a)x^2 - 3aL^2]$$

when $a < x < L$

$$M_x = R_1 x - P(x-a)$$

$$\triangle_x = \frac{Pa}{12EIL^3}(L-x)^2[(2L+x)a^2 - 3L^2 x]$$

BEAM FORMULAS
Case 10 — BEAM FIXED AT ONE END, SUPPORTED AT OTHER CONCENTRATED LOAD AT CENTER

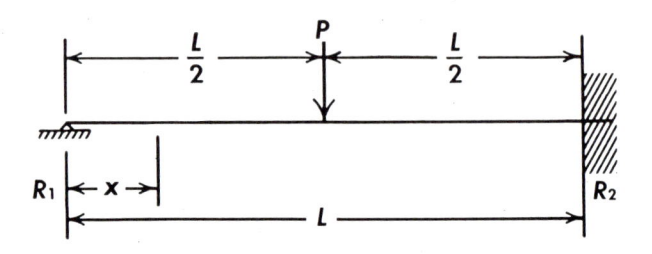

$$R_1 = \frac{5P}{16}$$

$$R_2 = \frac{11P}{16}$$

$$M_2 = M_{\text{max. negative}} = -\frac{3PL}{16}$$

at $x = \dfrac{L}{2}$

$$M_{\text{max. positive}} = \frac{5PL}{32}$$

$$\triangle = -\frac{7PL^3}{768EI}$$

when $x = \dfrac{L}{\sqrt{5}} = 0.4472L$

$$\triangle_{\text{max.}} = -0.009317 \frac{PL^3}{EI}$$

when $0 < x < \dfrac{L}{2}$

$$M_x = \frac{5Px}{16}$$

$$\triangle_x = \frac{Px}{96EI}(5x^2 - 3L^2)$$

when $\dfrac{L}{2} < x < L$

$$M_x = \frac{P}{16}(8L - 11x)$$

$$\triangle_x = \frac{P}{96EI}(L - x)^2(2L - 11x)$$

BEAM FIXED AT ONE END, SUPPORTED AT OTHER UNIFORMLY VARYING LOAD PARTIALLY DISTRIBUTED

BEAM FORMULAS Case 11

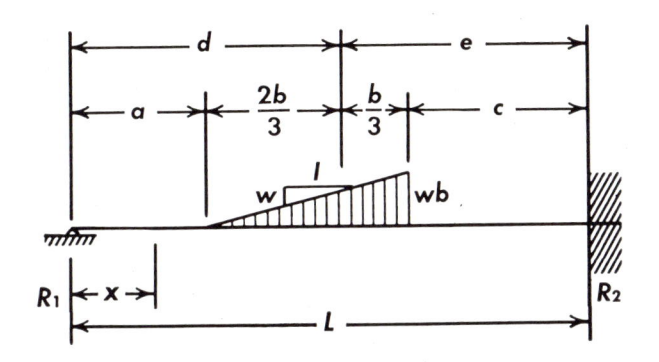

$$R_1 = \frac{wb^2}{1080L^3}[45ab^2 + 28b^3 + 270e^2(2L+d)]$$

$$R_2 = \frac{wb^2}{2} - R_1$$

$$M_2 = M_{max.\ negative} = R_1 L - \frac{wb^2 e}{2}$$

at $x = a + \sqrt{\frac{2R_1}{w}}$

$$M_{max.\ positive} = R_1\left(a + \frac{2}{3}\sqrt{\frac{2R_1}{w}}\right)$$

when $0 < x < a$

$M_x = R_1 x$

$$\triangle_x = \frac{x}{72EI}[12R_1(x^2 - 3L^2) + wb^2(b^2 + 18e^2)]$$

when $a < x < (a+b)$

$$M_x = R_1 x - \frac{w}{6}(x-a)^3$$

$$\triangle_x = \frac{1}{360EI}[60R_1(x^2 - 3L^2)x + 5wb^2(b^2 + 18e^2)x - 3w(x-a)^5]$$

when $(a+b) < x < L$

$$M_x = R_1 x - \frac{wb^2}{2}(x-d)$$

$$\triangle_x = \frac{1}{6EI}[3M_2(L-x)^2 + R_2(L-x)^3]$$

BEAM FORMULAS
Case 12
BEAM FIXED AT ONE END, SUPPORTED AT OTHER
UNIFORMLY VARYING LOAD
PARTIALLY DISTRIBUTED

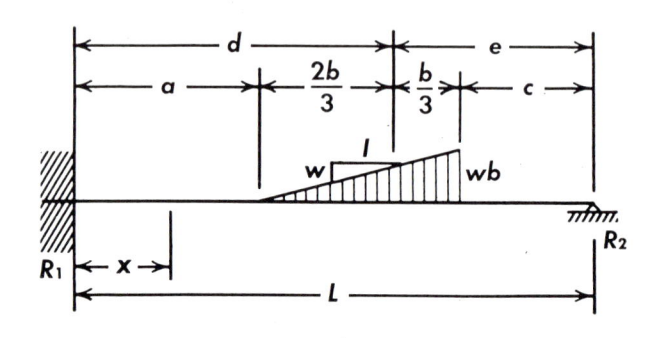

$$R_1 = \frac{wb^2}{1080L^3}(810eL^2 - 45b^2c - 17b^3 - 270e^3)$$

$$R_2 = \frac{wb^2}{2} - R_1$$

$$M_1 = M_{max.\ neg.} = \frac{wb^2}{1080L^2}[b^2(17b - 45c) - 270de(L+e)]$$

at $x = a + \sqrt{\dfrac{2R_1}{w}}$

$$M_{max.\ pos.} = M_1 + R_1\left(a + \frac{2}{3}\sqrt{\frac{2R_1}{w}}\right)$$

when $0 < x < a$

$$M_x = M_1 + R_1 x$$

$$\triangle_x = \frac{1}{6EI}(3M_1 x^2 + R_1 x^3)$$

when $a < x < (a+b)$

$$M_x = M_1 + R_1 x - \frac{w}{6}(x-a)^3$$

$$\triangle_x = \frac{1}{120EI}[60M_1 x^2 + 20R_1 x^3 - w(x-a)^5]$$

when $(a+b) < x < L$

$$M_x = M_1 + R_1 x - \frac{wb^2}{2}(x-d)$$

$$\triangle_x = \frac{1}{12EI}[6Mx^2 + 2R_1 x^3 - wb^2(x-d)^3$$

$$+ \frac{wb^4}{270}(45a + 28b - 45x)]$$

BEAM FIXED AT ONE END, SUPPORTED AT OTHER
UNIFORMLY VARYING LOAD

BEAM FORMULAS Case 13

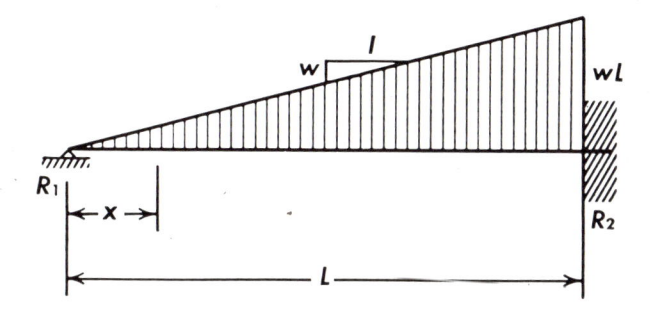

$$R_1 = \frac{wL^2}{10}$$

$$R_2 = \frac{2wL^2}{5}$$

$$M_2 = M_{\text{max. negative}} = -\frac{wL^3}{15}$$

at $x = \dfrac{L}{\sqrt{5}} = 0.4472L$

$$M_{\text{max. positive}} = \frac{wL^3}{15\sqrt{5}} = 0.02981 wL^3$$

$$\triangle_{\text{max.}} = -\frac{2wL^5}{375\sqrt{5}EI} = -0.002385\frac{wL^5}{EI}$$

when $0 < x < L$

$$M_x = \frac{w}{30}(3L^2x - 5x^3)$$

$$\triangle_x = -\frac{wx}{120EI}(L^2 - x^2)^2$$

BEAM FORMULAS
Case 14
**BEAM FIXED AT ONE END, SUPPORTED AT OTHER
UNIFORMLY VARYING LOAD**

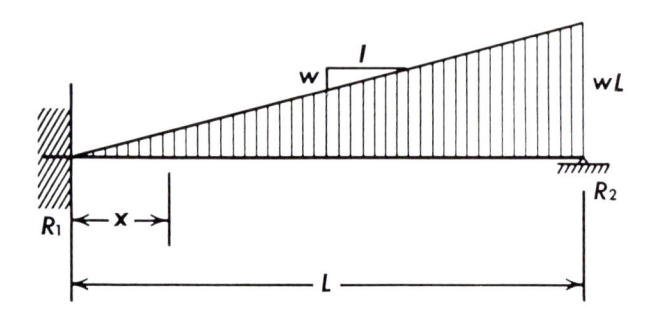

$$R_1 = \frac{9wL^2}{40}$$

$$R_2 = \frac{11wL^2}{40}$$

$$M_1 = M_{max.\ negative} = -\frac{7wL^3}{120}$$

at $x = \dfrac{3L}{2\sqrt{5}} = 0.6708L$

$$M_{max.\ positive} = \frac{wL^3}{120\sqrt{5}}(27 - 7\sqrt{5}) = 0.04229wL^3$$

at $x = 0.5975L$

$$\triangle_{max.} = -0.003048\frac{wL^5}{EI}$$

when $0 < x < L$

$$M_x = M_1 + R_1 x - \frac{wx^3}{6}$$

$$\triangle_x = \frac{x^2}{120EI}(60M_1 + 20R_1 x - wx^3)$$

BEAM SUPPORTED AT BOTH ENDS
UNIFORM LOAD PARTIALLY DISTRIBUTED

BEAM FORMULAS Case 15

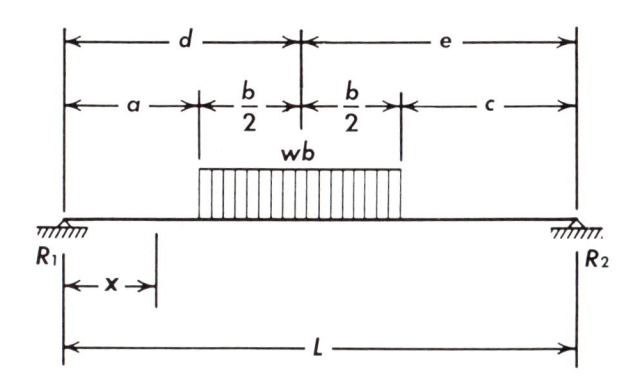

$$R_1 = \frac{wbe}{L}$$

$$R_2 = \frac{wbd}{L}$$

at $x = a + \dfrac{R_1}{w}$

$$M_{\text{max. positive}} = R_1\left(a + \frac{R_1}{2w}\right) = \frac{w}{2L^2}(2abeL + b^2e^2)$$

when $0 < x < a$

$$M_x = R_1 x = \frac{wbex}{L}$$

$$\triangle_x = \frac{wbex}{24EIL}(b^2 + 4e^2 - 4L^2 + 4x^2)$$

when $a < x < (a+b)$

$$M_x = R_1 x - \frac{w}{2}(x-a)^2$$

$$\triangle_x = \frac{w}{24EIL}\left[bex(b^2 + 4e^2 - 4L^2 + 4x^2) - L(x-a)^4\right]$$

BEAM FORMULAS
Case 16

BEAM SUPPORTED AT BOTH ENDS
UNIFORMLY DISTRIBUTED LOAD

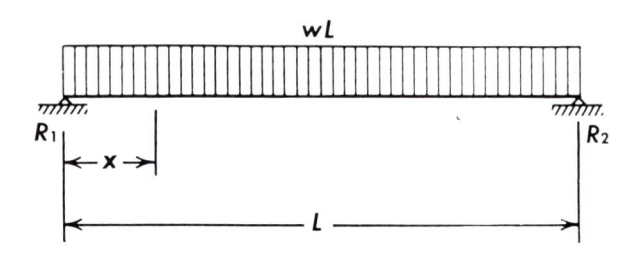

$$R_1 = R_2 = \frac{wL}{2}$$

at $x = \dfrac{L}{2}$

$$M_{\text{max. positive}} = \frac{wL^2}{8}$$

$$\triangle_{\text{max.}} = -\frac{5wL^4}{384EI}$$

when $0 < x < L$

$$M_x = \frac{wx}{2}(L-x)$$

$$\triangle_x = \frac{wx}{24EI}(2Lx^2 - L^3 - x^3)$$

BEAM SUPPORTED AT BOTH ENDS
CONCENTRATED LOAD AT ANY POINT

BEAM FORMULAS Case 17

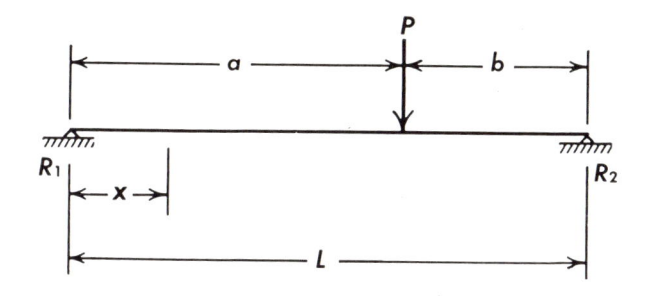

$$R_1 = \frac{Pb}{L}$$

$$R_2 = \frac{Pa}{L}$$

at $x = a$

$$M_{\text{max. positive}} = \frac{Pab}{L}$$

$$\triangle_a = -\frac{Pa^2b^2}{3EIL}$$

at $x = \sqrt{\dfrac{L^2 - b^2}{3}}$ when $a > b$

$$\triangle_{\text{max.}} = -\frac{Pb}{3EIL}\left(\frac{L^2 - b^2}{3}\right)^{\frac{3}{2}}$$

when $0 < x < a$

$$M_x = \frac{Pbx}{L}$$

$$\triangle_x = \frac{Pbx}{6EIL}(b^2 - L^2 + x^2)$$

BEAM FORMULAS
Case 18

BEAM SUPPORTED AT BOTH ENDS
CONCENTRATED LOAD AT CENTER

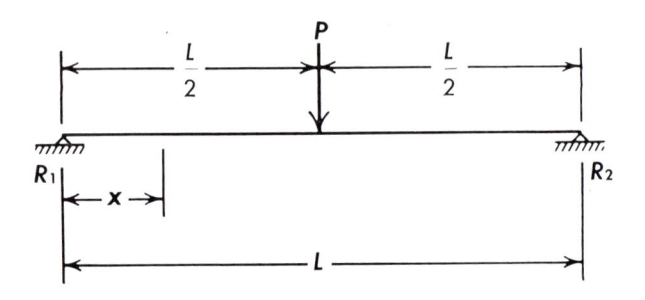

$$R_1 = R_2 = \frac{P}{2}$$

at $x = \frac{L}{2}$

$$M_{\text{max. positive}} = \frac{PL}{4}$$

$$\triangle_{\text{max.}} = -\frac{PL^3}{48EI}$$

when $0 < x \frac{L}{2}$

$$M_x = \frac{Px}{2}$$

$$\triangle_x = \frac{Px}{48EI}(4x^2 - 3L^2)$$

BEAM SUPPORTED AT BOTH ENDS
UNIFORMLY VARYING LOAD
PARTIALLY DISTRIBUTED

BEAM FORMULAS Case 19

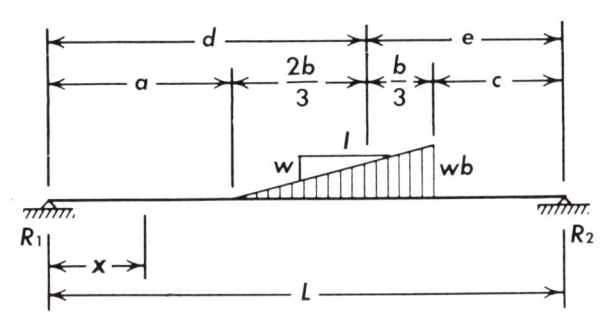

$$R_1 = \frac{wb^2 e}{2L}$$

$$R_2 = \frac{wb^2}{2} - R_1 = \frac{wb^2 d}{2L}$$

at $x = a + b\sqrt{\dfrac{e}{L}}$

$$M_{\text{max. pos.}} = \frac{wb^2 e}{6L}\left(3a + 2b\sqrt{\frac{e}{L}}\right)$$

when $0 < x < a$

$$M_x = R_1 x = \frac{wb^2 ex}{2L}$$

$$\triangle_x = \frac{wb^2 x}{3240 EIL}[45b^2 c + 17b^3 - 270de(L+e) + 270ex^2]$$

when $a < x < (a+b)$

$$M_x = \frac{w}{6L}[3b^2 ex - L(x-a)^3]$$

$$\triangle_x = \frac{w}{3240 EIL}\{b^2 x[45b^2 c + 17b^3 - 270de(L+e) + 270ex^2] - 27L(x-a)^5\}$$

when $(a+b) < x < L$

$$M_x = \frac{wb^2 d}{2L}(L-x)$$

$$\triangle_x = \frac{wb^2}{3240 EI}\left\{\frac{x}{L}[17b^3 - 45b^2(L-c) - 270e(L^2 - e^2) + 270ex^2] + b^2(45a + 28b) - 270(x-d)^3\right\}$$

BEAM FORMULAS
Case 20

**BEAM SUPPORTED AT BOTH ENDS
UNIFORMLY VARYING LOAD**

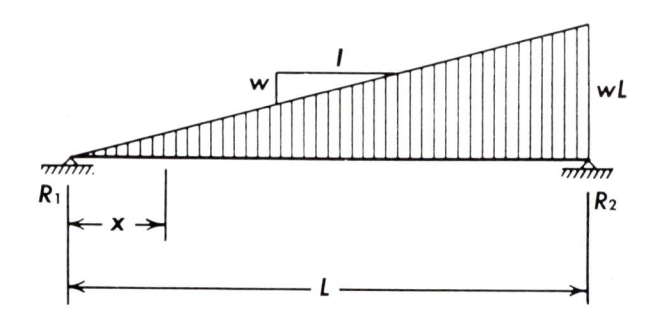

$$R_1 = \frac{wL^2}{6}$$

$$R_2 = \frac{wL^2}{3}$$

at $x = \dfrac{L}{\sqrt{3}} = 0.5774L$

$$M_{\text{max. positive}} = \frac{wL^3}{9\sqrt{3}} = 0.06415wL^3$$

at $x = L\sqrt{1 - \sqrt{\dfrac{8}{15}}} = 0.5193L$

$$\triangle_{\text{max.}} = -0.006522\frac{wL^5}{EI}$$

when $0 < x < L$

$$M_x = \frac{wx}{6}(L^2 - x^2)$$

$$\triangle_x = -\frac{wx}{360EI}(7L^4 - 10L^2x^2 + 3x^4)$$

CANTILEVER BEAM
UNIFORM LOAD PARTIALLY DISTRIBUTED

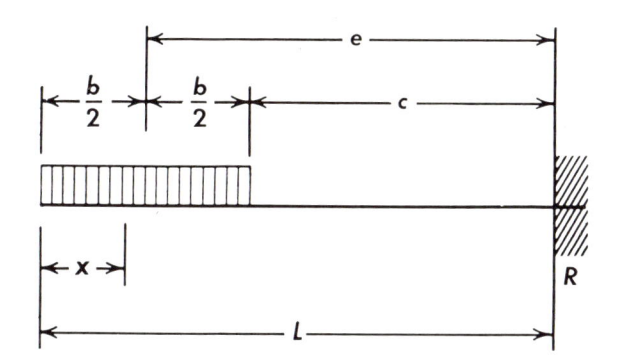

BEAM FORMULAS Case 21

$R = wb$

at $x = L$

$M_{max.} = -wbe$

at $x = 0$

$$\triangle_{max.} = \frac{wb}{48EI}(8e^3 - 24e^2L - b^3)$$

$$\theta = \frac{wb}{24EI}(b^2 + 12e^2)$$

when $0 < x < b$

$$M_x = -\frac{wx^2}{2}$$

$$\triangle_x = \frac{w}{48EI}[8be^3 - 24be^2(L-x) + 2b^3x - b^4 - 2x^4]$$

when $b < x < L$

$$M_x = \frac{wb}{2}(b - 2x)$$

$$\triangle_x = \frac{wb}{48EI}[8e^3 - 24e^2(L-x) - (2x-b)^3]$$

**BEAM FORMULAS
Case 22**

**CANTILEVER BEAM
UNIFORMLY DISTRIBUTED LOAD**

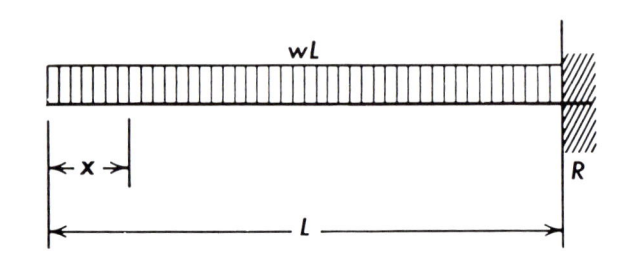

$R = wL$

at $x = L$

$$M_{max.} = -\frac{wL^2}{2}$$

at $x = 0$

$$\triangle_{max.} = -\frac{wL^4}{8EI}$$

$$\theta = \frac{wL^3}{6EI}$$

when $0 < x < L$

$$M_x = -\frac{wx^2}{2}$$

$$\triangle_x = \frac{w}{24EI}[L^3(4x-3L)-x^4]$$

CANTILEVER BEAM
CONCENTRATED LOAD AT FREE END

BEAM FORMULAS Case 23

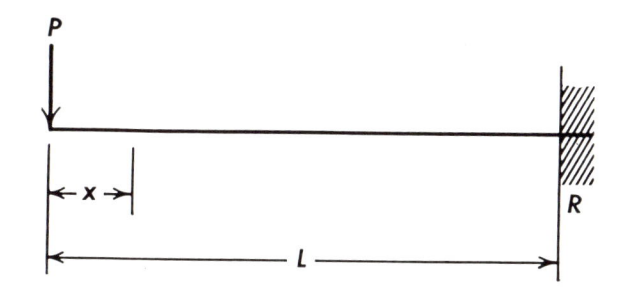

$R = P$

at $x = L$

$$M_{max.} = -PL$$

at $x = 0$

$$\triangle_{max.} = -\frac{PL^3}{3EI}$$

$$\theta = \frac{PL^2}{2EI}$$

when $0 < x < L$

$$M_x = -Px$$

$$\triangle_x = \frac{P}{6EI}(3L^2x - 2L^3 - x^3)$$

BEAM FORMULAS
Case 24

**CANTILEVER BEAM
UNIFORMLY VARYING LOAD
PARTIALLY DISTRIBUTED**

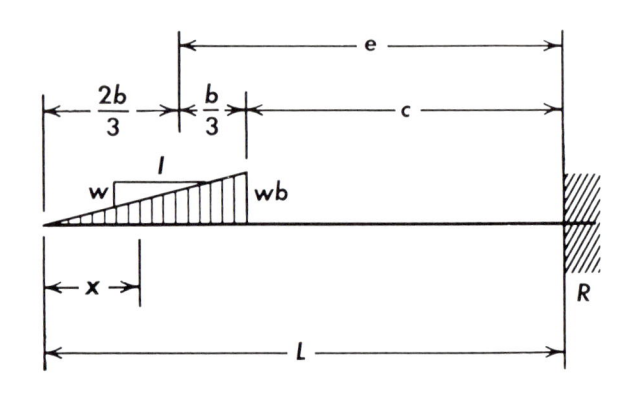

$$R = \frac{wb^2}{2}$$

at $x = L$

$$M_{max.} = -\frac{wb^2 e}{2}$$

at $x = 0$

$$\triangle_{max.} = \frac{wb^2}{1620EI}(135e^3 - 405Le^2 - 14b^3)$$

$$\theta = \frac{wb^2}{72EI}(b^2 + 18e^2)$$

when $0 < x < b$

$$M_x = -\frac{wx^3}{6}$$

$$\triangle_x = \frac{w}{3240EI}[270b^2 e^3 - 810b^2 e^2(L-x) + 45b^4 x - 28b^5 - 27x^5]$$

when $b < x < L$

$$M_x = -\frac{wb^2}{6}(3x - 2b)$$

$$\triangle_x = \frac{wb^2}{324EI}[27e^3 - 81e^2(L-x) - (3x-2b)^3]$$

CANTILEVER BEAM
UNIFORMLY VARYING LOAD

BEAM FORMULAS Case 25

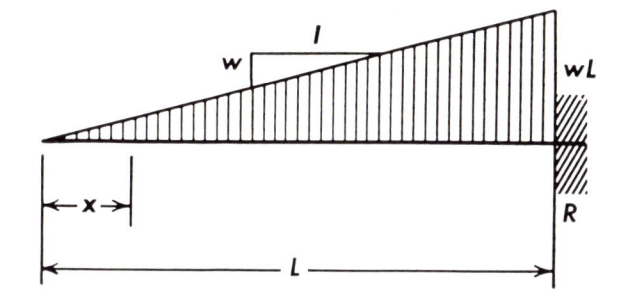

$R = \dfrac{wL^2}{2}$

at $x = L$

$M_{max.} = -\dfrac{wL^3}{6}$

at $x = 0$

$\triangle_{max.} = -\dfrac{wL^5}{30EI}$

$\theta_{max.} = \dfrac{wL^4}{24EI}$

when $0 < x < L$

$M_x = -\dfrac{wx^3}{6}$

$\triangle_x = \dfrac{w}{120EI}(5L^4x - 4L^5 - x^5)$

BEAM FORMULAS
Case 26

**CANTILEVER BEAM
UNIFORMLY VARYING LOAD
PARTIALLY DISTRIBUTED**

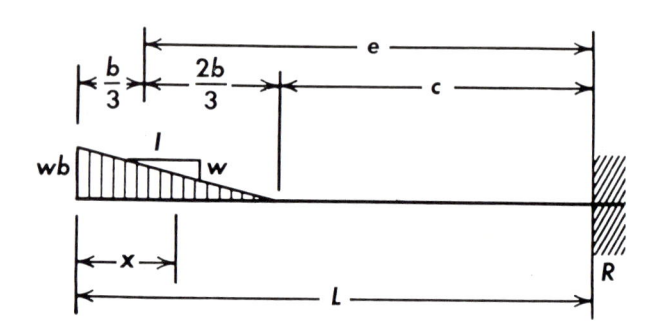

$$R = \frac{wb^2}{2}$$

at $x = L$

$$M_{max.} = -\frac{wb^2 e}{2}$$

at $x = 0$

$$\triangle_{max.} = -\frac{wb^2}{3240EI}[17b^3 + 270e^2(b+2e)]$$

$$\theta = \frac{wb^2}{72EI}(b^2 + 18e^2)$$

when $0 < x < b$

$$M_x = \frac{wx^2}{6}(x - 3b)$$

$$\triangle_x = \frac{w}{3240EI}[27x^4(x-5b) - 270b^2 e^2(b+2e-3x)$$

$$+ 45b^4 x - 17b^5]$$

when $b < x < L$

$$M_x = -\frac{wb^2}{2}\left(x - \frac{b}{3}\right)$$

$$\triangle_x = \frac{wb^2}{12EI}\left[e^3 - 3e^2(L-x) - \left(x - \frac{b}{3}\right)^3\right]$$

CANTILEVER BEAM
UNIFORMLY VARYING LOAD

BEAM FORMULAS Case 27

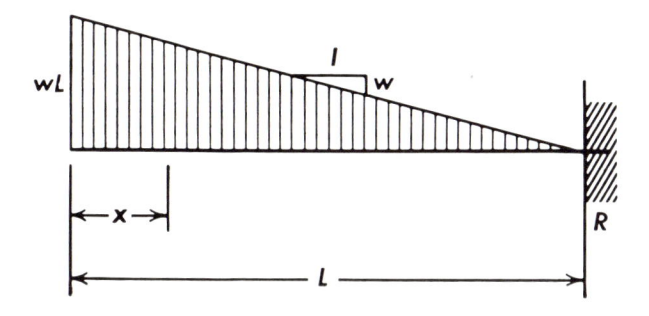

$$R = \frac{wL^2}{2}$$

at $x = L$

$$M_{max.} = -\frac{wL^3}{3}$$

at $x = 0$

$$\triangle_{max.} = -\frac{11wL^5}{120EI}$$

$$\theta_{max.} = \frac{wL^4}{8EI}$$

when $0 < x < L$

$$M_x = \frac{wx^2}{6}(x - 3L)$$

$$\triangle_x = \frac{w}{120EI}[L^4(15x - 11L) - x^4(5L - x)]$$

BEAM FORMULAS
Case 28

BEAM FIXED AT ONE END, SIMPLY SUPPORTED AT OTHER MOMENT APPLIED AT SUPPORTED END

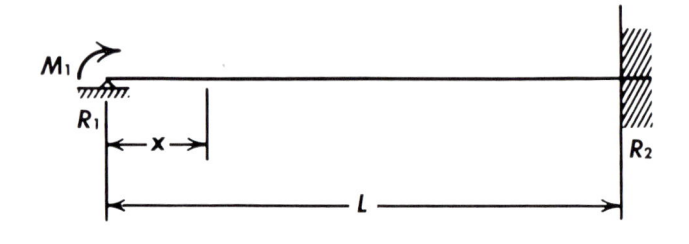

$$R_1 = -\frac{3M_1}{2L}$$

$$R_2 = -R_1 = \frac{3M_1}{2L}$$

$$M_1 = M_{\text{max. positive}} = M_1$$

$$M_2 = M_{\text{max. negative}} = -\frac{M_1}{2}$$

at $x = \dfrac{L}{3}$

$$\triangle_{\text{max.}} = -\frac{M_1 L^2}{27EI}$$

when $0 < x < L$

$$M_x = \frac{M_1}{2L}(2L - 3x)$$

$$\triangle_x = -\frac{M_1 x}{4EIL}(L - x)^2$$

BEAM SUPPORTED AT BOTH ENDS
MOMENT APPLIED AT ONE END

BEAM FORMULAS Case 29

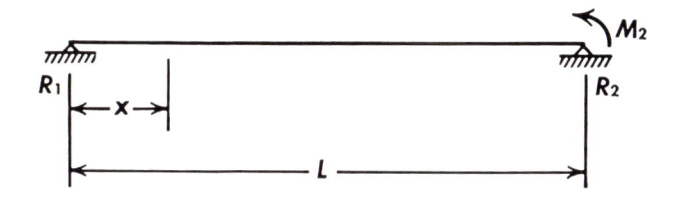

$$R_1 = \frac{M_2}{L}$$

$$R_2 = -R_1 = -\frac{M_2}{L}$$

$$M_2 = M_{\text{max. positive}}$$

at $x = \dfrac{L}{\sqrt{3}} = 0.5774L$

$$\triangle_{\text{max.}} = -\frac{M_2 L^2}{9\sqrt{3}EI} = -0.06415\frac{M_2 L^2}{EI}$$

when $0 < x < L$

$$M_x = \frac{M_2 x}{L}$$

$$\triangle_x = \frac{M_2 x}{6EIL}(x^2 - L^2)$$

**BEAM FORMULAS
Case 30**

**CANTILEVER BEAM
MOMENT APPLIED AT FREE END**

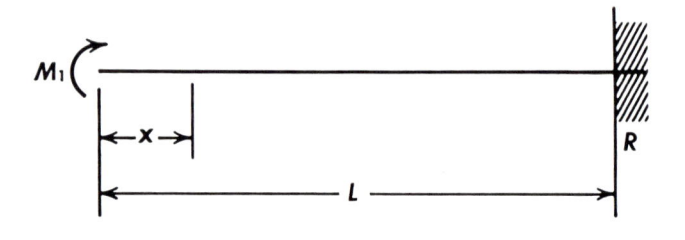

$R = 0$

at $x = L$

$M = M_1$

at $x = 0$

$$\triangle_{max.} = \frac{M_1 L^2}{2EI}$$

$$\theta = -\frac{M_1 L}{EI}$$

when $0 < x < L$

$$M_x = M_1$$

$$\triangle_x = \frac{M_1}{2EI}(L-x)^2$$

BEAM FIXED AT ONE END, SUPPORTED AT OTHER
MOMENT APPLIED AT ANY POINT

BEAM FORMULAS Case 31

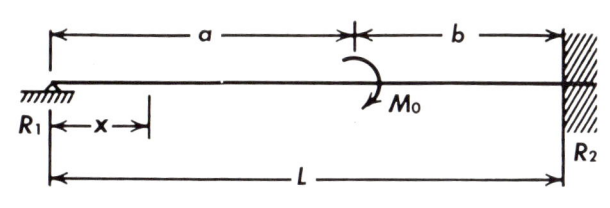

$$R_1 = -\frac{3M_0 b}{2L^3}(L+a)$$

$$R_2 = -R_1 = \frac{3M_0 b}{2L^3}(L+a)$$

$$M_2 = \frac{M_0}{2L^2}(3a^2 - L^2)$$

at $x = a_{(\text{right})}$

$$M_{\text{max. positive}} = R_1 a + M_0$$

when $a < 0.2776L$

$$M_{\text{max. negative}} = +M_2$$

when $a > 0.2776L$

$$M_{\text{max. negative}} = R_1 a$$

at $x = L\sqrt{\dfrac{3a-L}{3(L+a)}}$ if $a > \dfrac{L}{3}$

$$\triangle_{\text{max. positive}} = \frac{M_0 b}{6EI}\left[\frac{(3a-L)^3}{3(L+a)}\right]^{\frac{1}{2}}$$

at $x = L + \dfrac{2M_2}{R_2}$ if $a < 0.5774L$

$$\triangle_{\text{max. negative}} = \frac{2M_2{}^3}{3EIR_2{}^2}$$

when $0 < x < a$

$$M_x = R_1 x$$

$$\triangle_x = \frac{M_0 b x}{4EIL^3}[2a(L^2 - x^2) - b(L^2 + x^2)]$$

when $a < x < L$

$$M_x = R_1 x + M_0$$

$$\triangle_x = \frac{1}{6EI}[3M_2(L-x)^2 + R_2(L-x)^3]$$

BEAM FORMULAS
Case 32

**BEAM SUPPORTED AT BOTH ENDS
MOMENT APPLIED AT ANY POINT**

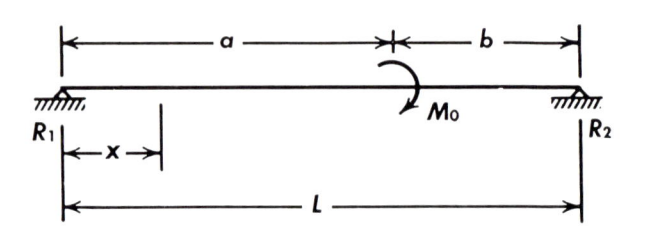

$$R_1 = -\frac{M_0}{L}$$

$$R_2 = \frac{M_0}{L}$$

at $x = a_{(left)}$

$$M_{max.\ negative} = R_1 a$$

at $x = a_{(right)}$

$$M_{max.\ positive} = R_1 a + M_0$$

at $x = \sqrt{\frac{L^2 - 3b^2}{3}}$ if $a > 0.4226L$

$$\triangle_{max.\ positive} = \frac{M_0}{3EIL}\left(\frac{L^2 - 3b^2}{3}\right)^{\frac{3}{2}}$$

at $x = L - \sqrt{\frac{L^2 - 3a^2}{3}}$ if $a < 0.5774L$

$$\triangle_{max.\ negative} = -\frac{M_0}{3EIL}\left(\frac{L^2 - 3a^2}{3}\right)^{\frac{3}{2}}$$

when $0 < x < a$

$$M_x = R_1 x$$

$$\triangle_x = -\frac{M_0 x}{6EIL}(3b^2 - L^2 + x^2)$$

when $a < x < L$

$$M_x = R_1 x + M_0$$

$$\triangle_x = \frac{M_0(L-x)}{6EIL}(3a^2 - 2Lx + x^2)$$

BEAM FIXED AT BOTH ENDS
MOMENT APPLIED AT ANY POINT

BEAM FORMULAS Case 33

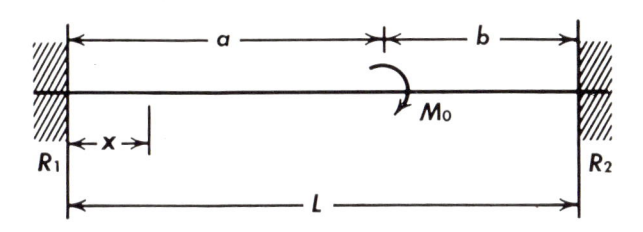

$$R_1 = -\frac{6M_0 ab}{L^3}$$

$$R_2 = -R_1 = \frac{6M_0 ab}{L^3}$$

$$M_1 = -\frac{M_0 b}{L^2}(L - 3a)$$

$$M_2 = -\frac{M_0 a}{L^2}(2L - 3a)$$

at $x = a_{(right)}$
$$M_{max.\ positive} = R_1 a + M_1 + M_0$$

at $x = a_{(left)}$
$$M_{max.\ negative} = R_1 a + M_1$$

at $x = -\frac{2M_1}{R_1}$ if $a > \frac{L}{3}$

$$\triangle_{max.\ positive} = \frac{2M_1^3}{3EIR_1^2}$$

at $x = L + \frac{2M_2}{R_2}$ if $a < \frac{2L}{3}$

$$\triangle_{max.\ negative} = \frac{2M_2^3}{3EIR_2^2}$$

when $0 < x < a$
$$M_x = R_1 x + M_1$$
$$\triangle_x = \frac{1}{6EI}(3M_1 x^2 + R_1 x^3)$$

when $a < x < L$
$$M_x = R_2(L - x) + M_2$$
$$\triangle_x = \frac{1}{6EI}[3M_2(L-x)^2 + R_2(L-x)^3]$$

BEAM FORMULAS
Case 34

CONTINUOUS BEAM, CONCENTRATED LOAD IN EACH SPAN; SPANS, LOADS AND SECTIONS DIFFERENT

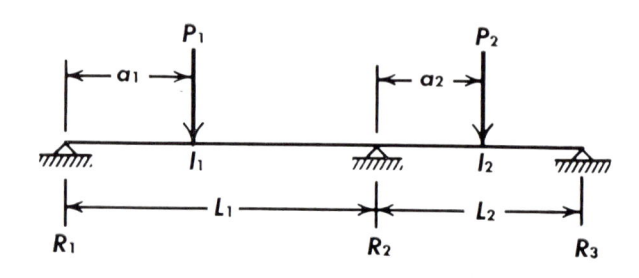

Letting $\dfrac{a_1}{L_1} = k_1$ and $\dfrac{a_2}{L_2} = k_2$

$$\frac{M_1 L_1}{I_1} + 2M_2\left(\frac{L_1}{I_1} + \frac{L_2}{I_2}\right) + \frac{M_3 L_2}{I_2} = \frac{P_1 L_1^2}{I_1}(k_1^3 - k_1)$$
$$+ \frac{P_2 L_2^2}{I_2}(3k_2^2 - k_2^3 - 2k_2)$$

BEAM FORMULAS
Case 35

CONTINUOUS BEAM, EACH SPAN UNIFORMLY LOADED; SPANS, LOADS AND SECTIONS DIFFERENT

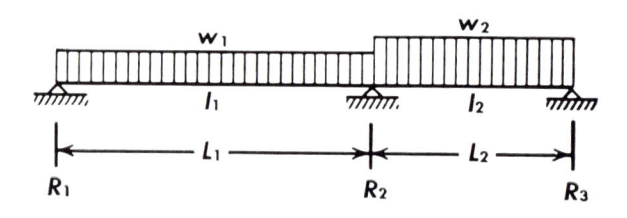

$$\frac{M_1 L_1}{I_1} + 2M_2\left(\frac{L_1}{I_1} + \frac{L_2}{I_2}\right) + \frac{M_3 L_2}{I_2} = -\frac{w_1 L_1^3}{4 I_1} - \frac{w_2 L_2^3}{4 I_2}$$

Characteristics of
USS High-Strength Steels

The United States Steel Corporation publishes a series of illustrated booklets and information sheets dealing with the properties of various USS High-Strength Steels, their fabricating characteristics and typical applications.

Excerpts of particular interest to design engineers are given in the following pages.

Copies of this literature may be obtained from any district sales office or from United States Steel Corporation, 525 William Penn Place, Pittsburgh, Pa.

USS COR-TEN STEEL

The premier corrosion-resistant high-strength, low-alloy steel intended primarily for weight reduction, or longer life, by means of greater strength and enhanced atmospheric corrosion resistance in applications involving cold forming and metal arc or spot welding.

MECHANICAL PROPERTIES	½ in. and Under in Thickness	Over ½ to 1½ in. incl.	Over 1½ to 3 in. incl.
Yield Point, min, psi	50,000	47,000	43,000
Tensile Strength, min, psi	70,000	67,000	63,000
Elong. in 2 in., min, per cent	22	—	24
Elong. in 8 in., min, per cent 0.180 in. and heavier	18	19	19
Cold Bend	180°$D=1t$	180°$D=2t$	180°$D=3t$

The minimum yield point and tensile strength requirements are 45,000 psi and 65,000 psi respectively, with 22% minimum elongation in 2" for cold rolled sheets, galvanized sheets, and hot rolled products when annealing or normalizing is specified, or in coils. The furnishing of cold rolled sheets to strength levels other than the above is subject to negotiation.

ASTM Standard Specimens, minimum number of tests and ductility modifications apply.

CHEMICAL COMPOSITION (For information purposes only)	C	Mn	P	S	Si	Cu	Cr	Ni
Composition Range, per cent	.12 max	.20/.50	.07/.15	.05 max	.25/.75	.25/.55	.30/1.25	.65 max
Typical Composition, per cent	.09	.38	.09	.033	.48	.41	.84	.28

FABRICATING PRACTICE FOR COLD FORMING

Thickness of Material	Suggested Min Inside Radius
Up to 1/16 in. incl.	1t
Over 1/16 to ¼ in. incl.	2t
Over ¼ to ½ in. incl.	3t

Hot forming is recommended for angle bending thicknesses over ½ inch.

September 1, 1955

USS COR-TEN STEEL AND STRUCTURAL CARBON STEELS
Comparative Properties and Engineering Data

MECHANICAL PROPERTIES ½ in. and Under in Thickness	USS COR-TEN STEEL	STRUCTURAL CARBON STEELS ASTM A7	ASTM A113 Grade B
Yield Point, min, psi	50,000	33,000	27,000
Tensile Strength, psi	70,000 min	60/72,000	50/62,000
Elong. in 2 in., min, per cent	22		
Elong. in 8 in., min, per cent, 0.180 in. and heavier	18	21	24
Cold Bend	$180°D = 1t$	$180°D = \frac{1}{2}t$	180° Flat
Resistance to atmospheric corrosion (comparative)	4 to 6	1 (or 2 with copper 0.20% min)	1 (or 2 with copper 0.20% min)
Compressive Yield Point, psi	Tensile Y.P.	Tensile Y.P.	Tensile Y.P.
Shearing Strength, psi	¾ T.S.	¾ T.S.	¾ T.S.
Modulus of Elasticity, psi	28/30,000,000	28/30,000,000	28/30,000,000
Endurance Limit (as rolled, avg), psi	42,000	28,000	26,000
Charpy Impact, keyhole notch (as rolled, room temp, avg), ft-lb	40	25	30
Coefficient of Expansion per degree F, 70 to 200 F	0.0000063	0.0000063	0.0000063

A booklet containing more detailed information regarding properties, fabrication and applications of COR-TEN steel is available upon request to any United States Steel Corporation sales office.

"USS" and "COR-TEN" are registered trademarks of United States Steel.

USS MAN-TEN STEEL

A high-strength manganese-copper steel intended primarily for weight reduction by means of greater strength in applications involving moderate forming. It is considered a weldable grade provided mild steel electrodes are used and good welding technique and workmanship are maintained. It is not considered suitable for spot welding.

MECHANICAL PROPERTIES	½ in. and Under in Thickness	Over ½ to 1½ in. incl.	Over 1½ to 3 in. incl.
Yield Point, min, psi	50,000	45,000	40,000
Tensile Strength, min, psi	75,000	70,000	65,000
Elong. in 2 in., min, per cent	20	—	22
Elong. in 8 in., min, per cent 0.180 in. and heavier	18	19	19
Cold Bend	$180°D = 1t$	$180°D = 2t$	$180°D = 3t$

The minimum yield point and tensile strength requirements will be reduced by 5,000 psi when annealing or normalizing is specified, or when furnished in coils.

ASTM Standard Specimens, minimum number of tests and ductility modifications apply.

CHEMICAL COMPOSITION (For information purposes only)	C	Mn	P	S	Si	Cu
Composition Range, per cent	.25 max	1.10/1.60	.045 max	.05 max	.30 max	.20 min
Typical Composition, per cent	.22	1.40	.020	.036	.07	.27

FABRICATING PRACTICE FOR COLD FORMING

Thickness of Material	Suggested Min Inside Radius
Up to ⅛ in. incl.	$2t$
Over ⅛ to ¼ in. incl.	$2½t$
Over ¼ to ½ in. incl.	$3½t$

Hot forming is recommended for angle bending thicknesses over ½ inch.

September 1, 1955

USS MAN-TEN STEEL AND STRUCTURAL CARBON STEELS
Comparative Properties and Engineering Data

MECHANICAL PROPERTIES ½ in. and Under in Thickness	USS MAN-TEN STEEL	STRUCTURAL CARBON STEELS ASTM A7	ASTM A113 Grade B
Yield Point, min, psi	50,000	33,000	27,000
Tensile Strength, psi	75,000 min	60/72,000	50/62,000
Elong. in 8 in., min, per cent, 0.180 in. and heavier	18	21	24
Cold Bend	$180°D = 1t$	$180°D = \frac{1}{2}t$	180° Flat
Resistance to atmospheric corrosion (comparative)	2	1 (or 2 with copper 0.20% min)	1 (or 2 with copper 0.20% min)
Compressive Yield Point, psi	Tensile Y.P.	Tensile Y.P.	Tensile Y.P.
Shearing Strength, psi	¾ T.S.	¾ T.S.	¾ T.S.
Modulus of Elasticity, psi	28/30,000,000	28/30,000,000	28/30,000,000
Endurance Limit (as rolled, avg), psi	39,000	28,000	26,000
Charpy Impact, keyhole notch (as rolled, room temp, avg), ft-lb	30	25	30
Coefficient of Expansion per degree F, 70 to 200 F	0.0000063	0.0000063	0.0000063

A booklet containing more detailed information regarding properties, fabrication and applications of MAN-TEN steel is available upon request to any United States Steel Corporation sales office.

"USS" and "MAN-TEN" are registered trademarks of United States Steel.

USS MAN-TEN (A242) STEEL
FOR RIVETED AND BOLTED BRIDGES, BUILDINGS AND TOWERS

A high-strength steel intended primarily for use in structural members of riveted and bolted bridges, buildings, and towers. The characteristics of USS Man-Ten (A242) Steel make it particularly applicable for structures of riveted construction requiring high strength with atmospheric corrosion resistance equal to that of copper steel.

MECHANICAL PROPERTIES	THICKNESS RANGES		
	¾ in. and under	Over ¾ to 1½ in. incl.	Over 1½ to 4 in. incl.
Yield Point, min, psi	50,000	46,000	42,000
Tensile Strength, min, psi	72,000	70,000	65,000
Elong. in 8 in., min, per cent	18	19	19
Elong. in 2 in., min, per cent	—	—	24
180° Cold Bend	$D=1t$ for thicknesses to ¾ in. incl. $D=1½t$ for thicknesses over ¾ to 1 in. incl. $D=2t$ for thicknesses over 1 to 1½ in. incl. $D=2½t$ for thicknesses over 1½ to 2 in. incl. $D=3t$ for thicknesses over 2 to 4 in. incl.		

ASTM Standard Specimens, minimum number of tests and ductility modifications apply.

CHEMICAL COMPOSITION, PER CENT (For information purposes only)		C	Mn	P	S	Si	Cu
ASTM A242	Ladle	.22 max	1.25 max	—	.05 max	—	—
	Check	.26 max	1.30 max	—	.063 max	—	—
USS Man-Ten A242	Ladle	.27 max*	1.10/1.60*	.04 max	.05 max	.30 max	.20/.35
	Check	.31 max*	1.65 max*	—	.063 max*	—	—

*Deviations from ASTM A242

FABRICATING PRACTICE FOR COLD FORMING

Thickness of Material	Suggested Min Inside Radius
Up to ¼ in. incl.	2½t
Over ¼ to ½ in. incl.	3½t

Hot forming is recommended for angle bending thicknesses over ½ inch.

In the welding of attachments, and in conditioning by welding, it is recommended that the low hydrogen type of electrode be used.

August 1, 1954

USS MAN-TEN (A242) STEEL AND STRUCTURAL CARBON STEEL
Comparative Properties and Engineering Data

MECHANICAL PROPERTIES ¾ in. and Under in Thickness	USS MAN-TEN (A242) STEEL	ASTM A7 STRUCTURAL CARBON STEEL
Yield Point, min, psi	50,000	33,000
Tensile Strength, psi	72,000 min	60/72,000
Elong. in 8 in., min, per cent	18	21
Cold Bend	$180°D = 1t$	$180°D = \frac{1}{2}t$
Resistance to atmospheric corrosion (comparative)	2	1 (or 2 with copper 0.20% min)
Compressive Yield Point, psi	Tensile Y.P.	Tensile Y.P.
Shearing Strength, psi	¾ T.S.	¾ T.S.
Modulus of Elasticity, psi	28/30,000,000	28/30,000,000
Endurance Limit (as rolled, avg), psi	39,000	28,000
Charpy Impact, keyhole notch (as rolled, room temp, avg), ft-lb	24	25
Coefficient of Expansion per degree F, 70 to 200 F	0.0000063	0.0000063

"USS" and "Man-Ten" are registered trademarks of United States Steel.

USS TRI-TEN "E" STEEL
MEETS ALL THE REQUIREMENTS OF ASTM A242

A high-strength low-alloy steel intended primarily for weight reduction by means of greater strength and toughness, in applications involving cold forming, metal-arc welding and moderately severe impacts in low temperature service, with atmospheric corrosion resistance equal to that of copper steel. USS Tri-Ten "E" is particularly applicable for structural members of metal-arc welded bridges, earth-moving equipment and similar applications.

MECHANICAL PROPERTIES	¾ in. and Under in Thickness	Over ¾ to 1½ in. incl.	Over 1½ to 4 in. incl.
Yield Point, min, psi	50,000	47,000	43,000
Tensile Strength, min, psi	70,000	67,000	63,000
Elong. in 2 in., min, per cent	22	—	24
Elong. in 8 in., min, per cent 0.180 in. and heavier	18	19	19
180° Cold Bend	\multicolumn{3}{l}{$D=1t$ for thicknesses to ¾ in. incl. $D=1\frac{1}{2}t$ for thicknesses over ¾ to 1 in. incl. $D=2t$ for thicknesses over 1 to 1½ in. incl. $D=2\frac{1}{2}t$ for thicknesses over 1½ to 2 in. incl. $D=3t$ for thicknesses over 2 to 4 in. incl.}		

For sheet and strip products, the minimum yield point and tensile strength requirements are 45,000 psi and 60,000 psi respectively, and minimum elongation in 2", 25%. In the case of plates, both the minimum yield point and tensile strength requirements will be reduced 5,000 psi when annealing or normalizing is specified, or when severe forming is involved.

ASTM Standard Specimens, minimum number of tests and ductility modifications apply.

CHEMICAL COMPOSITION (For information purposes only)	C	Mn	P	S	Si	Cu	V
Composition Range, per cent	.22 max	1.25 max	.04 max	.05 max	.30 max	.20 min	.02 min
Typical Composition, per cent	.18	1.14	.023	.031	.17	.28	.045
ASTM A242 REQUIREMENT							
Ladle	.22 max	1.25 max	..	.05 max	..	..	..
Check	.26 max	1.30 max	..	.063 max	..	..	..

FABRICATING PRACTICE FOR COLD FORMING

Thickness of Material	Suggested Min Inside Radius
Up to ¼ in. incl.	2t
Over ¼ to ½ in. incl.	3t

Hot forming is recommended for angle bending thicknesses over ½ inch.

July 15, 1955

USS TRI-TEN "E" STEEL AND STRUCTURAL CARBON STEEL
Comparative Properties and Engineering Data

MECHANICAL PROPERTIES ½ in. and Under in Thickness	USS TRI-TEN "E" STEEL	ASTM A7 STRUCTURAL CARBON STEEL
Yield Point, min, psi	50,000	33,000
Tensile Strength, psi	70,000 min	60/72,000
Elong. in 8 in., min, per cent, 0.180 in. and heavier	18	21
Cold Bend	$180°D = 1t$	$180°D = \frac{1}{2}t$
Resistance to atmospheric corrosion (comparative)	2	1 (or 2 with copper 0.20% min)
Compressive Yield Point, psi	Tensile Y.P.	Tensile Y.P.
Shearing Strength, psi	¾ T.S.	¾ T.S.
Modulus of Elasticity, psi	28/30,000,000	28/30,000,000
Endurance Limit (as rolled, avg), psi	42,000	28,000
Charpy Impact, keyhole notch (as rolled, room temp, avg), ft-lb	42	25
Coefficient of Expansion per degree F, 70 to 200 F	0.0000063	0.0000063

"USS" and "TRI-TEN" are registered trademarks of United States Steel.

USS TRI-TEN STEEL

A high-strength low-alloy steel intended primarily for weight reduction by means of greater strength and toughness, in applications involving cold forming, metal-arc welding and moderately severe impacts in low temperature service, with atmospheric corrosion resistance superior to that of copper steel.

MECHANICAL PROPERTIES	¾ in. and Under in Thickness	Over ¾ to 1½ in. incl.	Over 1½ to 4 in. incl.
Yield point, min, psi	50,000	46,000	42,000
Tensile Strength, min, psi	70,000	67,000	63,000
Elong. in 2 in., min, per cent	—	—	24
Elong. in 8 in., min, per cent 0.180 in. and heavier	18	19	19
180° Cold Bend	\multicolumn{3}{l	}{$D = 1t$ for thicknesses to ¾ in. incl. $D = 1\frac{1}{2}t$ for thickness over ¾ to 1 in. incl. $D = 2t$ for thicknesses over 1 to 1½ in. incl. $D = 2\frac{1}{2}t$ for thicknesses over 1½ to 2 in. incl. $D = 3t$ for thicknesses over 2 to 4 in. incl.}

The minimum yield point and tensile strength requirements will be reduced by 5,000 psi when the material is specified in the annealed or normalized conditions.

ASTM Standard Specimens, minimum number of tests and ductility modifications apply.

CHEMICAL COMPOSITION (For information purposes only)	C	Mn	P	S	Si	Cu	Ni
Composition Range, per cent	.25 max	1.35 max	.045 max	.05 max	.30 max	.30/.60	.40/.90
Typical Composition, per cent	.20	1.22	.021	.036	.17	.40	.60

FABRICATING PRACTICE FOR COLD FORMING

Thickness of Material	Suggested Min Inside Radius
Up to ¼ in. incl.	2t
Over ¼ to ½ in. incl.	3t

Hot forming is recommended for angle bending thicknesses over ½ inch.

July 15, 1955

USS TRI-TEN STEEL AND STRUCTURAL CARBON STEEL
Comparative Properties and Engineering Data

MECHANICAL PROPERTIES ½ in. and Under in Thickness	USS TRI-TEN STEEL	ASTM A7 STRUCTURAL CARBON STEEL
Yield Point, min, psi	50,000	33,000
Tensile Strength, psi	70,000 min	60/72,000
Elong. in 8 in., min, per cent, 0.180 in. and heavier	18	21
Cold Bend	$180°D = 1t$	$180°D = \tfrac{1}{2}t$
Resistance to atmospheric corrosion (comparative)	3	1 (or 2 with copper 0.20% min)
Compressive Yield Point, psi	Tensile Y.P.	Tensile Y.P.
Shearing Strength, psi	¾ T.S.	¾ T.S.
Modulus of Elasticity, psi	28/30,000,000	28/30,000,000
Endurance Limit (as rolled, avg), psi	42,000	28,000
Charpy Impact, keyhole notch (as rolled, room temp, avg), ft-lb	42	25
Coefficient of Expansion per degree F, 70 to 200 F	0.0000063	0.0000063

A booklet containing more detailed information regarding properties, fabrication and applications of TRI-TEN steel is available upon request to any United States Steel Corporation sales office.

"USS" and "TRI-TEN" are registered trademarks of United States Steel.

BIBLIOGRAPHY

The following papers pertaining to high-strength steels contain information on applications, designs and service results. Those marked with an asterisk are available upon request.

Low-Alloy Steels and Their Applications, by H. M. PRIEST, United States Steel Corporation. New York Section, American Welding Society, March 10, 1936. (Published, Journal, American Welding Society—May, 1936.)

Low-Alloy Structural Steels, by E. C. BAIN and F. T. LLEWELLYN, United States Steel Corporation, American Society of Civil Engineers, October 15, 1936. (Proceedings, October, 1936.)

Application in Car Construction of High Tensile Steels, by A. F. STUEBING, United States Steel Corporation. Car Department Officers' Association, September 29, 1937.

Physical Properties of Four Low-Alloy High Strength Steels, by W. L. COLLINS and T. J. DOLAN, University of Illinois. Proceedings, American Society for Testing Materials, Vol. 38, Part II, Pages 157-175, 1938. (Steel A is USS COR-TEN.)

*Light Weight Hoppers After Ten Years.** Railway Age, January 30, 1945.

The Fabrication of High Strength Steels, by C. E. LOOS, United States Steel Corporation. Steel Processing, December, 1945.

Modern Steels in Railroad Construction, by H. M. PRIEST, United States Steel Corporation. Railway Club of Pittsburgh, March 28, 1946.

Light Gage Steel Design Manual, American Iron and Steel Institute, January, 1949.

*Comparative Performance of USS COR-TEN and Copper Steel in Hopper Car Service,** United States Steel Corporation.

*Corrosion of Railroad Hopper Car Body Sheets,** by B. J. KELLY, United States Steel Corporation, Corrosion, June, 1951.

*Corrosion of Steels,** United States Steel Corporation.

Effect of Composition of Steel on the Performance of Organic Coatings in Atmospheric Exposure, by F. L. LA QUE and JAMES A. BOYLAN. National Association of Corrosion Engineers, March, 1953.

Effecting Economies with High-Strength Low-Alloy Steels, by A. F. STUEBING, United States Steel Corporation. Basic Materials Conference, June 16, 1953.

*Corrosion Resistance of High-Strength Low-Alloy Steels as Influenced by Composition and Environment,** by C. P. LARRABEE, United States Steel Corporation. Corrosion, August, 1953.

*High-Strength, Low-Alloy Steels,** Material and Methods Manual 102, February, 1954.